Microsoft® Excel® 2013

Basic | Intermediate | Advanced

Microsoft® Excel® 2013

Basic | Intermediate | Advanced

Lynn Wermers

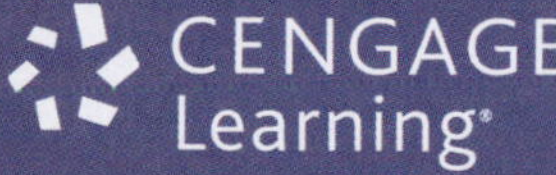

Australia • Brazil • Mexico • Singapore • United Kingdom • United States

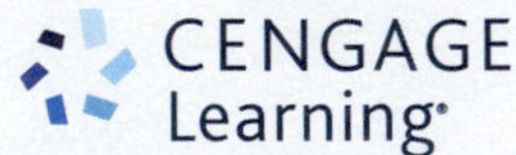

Illustrated Course Guide: Microsoft® Excel® 2013 Intermediate
Lynn Wermers

Senior Product Manger: Marjorie Hunt

Associate Product Manager: Amanda Lyons

Senior Content Developer: Christina Kling-Garrett

Content Developer: Megan Chrisman

Marketing Manager: Gretchen Swann

Developmental Editor: Barbara Clemens

Full-Service Project Management: GEX Publishing Services

Copyeditor: Kathy Orrino

Proofreader: Brandy Lilly

Indexer: Alexandra Nickerson

QA Manuscript Reviewers: John Freitas, Jeff Schwartz, Danielle Shaw, Susan Pedicini, Susan Whalen

Print Buyer: Fola Orekoya

Cover Designer: GEX Publishing Services

Cover Artist: © Katerina Havelkova/Shutterstock

Composition: GEX Publishing Services

Library of Congress Control Number: 2013953083
ISBN-13: 978-1-285-09340-6
ISBN-10: 1-285-09340-2

Cengage Learning
200 First Stamford Place, 4th Floor
Stamford, CT 06902
USA

Cengage Learning is a leading provider of customized learning solutions with office locations around the globe, including Singapore, the United Kingdom, Australia, Mexico, Brazil, and Japan. Locate your local office at: **www.cengage.com/global**

Cengage Learning products are represented in Canada by Nelson Education, Ltd.

For your course and learning solutions, visit **www.cengage.com**

Purchase any of our products at your local college store or at our preferred online store **www.cengagebrain.com**

Printed in the United States of America
1 2 3 4 5 6 7 19 18 17 16 15 14

Brief Contents

Contents

Preface

Welcome to *Illustrated Course Guide: Microsoft Excel 2013 Intermediate.* This book has a unique design: Each skill is presented on two facing pages, with steps on the left and screens on the right. The layout makes it easy to learn a skill without having to read a lot of text and flip pages to see an illustration.

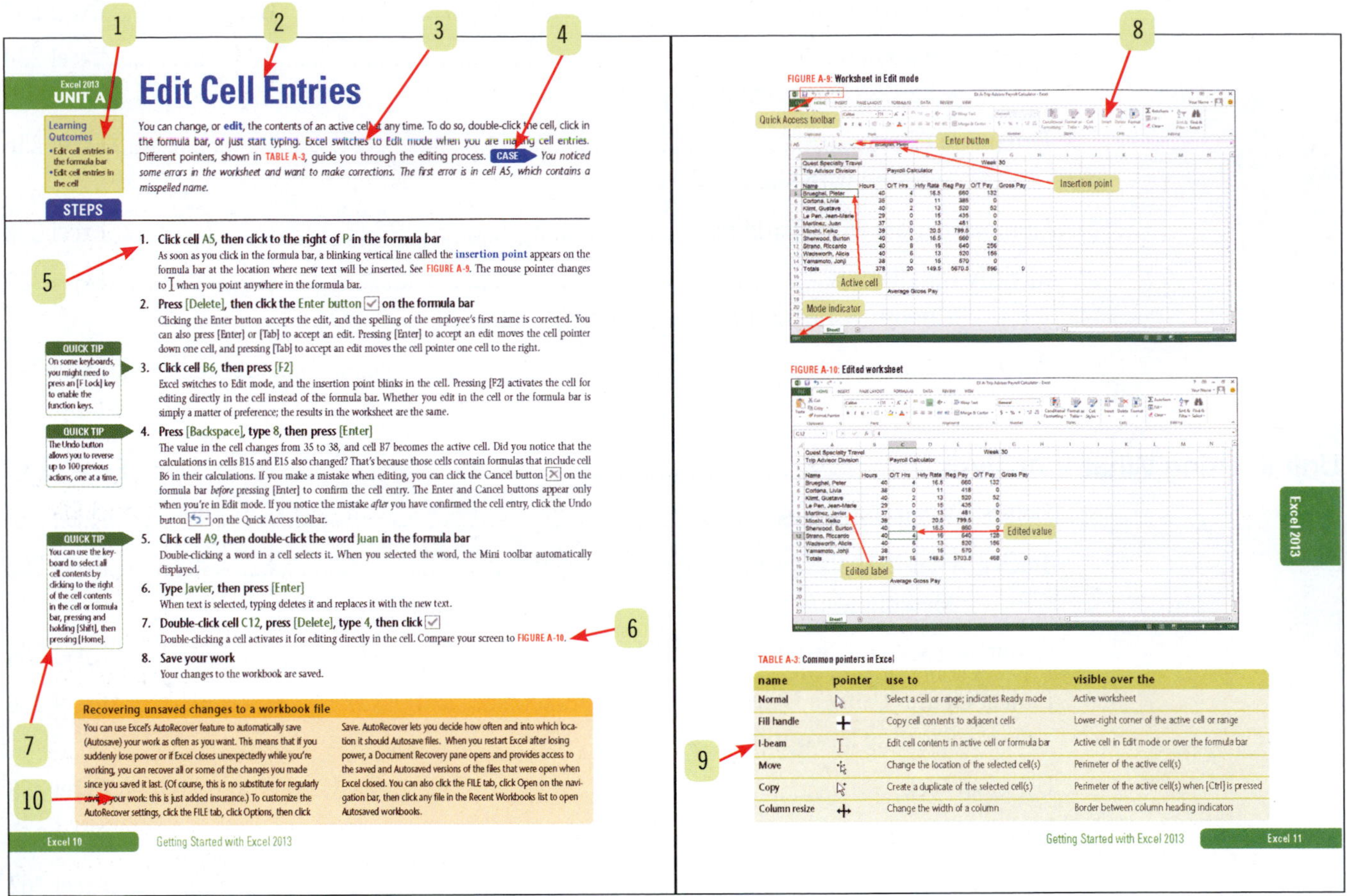
Excel 2013 UNIT A

Learning Outcomes
• Edit cell entries in the formula bar
• Edit cell entries in the cell

Edit Cell Entries

You can change, or **edit**, the contents of an active cell at any time. To do so, double-click the cell, click in the formula bar, or just start typing. Excel switches to Edit mode when you are making cell entries. Different pointers, shown in TABLE A-3, guide you through the editing process. CASE *You noticed some errors in the worksheet and want to make corrections. The first error is in cell A5, which contains a misspelled name.*

STEPS

1. **Click cell A5, then click to the right of P in the formula bar**
   As soon as you click in the formula bar, a blinking vertical line called the **insertion point** appears on the formula bar at the location where new text will be inserted. See FIGURE A-9. The mouse pointer changes to I when you point anywhere in the formula bar.
2. **Press [Delete], then click the Enter button on the formula bar**
   Clicking the Enter button accepts the edit, and the spelling of the employee's first name is corrected. You can also press [Enter] or [Tab] to accept an edit. Pressing [Enter] to accept an edit moves the cell pointer down one cell, and pressing [Tab] to accept an edit moves the cell pointer one cell to the right.
3. **Click cell B6, then press [F2]**
   Excel switches to Edit mode, and the insertion point blinks in the cell. Pressing [F2] activates the cell for editing directly in the cell instead of the formula bar. Whether you edit in the cell or the formula bar is simply a matter of preference; the results in the worksheet are the same.
4. **Press [Backspace], type 8, then press [Enter]**
   The value in the cell changes from 35 to 38, and cell B7 becomes the active cell. Did you notice that the calculations in cells B15 and E15 also changed? That's because those cells contain formulas that include cell B6 in their calculations. If you make a mistake when editing, you can click the Cancel button on the formula bar *before* pressing [Enter] to confirm the cell entry. The Enter and Cancel buttons appear only when you're in Edit mode. If you notice the mistake *after* you have confirmed the cell entry, click the Undo button on the Quick Access toolbar.
5. **Click cell A9, then double-click the word Juan in the formula bar**
   Double-clicking a word in a cell selects it. When you selected the word, the Mini toolbar automatically displayed.
6. **Type Javier, then press [Enter]**
   When text is selected, typing deletes it and replaces it with the new text.
7. **Double-click cell C12, press [Delete], type 4, then click**
   Double-clicking a cell activates it for editing directly in the cell. Compare your screen to FIGURE A-10.
8. **Save your work**
   Your changes to the workbook are saved.

QUICK TIP
On some keyboards, you might need to press an [F Lock] key to enable the function keys.

QUICK TIP
The Undo button allows you to reverse up to 100 previous actions, one at a time.

QUICK TIP
You can use the keyboard to select all cell contents by clicking to the right of the cell contents in the cell or formula bar, pressing and holding [Shift], then pressing [Home].

Recovering unsaved changes to a workbook file

You can use Excel's AutoRecover feature to automatically save (Autosave) your work as often as you want. This means that if you suddenly lose power or if Excel closes unexpectedly while you're working, you can recover all or some of the changes you made since you saved it last. (Of course, this is no substitute for regularly saving your work: this is just added insurance.) To customize the AutoRecover settings, click the FILE tab, click Options, then click Save. AutoRecover lets you decide how often and into which location it should Autosave files. When you restart Excel after losing power, a Document Recovery pane opens and provides access to the saved and Autosaved versions of the files that were open when Excel closed. You can also click the FILE tab, click Open on the navigation bar, then click any file in the Recent Workbooks list to open Autosaved workbooks.

Excel 10 Getting Started with Excel 2013

FIGURE A-9: Worksheet in Edit mode

FIGURE A-10: Edited worksheet

TABLE A-3: Common pointers in Excel

name	pointer	use to	visible over the
Normal		Select a cell or range; indicates Ready mode	Active worksheet
Fill handle	+	Copy cell contents to adjacent cells	Lower-right corner of the active cell or range
I-beam	I	Edit cell contents in active cell or formula bar	Active cell in Edit mode or over the formula bar
Move		Change the location of the selected cell(s)	Perimeter of the active cell(s)
Copy		Create a duplicate of the selected cell(s)	Perimeter of the active cell(s) when [Ctrl] is pressed
Column resize		Change the width of a column	Border between column heading indicators

Getting Started with Excel 2013 Excel 11

1 New! Learning Outcomes box lists measurable learning goals for which a student is accountable in that lesson.

2 Each two-page lesson focuses on a single skill.

3 Introduction briefly explains why the lesson skill is important.

4 A case scenario motivates the steps and puts learning in context.

5 Step-by-step instructions and brief explanations guide students through each hands-on lesson activity.

6 New! Figure references are now in red bold to help students refer back and forth between the steps and screenshots.

7 Tips and troubleshooting advice, right where you need it–next to the step itself.

8 New! Larger screenshots with green callouts keep students on track as they complete steps.

9 Tables provide summaries of helpful information such as button references or keyboard shortcuts.

10 Clues to Use are yellow boxes that provide useful information related to the lesson skill.

This book is an ideal learning tool for a wide range of learners—the "rookies" will find the clean design easy to follow and focused with only essential information presented, and the "hotshots" will appreciate being able to move quickly through the lessons to find the information they need without reading a lot of text. The design also makes this a great reference after the course is over! See the illustration on the left to learn more about the pedagogical and design elements of a typical lesson.

What's New in this Edition

- **Coverage** — Coverage of Excel 2013 helps students learn intermediate level skills including enhancing charts, managing and analyzing worksheet data, using What-If analysis, and more.
- **New! Learning Outcomes** — Each lesson displays a green Learning Outcomes box that lists skills-based or knowledge-based learning goals for which students are accountable. Each Learning Outcome maps to a variety of learning activities and assessments. (See the *New! Learning Outcomes* section on page xiii for more information.)
- **New! Updated Design** — This edition features many new design improvements to engage students — including larger lesson screenshots with green callouts placed on top, and a refreshed Unit Opener page.
- **New! Independent Challenge 4: Explore** — This new case-based assessment activity allows students to explore new skills and use creativity to solve a problem or create a project.

Assignments

This book includes a wide variety of high quality assignments you can use for practice and assessment. Assignments include:

- **Concepts Review** — Multiple choice, matching, and screen identification questions.
- **Skills Review** — Step-by-step, hands-on review of every skill covered in the unit.
- **Independent Challenges 1–3** — Case projects requiring critical thinking and application of the unit skills. The Independent Challenges increase in difficulty. The first one in each unit provides the most hand-holding; the subsequent ones provide less guidance and require more critical thinking and independent problem solving.
- **Independent Challenge 4: Explore** — Case projects that let students explore new skills that are related to the core skills covered in the unit and are often more open ended, allowing students to use creativity to complete the assignment.
- **Visual Workshop** — Critical thinking exercises that require students to create a project by looking at a completed solution; they must apply the skills they've learned in the unit and use critical thinking skills to create the project from scratch.

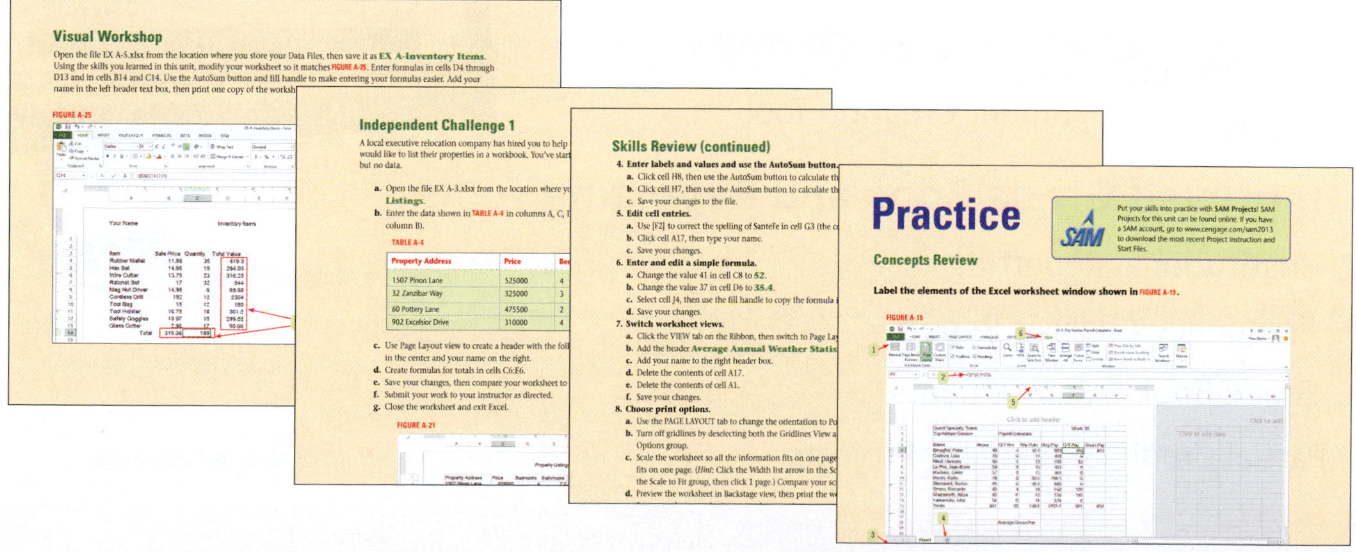

WHAT'S NEW FOR SAM 2013?

Get your students workplace ready with

The market-leading assessment and training solution for Microsoft Office

SAM 2013

Exciting New Features and Content

- Computer Concepts Trainings and Assessments *(shown on monitor)*
- Student Assignment Calendar
- All New SAM Projects
- Mac Hints
- More MindTap Readers

More Efficient Course Setup and Management Tools

- Individual Assignment Tool
- Video Playback of Student Clickpaths
- Express Assignment Creation Tool

Improved Grade Book and Reporting Tools

- Institutional Reporting
- Frequency Analysis Report
- Grade Book Enhancements
- Partial Credit Grading for Projects

SAM is sold separately.

SAM's active, hands-on environment helps students master Microsoft Office skills and computer concepts that are essential to academic and career success.

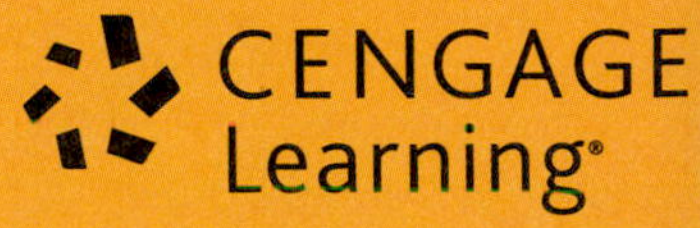

New! Learning Outcomes

Every 2-page lesson in this book now contains a green **Learning Outcomes box** that states the learning goals for that lesson.

> **Learning Outcomes**
> - Scroll the Start screen
> - Display the Charms bar
> - Switch between Start screen and desktop

- **What is a learning outcome?** A learning outcome states what a student is expected to know or be able to do after completing a lesson. Each learning outcome is skills-based or knowledge-based and is *measurable*. Learning outcomes map to learning activities and assessments.
- **How do students benefit from learning outcomes?** Learning outcomes tell students exactly what skills and knowledge they are *accountable* for learning in that lesson. This helps students study more efficiently and effectively and makes them more active learners.
- **How do instructors benefit from learning outcomes?** Learning outcomes provide clear, measurable, skills-based learning goals that map to various high-quality learning activities and assessments. A **Learning Outcomes Map**, available for each unit in this book, maps every learning outcome to the learning activities and assessments shown below.

Learning Outcomes Map to These Learning Activities:

1. **Book lessons:** Step-by-step tutorial on one skill presented in a two-page learning format
2. **SAM Training:** Short animations and hands-on practice activities in simulated environment *(SAM is sold separately.)*

Learning Outcomes Map to These Assessments:

1. **End-of-Unit Exercises:** **Concepts Review** (screen identification, matching, multiple choice); **Skills Review** (hands-on review of each lesson); **Independent Challenges** (hands-on, case-based review of specific skills); **Visual Workshop** (activity that requires student to build a project by looking at a picture of the final solution).
2. **Exam View Test Banks**: Objective-based questions you can use for online or paper testing.
3. **SAM Assessment:** Performance-based assessment in a simulated environment. *(SAM is sold separately.)*
4. **SAM Projects:** Auto-graded projects for Word, Excel, Access, and PowerPoint that students create. *(SAM is sold separately.)*
5. **Extra Independent Challenges**: Extra case-based exercises available in the Instructor Resources that cover various skills.

Learning Outcomes Map

A **Learning Outcomes Map**, contained in the Instructor Resources, provides a listing of learning activities and assessments for each learning outcome in the book.

Learning Outcomes Map
Microsoft Excel 2013 Illustrated Complete
Unit G

KEY:
IC=Independent Challenge
EIC=Extra Independent Challenge
VW=Visual Workshop

	Concepts Review	Skills Review	IC1	IC2	IC3	IC4	VW	EIC 1	EIC 2	Test Bank	SAM Assessment	SAM Projects	SAM Training
Plan a table													
Plan the data organization for a table	✓			✓						✓			
Plan the data elements for a table	✓			✓						✓			
Create and format a table													
Create a table		✓	✓	✓	✓	✓	✓			✓		✓	
Format a table		✓	✓	✓	✓	✓	✓			✓	✓	✓	✓
Add table data													
Add fields to a table		✓		✓	✓					✓	✓		✓
Add records to a table		✓		✓	✓					✓	✓		✓
Find and replace table data													
Find data in a table		✓	✓							✓	✓	✓	✓
Replace data in a table		✓	✓		✓					✓	✓	✓	✓
Delete table data													
Delete a table field		✓			✓					✓			
Delete a table row		✓			✓					✓	✓		✓
Remove duplicate data from a table		✓	✓										
Sort table data													
Sort a table in ascendi		✓	✓										

Instructor Resources

This book comes with a wide array of high-quality technology-based, teaching tools to help you teach and to help students learn. The following teaching tools are available for download at our Instructor Companion Site. Simply search for this text at *login.cengage.com.* An instructor login is required.

- **New! Learning Outcomes Map** — A detailed grid for each unit (in Excel format) shows the learning activities and assessments that map to each learning outcome in that unit.
- **Instructor's Manual** — Available as an electronic file, the Instructor's Manual includes lecture notes with teaching tips for each unit.
- **Sample Syllabus** — Prepare and customize your course easily using this sample course outline.
- **PowerPoint Presentations** — Each unit has a corresponding PowerPoint presentation covering the skills and topics in that unit that you can use in lectures, distribute to your students, or customize to suit your course.
- **Figure Files** — The figures in the text are provided on the Instructor Resources site to help you illustrate key topics or concepts. You can use these to create your own slide shows or learning tools.
- **Solution Files** — Solution Files are files that contain the finished project that students create or modify in the lessons or end-of-unit material.
- **Solutions Document** — This document outlines the solutions for the end-of-unit Concepts Review, Skills Review, Independent Challenges and Visual Workshops. An Annotated Solution File and Grading Rubric accompany each file and can be used together for efficient grading.
- **ExamView Test Banks** — ExamView is a powerful testing software package that allows you to create and administer printed, computer (LAN-based), and Internet exams. Our ExamView test banks include questions that correspond to the skills and concepts covered in this text, enabling students to generate detailed study guides that include page references for further review. The computer-based and Internet testing components allow students to take exams at their computers, and also save you time by grading each exam automatically.

Key Facts About Using This Book

Data Files are needed: To complete many of the lessons and end-of-unit assignments, students need to start from partially completed Data Files, which help students learn more efficiently. By starting out with a Data File, students can focus on performing specific tasks without having to create a file from scratch. All Data Files are available as part of the Instructor Resources. Students can also download Data Files themselves for free at cengagebrain.com. (For detailed instructions, go to www.cengage.com/ct/studentdownload.)

System requirements: This book was developed using Microsoft Office 2013 Professional running on Windows 8. Note that Windows 8 is not a requirement for the units on Microsoft Office; Office 2013 runs virtually the same on Windows 7 and Windows 8. Please see Important Notes for Windows 7 Users on the next page for more information.

Screen resolution: This book was written and tested on computers with monitors set at a resolution of 1366 x 768. If your screen shows more or less information than the figures in this book, your monitor is probably set at a higher or lower resolution. If you don't see something on your screen, you might have to scroll down or up to see the object identified in the figure.

Tell Us What You Think!

We want to hear from you! Please email your questions, comments, and suggestions to the Illustrated Series team at: **illustratedseries@cengage.com**

Important Notes for Windows 7 Users

The screenshots in this book show Microsoft Office 2013 running on Windows 8. However, if you are using Microsoft Windows 7, you can still use this book because Office 2013 runs virtually the same on both platforms. There are only two differences that you will encounter if you are using Windows 7. Read this section to understand the differences.

Dialog boxes

If you are a Windows 7 user, dialog boxes shown in this book will look slightly different than what you see on your screen. Dialog boxes for Windows 7 have a light blue title bar, instead of a medium blue title bar. However, beyond this superficial difference in appearance, the options in the dialog boxes across platforms are the same. For instance, the screen shots below show the Font dialog box running on Windows 7 and the Font dialog box running on Windows 8.

FIGURE 1: Font dialog box in Windows 7

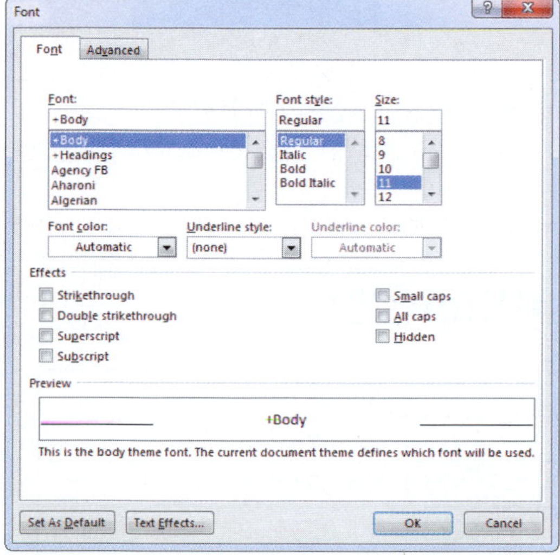

FIGURE 2: Font dialog box in Windows 8

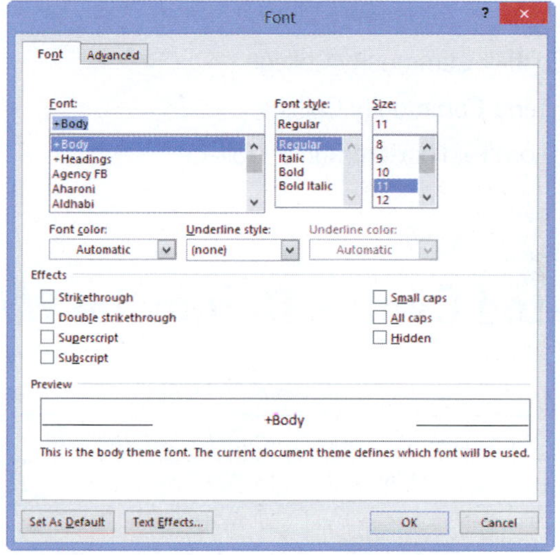

Alternate Steps for Starting an App in Windows 7

Nearly all of the steps in this book work exactly the same for Windows 7 users. However, starting an app (or program/application) requires different steps for Windows 7. The steps below show the Windows 7 steps for starting an app. (Note: Windows 7 alternate steps also appear in red Trouble boxes next to any step in the book that requires starting an app.)

Starting an app (or program/application) using Windows 7

1. Click the **Start button** on the taskbar to open the Start menu.
2. Click **All Programs**, then click the **Microsoft Office 2013 folder**. See Figure 3.
3. Click the app you want to use (such as **Excel 2013**).

FIGURE 3: Starting an app using Windows 7

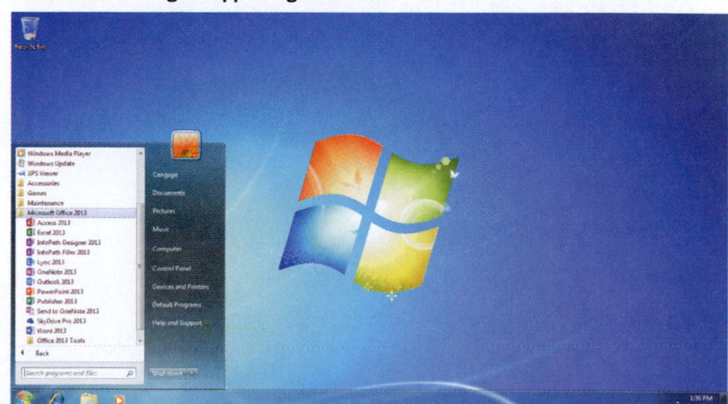

Acknowledgements

Author Acknowledgements

Thanks to Barbara Clemens for her insightful contributions, invaluable feedback, great humor, and patience. Thanks also to Christina Kling-Garrett for her encouragement and support in guiding and managing this project.

–Lynn Wermers

Advisory Board Acknowledgements

We thank our Illustrated Advisory Board who gave us their opinions and guided our decisions as we developed all of the new editions for Microsoft Office 2013.

Merlin Amirtharaj, Stanly Community College

Londo Andrews, J. Sargeant Reynolds Community College

Rachelle Hall, Glendale Community College

Terri Helfand, Chaffey Community College

Sheryl Lenhart, Terra Community College

Dr. Jose Nieves, Lord Fairfax Community College

Illustrated Course Guides for Microsoft Office 2013

Illustrated Course Guide: Microsoft Word 2013 Basic	978-1-285-09336-9
Illustrated Course Guide: Microsoft Word 2013 Intermediate	978-1-285-09337-6
Illustrated Course Guide: Microsoft Word 2013 Advanced	978-1-285-09338-3
Illustrated Course Guide: Microsoft Excel 2013 Basic	978-1-285-09339-0
Illustrated Course Guide: Microsoft Excel 2013 Intermediate	978-1-285-09340-6
Illustrated Course Guide: Microsoft Excel 2013 Advanced	978-1-285-09341-3
Illustrated Course Guide: Microsoft Access 2013 Basic	978-1-285-09342-0
Illustrated Course Guide: Microsoft Access 2013 Intermediate	978-1-285-09343-7
Illustrated Course Guide: Microsoft Access 2013 Advanced	978-1-285-09344-4
Illustrated Course Guide: Microsoft PowerPoint 2013 Basic	978-1-285-09345-1
Illustrated Course Guide: Microsoft PowerPoint 2013 Advanced	978-1-285-09346-8

Managing Workbook Data

CASE Kate Morgan, the vice president of sales at Quest Specialty Travel, asks for your help in analyzing yearly sales data from the Canadian branches. When the analysis is complete, she will distribute the workbook for branch managers to review.

Unit Objectives

After completing this unit, you will be able to:

- View and arrange worksheets
- Protect worksheets and workbooks
- Save custom views of a worksheet
- Add a worksheet background
- Prepare a workbook for distribution
- Insert hyperlinks
- Save a workbook for distribution
- Group worksheets

Files You Will Need

EX F-1.xlsx
EX F-2.xlsx
EX F-3.jpg
EX F-4.xlsx
EX F-5.xlsx
EX F-6.xlsx
EX F-7.xlsx
EX F-8.jpg
EX F-Classifications.xlsx
EX F-Expenses.xlsx
EX F-Hardware.xlsx
EX F-Logo.gif
EX F-Price Information.xlsx
EX F-Toronto Sales.xlsx

View and Arrange Worksheets

Learning Outcomes
- Compare worksheet data by arranging worksheets
- View and hide instances of a workbook

As you work with workbooks made up of multiple worksheets, you might need to compare data in the various sheets. To do this, you can view each worksheet in its own workbook window, called an **instance**, and display the windows in an arrangement that makes it easy to compare data. When you work with worksheets in separate windows, you are working with different views of the same workbook; the data itself remains in one file. **CASE** *Kate asks you to compare the monthly store sales totals for the Toronto and Vancouver branches. Because the sales totals are on different worksheets, you want to arrange the worksheets side by side in separate windows.*

STEPS

1. **Start Excel, open the file EX F-1.xlsx from the location where you store your Data Files, then save it as EX F-Store Sales**
2. **With the Toronto sheet active, click the VIEW tab, then click the New Window button in the Window group**
   There are now two instances of the Store Sales workbook open. You can see them when you place the mouse pointer over the Excel icon on the task bar: EX F-Store Sales.xlsx:1 and EX F-Store Sales.xlsx:2. The EX F-Store Sales.xlsx:2 window appears in the title bar, indicating that it's the active instance.
3. **Click the Vancouver sheet tab, click the VIEW tab, click the Switch Windows button in the Window group, then click EX F-Store Sales.xlsx:1**
   The EX F-Store Sales.xlsx:1 instance is active. The Toronto sheet is active in the EX F-Store Sales.xlsx:1 workbook, and the Vancouver sheet is active in the EX F-Store Sales.xlsx:2 workbook.
4. **Click the Arrange All button in the Window group**
   The Arrange Windows dialog box, shown in **FIGURE F-1**, lets you choose how to display the instances. You want to view the workbooks next to each other.
5. **Click the Vertical option button to select it, then click OK**
   The windows are arranged next to each other, as shown in **FIGURE F-2**. The second instance of the workbook opens at a zoom of 100%, not the 120% zoom of the workbook. You can activate a workbook by clicking one of its cells. You can also view only one of the workbooks by hiding the one you do not wish to see.
6. **Scroll horizontally to view the data in the EX F-Store Sales.xlsx:1 workbook, click anywhere in the EX F-Store Sales.xlsx:2 workbook, scroll horizontally to view the data in the EX F-Store Sales.xlsx:2 workbook, then click the Hide button in the Window group**
   When you hide the second instance, only the EX F-Store Sales.xlsx:1 workbook is visible.
7. **In the EX F-Store Sales.xlsx:1 window, click the Unhide button in the Window group; click EX F-Store Sales.xlsx:2 if necessary in the Unhide dialog box, then click OK**
   The EX F-Store Sales.xlsx:2 instance appears.
8. **Close the EX F-Store Sales.xlsx:2 instance, then maximize the Toronto worksheet in the EX F-Store Sales.xlsx workbook**
   Closing the EX F-Store Sales.xlsx:2 instance leaves only the first instance open. Its name in the title bar returns to EX F-Store Sales.xlsx.

QUICK TIP
You can use the View Side by Side button in the Window group to arrange the windows in their previous configuration. The Synchronous Scrolling button below the View Side by Side button is active by default, allowing you to scroll through the arranged worksheets simultaneously.

QUICK TIP
You can also hide a worksheet by right-clicking its sheet tab and clicking Hide on the shortcut menu. To display the hidden sheet, right-click any sheet tab, click Unhide, in the Unhide dialog box, select the sheet, then click OK.

FIGURE F-1: Arrange Windows dialog box

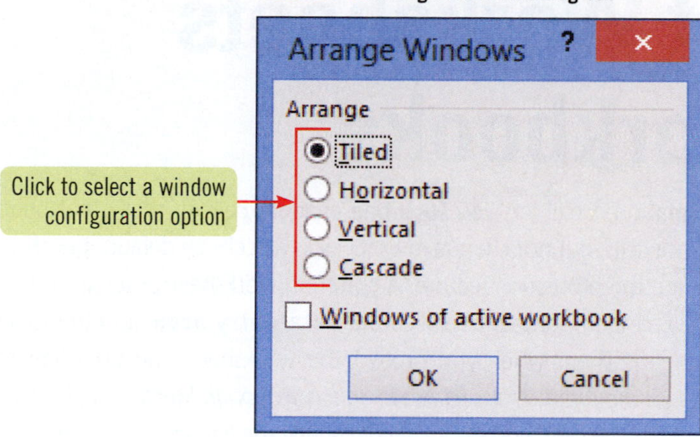

FIGURE F-2: Windows instances displayed vertically

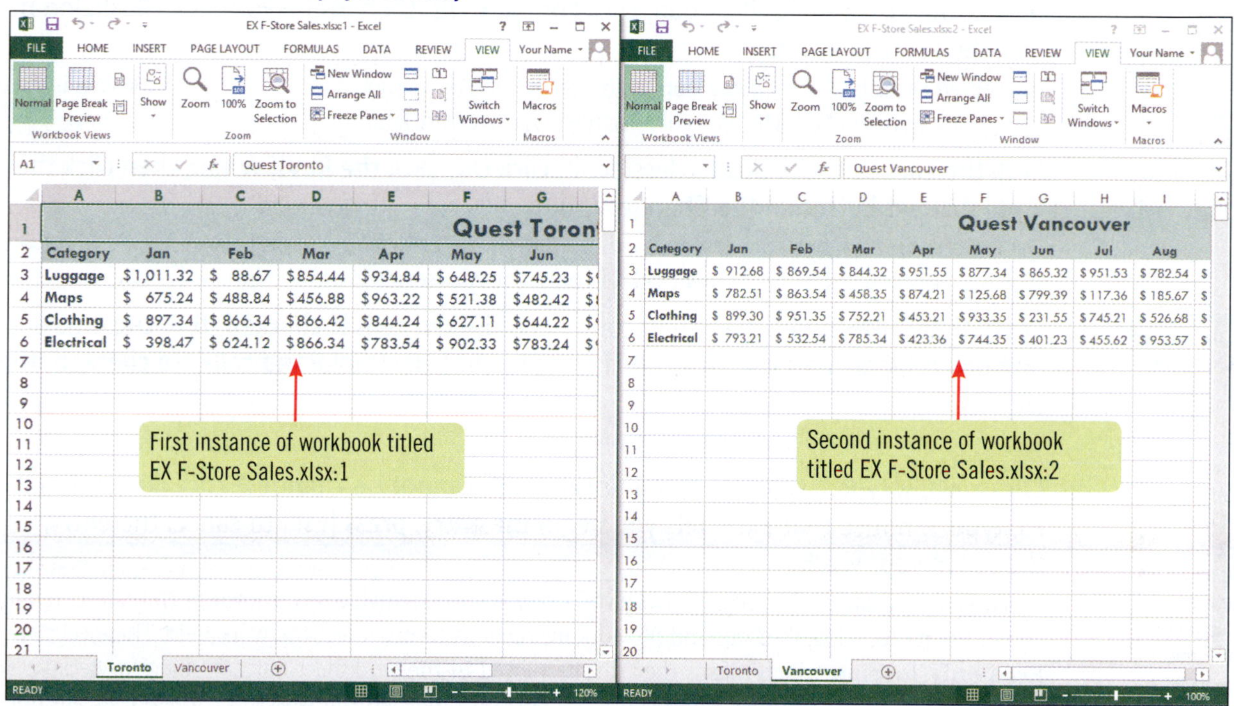

Splitting the worksheet into multiple panes

Excel lets you split the worksheet area into vertical and/or horizontal panes, so that you can click inside any one pane and scroll to locate information in that pane while the other panes remain in place, as shown in FIGURE F-3. To split a worksheet area into multiple panes, click a cell below and to the right of where you want the split to appear, click the VIEW tab, then click the Split button in the Window group. You can also split a worksheet into only two panes by selecting the row or column below or to the right of where you want the split to appear, clicking the VIEW tab, then clicking Split in the Window group. To remove a split, click the VIEW tab, then click Split in the Windows group.

FIGURE F-3: Worksheet split into two horizontal and two vertical panes

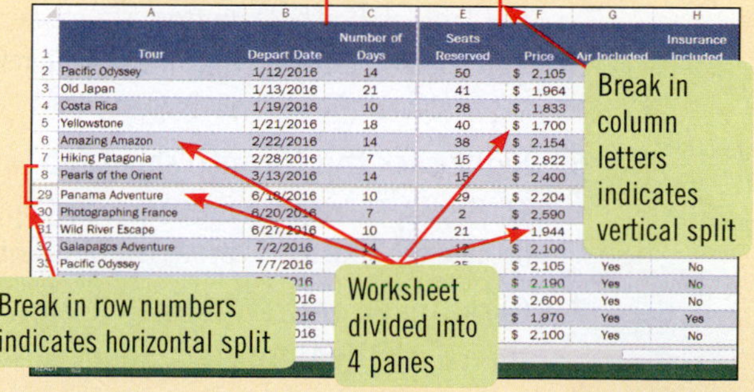

Excel 2013
UNIT F

Protect Worksheets and Workbooks

Learning Outcomes
- Protect worksheet data by locking cells
- Create a data entry area on a worksheet by unlocking cells
- Protect a workbook using Read-only format

To protect sensitive information, Excel lets you **lock** one or more cells so that other people can view the values and formulas in those cells, but not change it. Excel locks all cells by default, but this locking does not take effect until you activate the protection feature. A common worksheet protection strategy is to unlock cells in which data will be changed, sometimes called the **data entry area**, and to lock cells in which the data should not be changed. Then, when you protect the worksheet, the unlocked areas can still be changed. CASE *Because the Toronto sales figures for January through March have been finalized, Kate asks you to protect that worksheet area. That way, users cannot change the figures for those months.*

STEPS

QUICK TIP
You can also lock a cell by clicking the Format button in the Cells group of the HOME tab, then clicking Lock Cell on the shortcut menu.

1. **On the Toronto sheet, select the range E3:M6, click the HOME tab, click the Format button in the Cells group, click Format Cells, then in the Format Cells dialog box click the Protection tab**

   The Locked check box in the Protection tab is already checked, as shown in FIGURE F-4. All the cells in a new workbook start out locked. The protection feature is inactive by default.

2. **Click the Locked check box to deselect it, click OK, click the REVIEW tab, then click the Protect Sheet button in the Changes group**

   The Protect Sheet dialog box opens, as shown in FIGURE F-5. The default options protect the worksheet while allowing users to select locked or unlocked cells only. You choose not to use a password.

QUICK TIP
To hide any formulas that you don't want to be visible, select the cells that contain formulas that you want to hide, open the Format Cells dialog box, then click the Hidden check box on the Protection tab to select it. The formula will be hidden after the worksheet is protected.

3. **Verify that Protect worksheet and contents of locked cells is checked, that the password text box is blank, and that Select locked cells and Select unlocked cells are checked, then click OK**

   You are ready to test the new worksheet protection.

4. **Click cell B3, type 1 to confirm that locked cells cannot be changed, click OK, click cell F3, type 1, notice that Excel lets you begin the entry, press [Esc] to cancel the entry, then save your work**

   When you try change a locked cell on a protected worksheet, a dialog box, shown in FIGURE F-6, reminds you of the protected cell's status and provides instructions to unprotect the worksheet. These cells are in **Read-only format**, which means they can be viewed in the worksheet but not changed. Because you unlocked the cells in columns E through M before you protected the worksheet, these cells are not in read-only format and you can change these cells. You decide to add more protection by protecting the workbook from changes to the workbook's structure, but decide not to require a password.

5. **Click the Protect Workbook button in the Changes group, in the Protect Structure and Windows dialog box, make sure the Structure check box is selected, verify that the password text box is blank, then click OK**

   The Protect Workbook button is a toggle, which means it's like an on/off switch. When it is green, the workbook is protected. Clicking it again removes the green color indicating the protection is removed from the workbook. You are ready to test the new workbook protection.

6. **Right-click the Toronto sheet tab**

   The Insert, Delete, Rename, Move or Copy, Tab Color, Hide, and Unhide menu options are not available because the structure is protected. You decide to remove the workbook and worksheet protections.

7. **Click the Protect Workbook button in the Changes group to turn off the protection, then click the Unprotect Sheet button to remove the worksheet protection**

FIGURE F-4: Protection tab in Format Cells dialog box

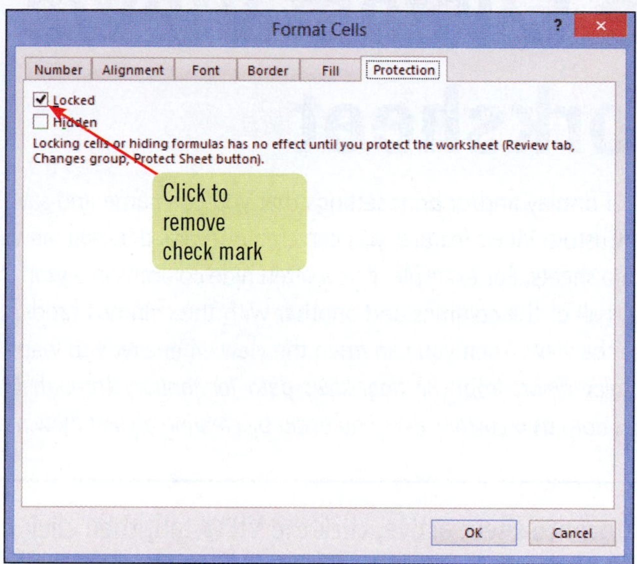

FIGURE F-5: Protect Sheet dialog box

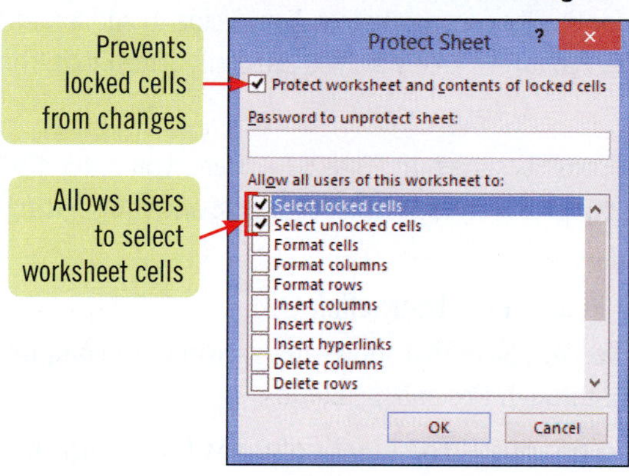

FIGURE F-6: Reminder of protected worksheet status

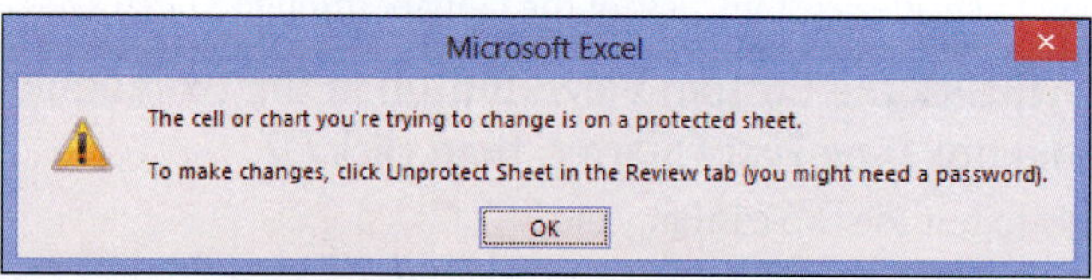

Freezing rows and columns

As the rows and columns of a worksheet fill up with data, you might want to Freeze panes to hold headers in place so you can see them as you scroll through the worksheet. Freezing panes is similar to splitting panes except that the panes do not move, so you can keep column or row labels in view as you scroll. **Panes** are the columns and rows that **freeze**, or remain in place, while you scroll through your worksheet. To freeze panes, click the first cell in the area you want to scroll, click the VIEW tab, click the Freeze Panes button in the Window group, then click Freeze Panes. Excel freezes the columns to the left and the rows above the selected cell as shown in FIGURE F-7. You can also select Freeze Top Row or Freeze First Column to freeze the top row or left worksheet column. To unfreeze panes, click the VIEW tab, click Freeze panes, then click Unfreeze Panes.

FIGURE F-7: Worksheet with top row and left column frozen

	A	D	E	F	G	H
1	Tour	Seat Capacity	Seats Reserved	Price	Air Included	Insurance Included
8	Pearls of the Orient	45	15	$ 2,400	Yes	No
9	Silk Road Travels	23	19	$ 2,031	Yes	Yes
10	Photographing France	20	20	$ 1,541	Yes	Yes
11	Green Adventures in Ecuador	25	22	$ 2,450	No	No
12	African National Parks	12	10	$ 3,115	Yes	Yes
13	Experience Cambodia	35	21	$ 2,441	Yes	No
14	Old Japan	47	30	$ 1,900	Yes	No
15	Costa Rica	30	20	$ 2,800	Yes	Yes
16	Yellowstone	51	31	$ 1,652	Yes	Yes
17	Amazing Amazon	43	30	$ 2,133	No	No
18	Catalonia Adventure	51	30	$ 2,587	Yes	No
19	Treasures of Ethiopia	41	15	$ 1,638	Yes	Yes
20	Monasteries of Bulgaria	19	11	$ 1,663	Yes	Yes
21	Biking in France	12	10	$ 1,635	No	No
22	Magnificent Montenegro	48	4	$ 1,890	No	No
23	Catalonia Adventure	51	15	$ 2,100	Yes	No

2016 Tours

READY

Break in column letters and row numbers indicates first column and first row are frozen

Excel 2013
UNIT F

Learning Outcomes
- Create different views of worksheet data using custom views
- Display different views of worksheet data using custom views

Save Custom Views of a Worksheet

A **view** is a set of display and/or print settings that you can name and save, then access at a later time. By using the Excel Custom Views feature, you can create several different views of a worksheet without having to create separate sheets. For example, if you often hide columns in a worksheet, you can create two views, one that displays all of the columns and another with the columns hidden. You set the worksheet display first, then name the view. Then you can open the view whenever you want. **CASE** *Because Kate wants to generate a sales report from the final sales data for January through March, she asks you to save the first-quarter sales data as a custom view. You begin by creating a view showing all of the worksheet data.*

STEPS

1. **With the Toronto sheet active, click the VIEW tab, then click the Custom Views button in the Workbook Views group**
   The Custom Views dialog box opens. Any previously defined views for the active worksheet appear in the Views box. No views are defined for the Toronto worksheet. You decide to add a named view for the current view, which shows all the worksheet columns. That way, you can easily return to it from any other views you create.

QUICK TIP
To delete views from the active worksheet, select the view in the Custom Views dialog box, then click Delete.

2. **Click Add**
   The Add View dialog box opens, as shown in **FIGURE F-8**. Here, you enter a name for the view and decide whether to include print settings and hidden rows, columns, and filter settings. You want to include these options, which are already selected.
3. **In the Name box, type Year Sales, then click OK**
   You have created a view called Year Sales that shows all the worksheet columns. You want to set up another view that will hide the April through December columns.
4. **Drag across the column headings to select columns E through M, right-click the selected area, then click Hide on the shortcut menu**
   You are ready to create a custom view of the January through March sales data.
5. **Click cell A1, click the Custom Views button in the Workbook Views group, click Add, in the Name box type First Quarter, then click OK**
   You are ready to test the two custom views.

TROUBLE
If you receive the message "Some view settings could not be applied", turn off worksheet protection by clicking the Unprotect Sheet button in the Changes group of the REVIEW tab.

6. **Click the Custom Views button in the Workbook Views group, click Year Sales in the Views list, then click Show**
   The Year Sales custom view displays all of the months' sales data. Now you are ready to test the First Quarter custom view.
7. **Click the Custom Views button in the Workbook Views group, then with First Quarter in the Custom Views dialog box selected, click Show**
   Only the January through March sales figures appear on the screen, as shown in **FIGURE F-9**.
8. **Return to the Year Sales view, then save your work**

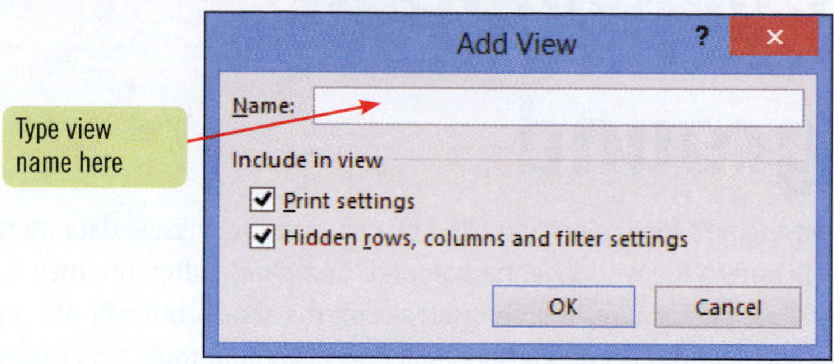

FIGURE F-8: Add View dialog box

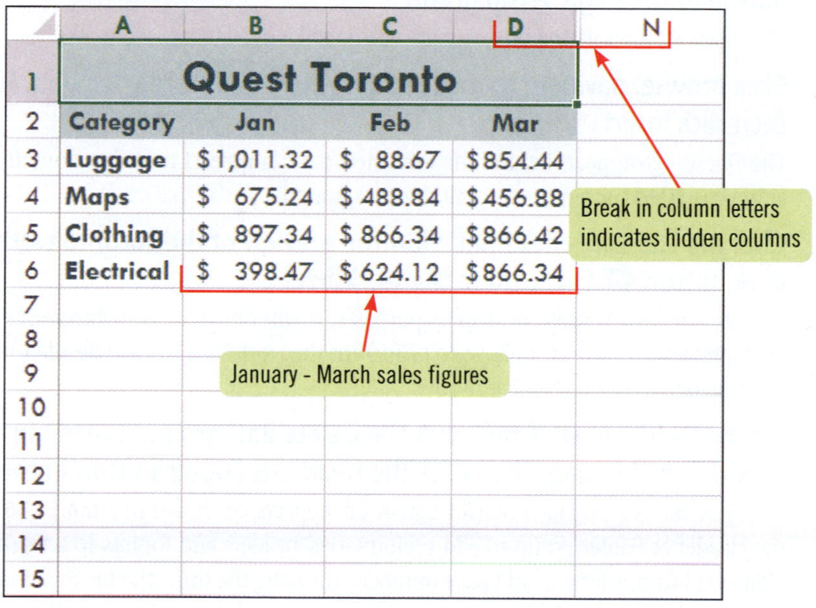

FIGURE F-9: First Quarter view

Using Page Break Preview

The vertical and horizontal dashed lines in the Normal view of worksheets represent page breaks. Excel automatically inserts a page break when your worksheet data doesn't fit on one page. These page breaks are **dynamic**, which means they adjust automatically when you insert or delete rows and columns and when you change column widths or row heights. Everything to the left of the first vertical dashed line and above the first horizontal dashed line is printed on the first page. You can manually add or remove page breaks by clicking the PAGE LAYOUT tab, clicking the Breaks button in the Page Setup group, then clicking the appropriate command. You can also view and change page breaks manually by clicking the VIEW tab, then clicking the Page Break Preview button in the Workbook Views group, or by clicking the Page Break Preview button on the status bar, then clicking OK. You can drag the blue page break lines to the desired location. Some cells may temporarily display ##### while you are in Page Break Preview. If you drag a page break to the right to include more data on a page, Excel shrinks the type to fit the data on that page. To exit Page Break Preview, click the Normal button in the Workbook Views group.

Add a Worksheet Background

Learning Outcomes
- Add a background to a worksheet
- Add a watermark to a worksheet

In addition to using a theme's font colors and fills, you can make your Excel data more attractive on the screen by adding a picture to the worksheet background. Companies often use their logo as a worksheet background. A worksheet background will be displayed on the screen but will not print with the worksheet. If you want to add a worksheet background that appears on printouts, you can add a **watermark**, a translucent background design that prints behind your data. To add a watermark, you add the image to the worksheet header or footer. CASE *Kate asks you to add the Quest logo to the printed background of the Toronto worksheet. But first she wants to see it as a nonprinting background.*

STEPS

1. **With the Toronto sheet active, click the PAGE LAYOUT tab, then click the Background button in the Page Setup group**

   The Insert Pictures dialog box opens.

2. **Click Browse, navigate to the location where you store your Data Files, click EX F-Logo.gif, then click Insert**

   The Quest logo appears behind the worksheet data. It appears twice horizontally on your screen because the graphic is **tiled**, or repeated, to fill the background.

3. **Click the FILE tab, click Print, view the preview of the Toronto worksheet, then click the Back button to return to the worksheet**

   Because the logo is only for display purposes, it will not print with the worksheet, so is not visible in the Print preview. You want the logo to print with the worksheet, so you decide to remove the background and add the logo to the worksheet header.

4. **On the PAGE LAYOUT tab, click the Delete Background button in the Page Setup group, click the INSERT tab, then click the Header & Footer button in the Text group**

   The HEADER & FOOTER TOOLS DESIGN tab appears, as shown in FIGURE F-10. You can use the buttons in the Header & Footer group to add preformatted headers and footers to a worksheet. The Header & Footer Elements buttons let you add page numbers, the date, the time, the file location, names, and pictures to the header or footer. The Navigation group buttons move the insertion point from the header to the footer and back. You want to add a picture to the header.

5. **Click in the center section of the header to place the insertion point, click the Picture button in the Header & Footer Elements group, click Browse, then navigate to the location where you store your Data Files, click EX F-Logo.gif, then click Insert**

   A code representing a picture, "&[Picture]", appears in the center of the header.

6. **Click cell A1, then click the Normal button on the Status Bar**

   You want to scale the worksheet data to print on one page.

7. **Click the PAGE LAYOUT tab, click the Width list arrow in the Scale to Fit group, click 1 page, click the Height list arrow in the Scale to Fit group, click 1 page, then preview the worksheet**

   Your worksheet should look like FIGURE F-11.

8. **Return to the worksheet, click the HOME tab, then save the workbook**

QUICK TIP
You can also scale the worksheet to fit on one page by clicking the FILE tab, clicking Print, clicking the No Scaling list arrow, then clicking Fit Sheet on One Page.

FIGURE F-10: HEADER & FOOTER TOOLS DESIGN tab

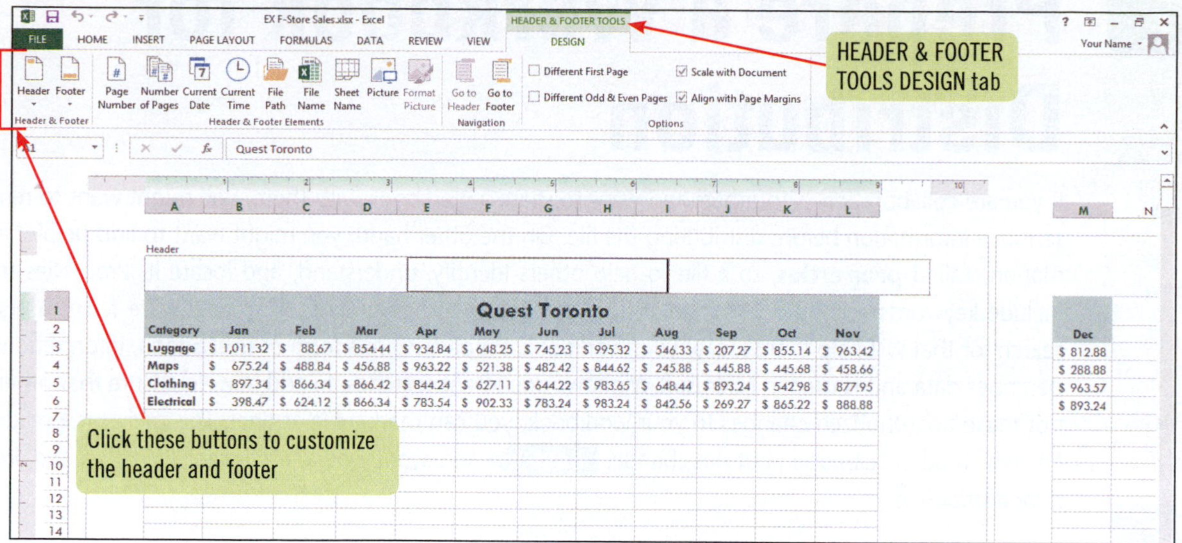

FIGURE F-11: Preview of Toronto worksheet with logo in the background

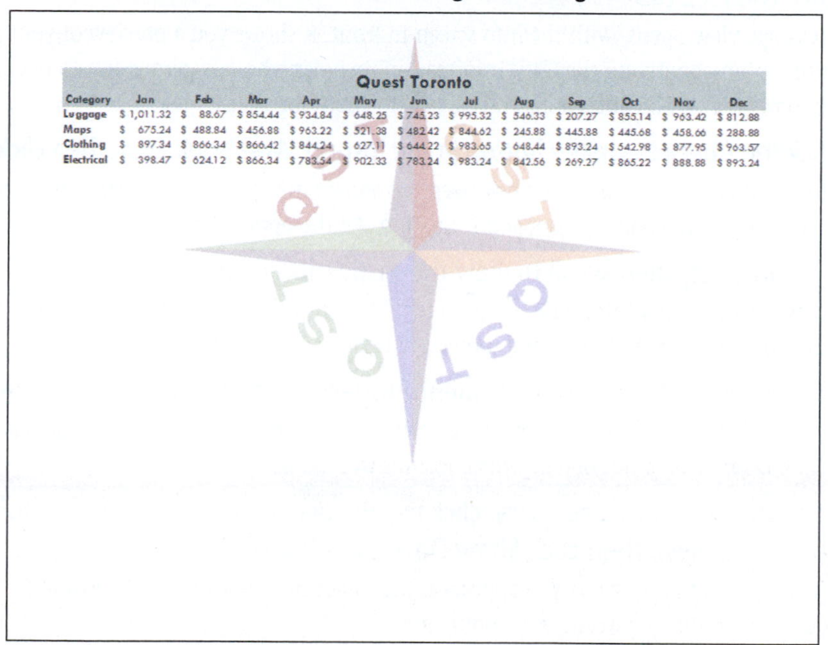

Working with Screenshots in Excel

You can paste an image of an open file, called a **screenshot**, into an Excel workbook or another Office document. This pastes the screenshot into your document as an image that you can move, copy, or edit. To insert a screenshot, click the INSERT tab, click the Screenshot button in the Illustrations group to see a gallery of other currently open windows, then click on one of the available windows in the gallery. This pastes a screen shot of the window you clicked into the current Excel document. You can also click the Screen Clipping button in the gallery to select and paste an area from an open window. Once you have created a screenshot and positioned it in your worksheet, you can modify it using tools on the PICTURE TOOLS FORMAT tab. This tab appears when the screenshot object is selected. You can change the overall visual style of the image by clicking the More button in the Picture Styles group, then clicking a style. In the Picture Styles group you can also use the Picture Effects button to apply a visual effect to the image, the Picture Border button to enhance the border surrounding the image, and the Picture Layout button to convert the image to a SmartArt Graphic. The Picture Tools tab also has other tools to correct images. For example, you can sharpen and soften an image and make corrections for brightness and contrast by clicking the Corrections button in the Adjust group. Clicking a choice in the Sharpen/Soften section allows you to change the visual acuity of the image and choosing an option in the Brightness/Contrast section adjusts the lightness of an image.

Prepare a Workbook for Distribution

Learning Outcomes
- Add keywords to a worksheet using the Document Panel
- Review a file for problems using the Inspect Document feature
- Protect a workbook by using Mark as Final status

If you are collaborating with others and want to share a workbook with them, you might want to remove sensitive information before distributing the file. On the other hand, you might want to add helpful information, called **properties**, to a file to help others identify, understand, and locate it. Properties might include keywords, the author's name, a title, the status, and comments. **Keywords** are terms users can search for that will help them locate your workbook. Properties are a form of **metadata**, information that describes data and is used in Microsoft Windows document searches. In addition, to ensure that others do not make unauthorized changes to your workbook, you can mark a file as final. This makes it a read-only file, which others can open but not change. **CASE** *Kate wants you to protect the workbook and prepare it for distribution.*

STEPS

1. **Click the FILE tab**

   Backstage view opens, with the Info screen in front. It shows you a preview of your printed worksheet and information about your file. This information includes who has permission to open, copy, or change your workbook. It also includes tools you can use to check for security issues.

> **TROUBLE**
> If asked to save your file, click Yes.

2. **Click the Check for Issues button in the Inspect Workbook area, then click Inspect Document**

   The Document Inspector dialog box opens, as shown in FIGURE F-12. It lists items from which you can have Excel evaluate hidden or personal information. All the options are selected by default.

3. **Click Inspect, then scroll to view the inspection results**

   Areas with personal information have a red "!" in front of them. Headers and footers is also flagged. You want to keep the file's header and footer and remove personal information.

> **QUICK TIP**
> You can view a file's summary information by clicking the FILE tab and reviewing the information on the right side of the information area.

4. **Click Remove All next to Document Properties and Personal Information, then click Close**

   You decide to add keywords to help the sales managers find the worksheet. The search words "Toronto" or "Vancouver" would be good keywords for this workbook.

5. **Click the File tab if necessary, click the Properties list arrow on the right side of Backstage view, then click Show Document Panel**

   The Document Properties Panel appears at the top of the worksheet, as shown in FIGURE F-13. You decide to add a title, status, keywords, and comments.

> **QUICK TIP**
> If asked if you want to turn on AutoComplete, click Yes.

6. **In the Title text box type Store Sales, in the Keywords text box type Toronto Vancouver store sales, in the Status text box type DRAFT, then in the Comments text box type The first-quarter figures are final., then click the Close button on the Document Properties Panel**

   You are ready to mark the workbook as final.

7. **Click the FILE tab, click the Protect Workbook button in the Info area, click Mark as Final, click OK, then click OK again**

   "[Read-Only]" appears in the title bar indicating the workbook is saved as a read-only file. A yellow bar also appears below the tabs indicating the workbook is marked as final. The yellow bar also has an Edit Anyway button.

8. **Click the HOME tab, click cell B3, type 1 to confirm that the cell cannot be changed, click the Edit Anyway button above the formula bar, then save the workbook**

   Marking a workbook as final is not a strong form of workbook protection because a workbook recipient can remove this Final status. By clicking Edit Anyway, you remove the read-only status, which makes the workbook editable again.

FIGURE F-12: Document Inspector dialog box

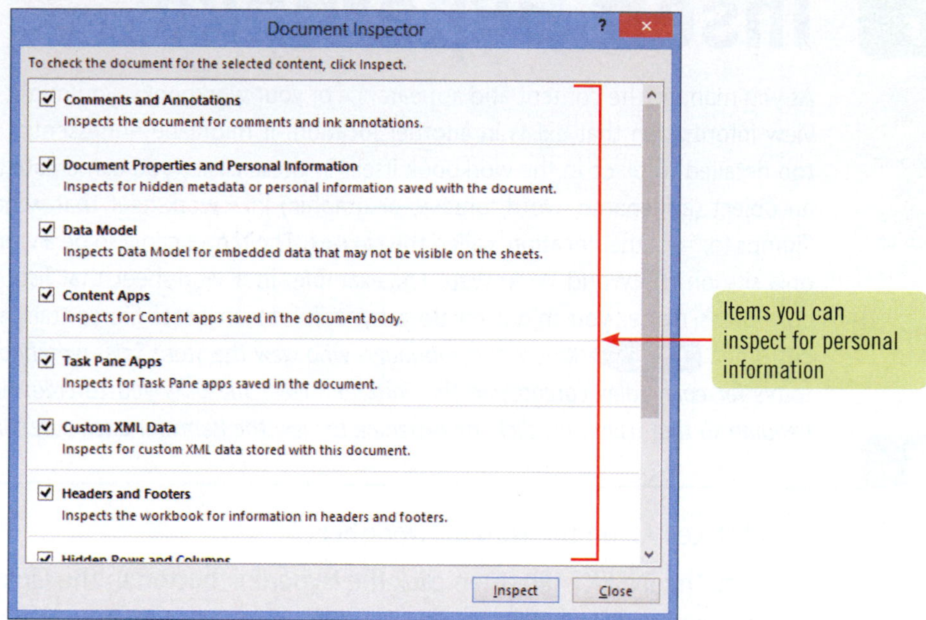

FIGURE F-13: Document Properties panel

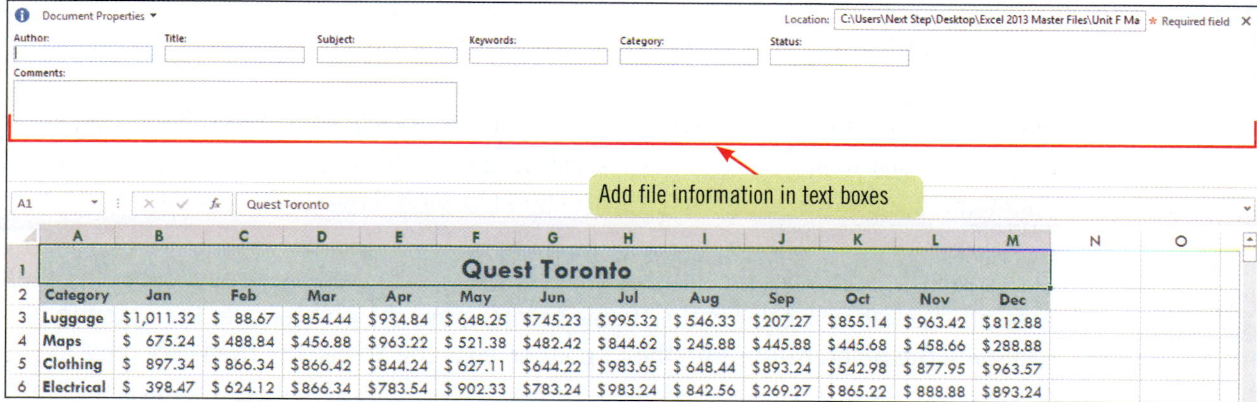

Sharing a workbook using SkyDrive

Once you set up a Windows Live account you can save your Excel files "to the cloud" (meaning on the Internet) using SkyDrive. This allows you to access your Excel files from any computer and share Excel files with others. When saving an Excel file to the cloud, click the FILE tab, click Save As, then click the SkyDrive, which is the default location and the first location listed under Places on the Save As tab. After you save an Excel file to your SkyDrive, you can share it by clicking the FILE tab, clicking Share, entering the email addresses of the people you wish to invite to share the file, and clicking Share. An email with a link to the Excel file on your SkyDrive will be sent to the addresses you entered. The recipients can open and edit the file using the Excel Web App. The Share option also allows you to get a link to your Excel file on your SkyDrive, post a workbook to social networks, and email your workbook.

Insert Hyperlinks

Learning Outcomes
- Link to workbooks and websites by adding hyperlinks
- Add screentips to a hyperlink

As you manage the content and appearance of your workbooks, you might want the workbook user to view information that exists in another location. It might be nonessential information or data that is too detailed to place in the workbook itself. In these cases, you can create a hyperlink. A **hyperlink** is an object (a filename, word, phrase, or graphic) in a worksheet that, when you click it, displays, or "jumps to," another location, called the **target**. The target can also be a worksheet, another document, or a site on the World Wide Web. For example, in a worksheet that lists customer invoices, at each customer's name, you might create a hyperlink to an Excel file containing payment terms for each customer. **CASE** *Kate wants managers who view the Store Sales workbook to be able to view the item totals for each sales category in the Toronto sheet. She asks you to create a hyperlink at the Category heading so that users can click the hyperlink to view the items for each category.*

STEPS

1. **Click cell A2 on the Toronto worksheet**
2. **Click the INSERT tab, then click the Hyperlink button in the Links group**

   The Insert Hyperlink dialog box opens, as shown in FIGURE F-14. The icons under "Link to" on the left side of the dialog box let you select the type of location to where you want the link jump: an existing file or Web page, a place in the same document, a new document, or an e-mail address. Because you want the link to display an already-existing document, the selected first icon, Existing File or Web Page, is correct, so you won't have to change it.
3. **Click the Look in list arrow, navigate to the location where you store your Data Files if necessary, then click EX F-Toronto Sales.xlsx in the file list**

   The filename you selected and its path appear in the Address text box. This is the document users will see when they click the hyperlink. You can also specify the ScreenTip that users see when they hold the pointer over the hyperlink.
4. **Click the ScreenTip button, type Items in each category, click OK, then click OK again**

   Cell A2 now contains underlined yellow text, indicating that it is a hyperlink. The color of a hyperlink depends on the worksheet theme colors. You need to change the text color of the hyperlink text so it is visible on the gray background.
5. **Click the HOME tab, click the Font Color list arrow in the Font group, click the Green, Accent 5, Darker 50% color in the Theme Colors, move the pointer over the Category text, until the pointer turns into the pointer, view the ScreenTip, then click once**

   After you click, the EX F-Toronto Sales workbook opens, displaying the Sales sheet, as shown in FIGURE F-15.
6. **Close the EX F-Toronto Sales workbook, click Don't Save if necessary, then save the EX F-Store Sales workbook**

QUICK TIP
To remove a hyperlink or change its target, right-click it, then click Remove Hyperlink or Edit Hyperlink.

QUICK TIP
If you link to a Web page, you must be connected to the Internet to test the link.

Working with Headers and Footers

You may want to add a different header or footer to the first page of your worksheet. You can do this by clicking the INSERT tab on the Ribbon, clicking the Header & Footer button in the Text group, clicking the HEADER & FOOTER TOOLS DESIGN tab on the Ribbon, then clicking the Different First Page check box in the Options group to select it. A text indicator (that changes to 'First Page Header' from 'Header') appears in the header/footer area on the Page Layout view, indicating that you are creating a different first page header/footer. You can also have different headers or footers on odd and even pages of your worksheet by clicking the Different Odd & Even Pages check box to select it. In the Options group of the HEADER & FOOTER TOOLS DESIGN tab, you can also change the header and footer size by clicking the Scale with Document check box to select it, if you want the headers/footers to use the same scale and font size that are used in the worksheet. You can use the Align with Page Margins check box to place the header or footer at the margins of the worksheet. You can also add the name of the worksheet by clicking the Sheet Name button in the Header and Footer Elements group of the HEADER & FOOTER TOOLS DESIGN tab.

FIGURE F-14: Insert Hyperlink dialog box

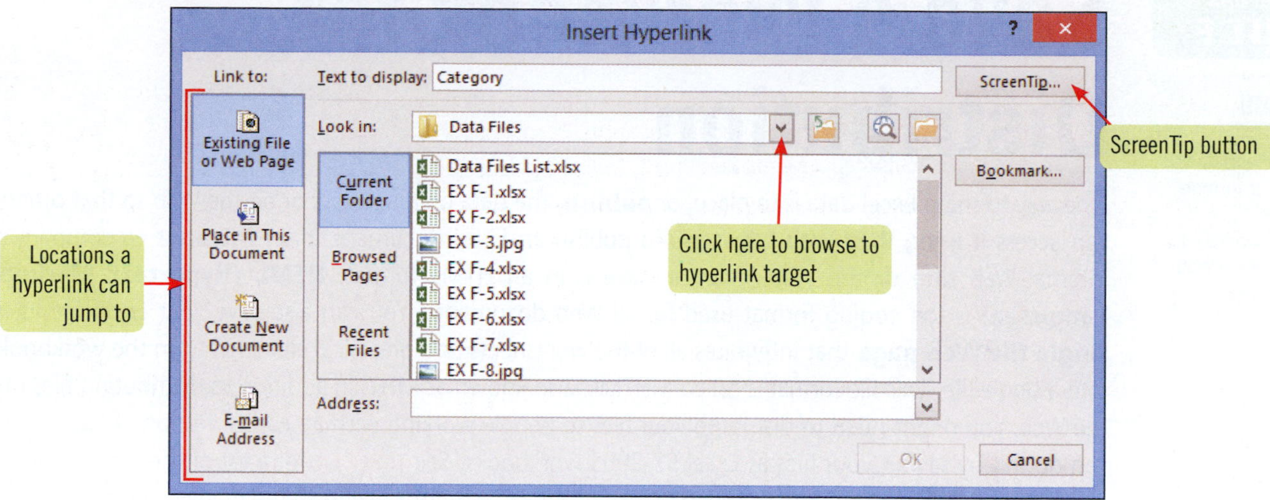

FIGURE F-15: Target document

	A	B	C
1	Quest Toronto		
2	Travel Store Sales		
3	Item	Total Sales	Category
4	PopOut Maps	$ 1,729.81	Maps
5	Smart Packing Books	$ 3,874.22	Maps
6	Airport Guides	$ 4,821.33	Maps
7	Pack It Guides	$ 1,114.65	Maps
8	Computer Case	$ 1,855.65	Luggage
9	Backpack	$ 1,836.91	Luggage
10	Plane Slippers	$ 1,099.15	Clothing
11	Travel Socks	$ 1,108.16	Clothing
12	Men's Sandals	$ 1,103.14	Clothing
13	Women's Sandals	$ 1,954.19	Clothing
14	Hats	$ 975.44	Clothing
15	Men's T-Shirts	$ 3,111.76	Clothing
16	Women's T-Shirts	$ 1,108.41	Clothing
17	Converter	$ 1,798.53	Electrical
18	Phone Charger	$ 1,108.41	Electrical

Sales

READY

Using research tools

You can access resources online and locally on your computer using the Research task pane. To open the Research task pane, click the REVIEW tab, then click the Research button in the Proofing group. The Search for text box in the Research pane lets you enter a research topic. The Research pane has a drop-down list of the resources available to search for your topic. You can use this list to access resources such as a thesaurus, a dictionary, financial web sites, and research web sites. You can also access a Thesaurus task pane using the Thesaurus button on the REVIEW tab in the Proofing group.

Excel 2013
UNIT F

Learning Outcomes
- Save a workbook in earlier formats of Excel
- Save a workbook in single file Web page format

Save a Workbook for Distribution

One way to share Excel data is to place, or **publish**, the data on a network or on the Web so that others can access it using their Web browsers. To publish an Excel document to an **intranet** (a company's internal Web site) or the Web, you can save it in an HTML format. **HTML (Hypertext Markup Language)** is the coding format used for all Web documents. You can also save your Excel file as a **single-file Web page** that integrates all of the worksheets and graphical elements from the workbook into a single file. This file format is called MHTML, also known as MHT. In addition to distributing files on the Web, you might need to distribute your files to people working with an earlier version of Excel. You can do this by saving your files as Excel 97-2003 workbooks. See TABLE F-1 for a list of the most popular formats. **CASE** *Kate asks you to create a workbook version that managers running an earlier Excel version can use. She also asks you to save the EX F-Store Sales workbook in MHT format so she can publish it on the Quest intranet.*

STEPS

QUICK TIP
You can also export an Excel file into another format by clicking the FILE tab, clicking Export, clicking Change File Type, then clicking a file type.

1. **Click the FILE tab, click Save As, click Browse, navigate to the location where you store your Data Files, click the Save as type list arrow in the Save As dialog box, click Excel 97-2003 Workbook (*.xls), then click Save**
   The Compatibility Checker dialog box opens. It alerts you to the features that will be lost or converted by saving in the earlier format. Some Excel 2013 features are not available in earlier versions of Excel.
2. **Click Continue, close the workbook, then reopen the EX F-Store Sales.xls workbook**
   "[Compatibility Mode]" appears in the title bar, as shown in FIGURE F-16. Compatibility mode prevents you from including Excel features in your workbook that are not supported in Excel 97-2003 workbooks. To exit compatibility mode, you need to convert your file to the Excel 2013 format.

QUICK TIP
To ensure that your workbook is displayed the same way on different computer platforms and screen settings, you can publish it in PDF format by clicking File, clicking Export, then clicking Create PDF/XPS Document. TABLE F-1 provides additional information about the PDF format.

3. **Click the FILE tab, click Info, click the Convert button, click Save, click Yes if you are asked if you want to replace the existing file, then click Yes to close and reopen the workbook**
   The title bar no longer displays "[Compatibility Mode]" and the file has been changed to the .xlsx format. You still need to save the file for Web distribution.
4. **Click the FILE tab, click Save As, in the Save As dialog box navigate to the location where you store your Data Files if necessary, change the filename to sales, then click the Save as type list arrow and click Single File Web Page (*.mht, *.mhtml)**
   The Save as type list box indicates that the workbook is to be saved as a Single File Web Page, which is in MHTML or MHT format. To avoid problems when publishing your pages to a Web server, it is best to use lowercase characters, omit special characters and spaces, and limit your filename to eight characters with an additional three-character extension.
5. **Click Save, then click Yes**
   The dialog box indicated that some features may not be retained in the Web page file. Excel saves the workbook as an MHT file in the location you specified. The MHT file is open on your screen. See FIGURE F-17. It's a good idea to open an MHT file in your browser to see how it will look to viewers.

QUICK TIP
Your browser may display a message telling you that active content is restricted. Active content is interactive and usually in the form of small programs. These programs can present a security threat and you should allow the active content only if you trust the source of the file.

6. **Close the sales.mht file in Excel, start your browser, open the sales.mht file by double-clicking it in the location where you store your Data Files, click the Vancouver sheet tab, then close your browser window**

FIGURE F-16: Workbook in compatibility mode

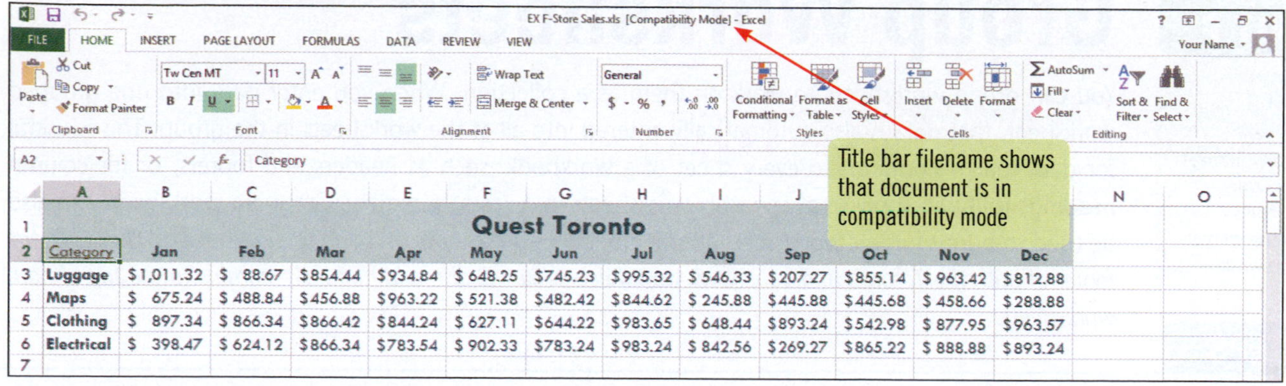

FIGURE F-17: Workbook saved as a single file Web page

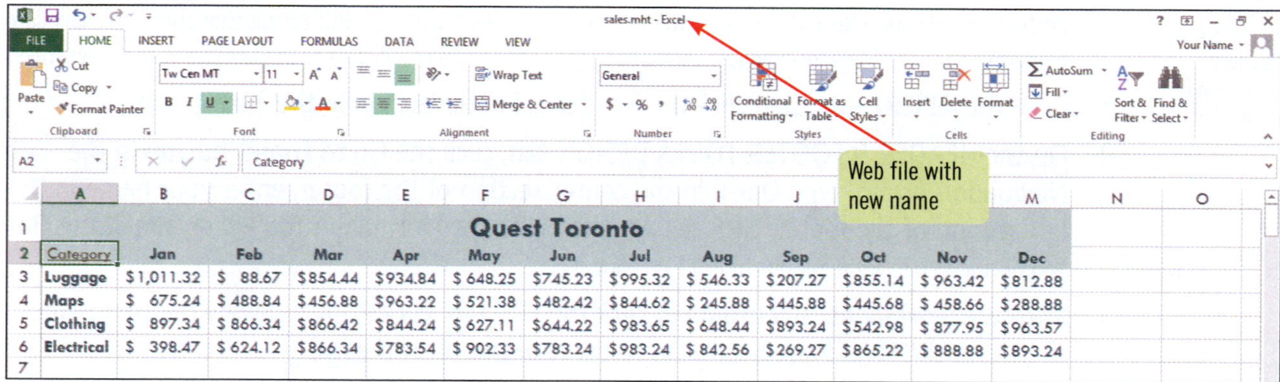

TABLE F-1: Workbook formats

type of file	file extension(s)	used for
Macro-enabled workbook	.xlsm	Files that contain macros
Excel 97 – 2003 workbook	.xls	Working with people using older versions of Excel
Single file Web page	.mht, .mhtml	Web sites with multiple pages and graphics
Web page	.htm, .html	Simple single-page Web sites
Excel template	.xltx	Excel files that will be reused with small changes
Excel macro-enabled template	.xltm	Excel files that will be used again and contain macros
PDF (Portable document format)	.pdf	Files with formatting that needs to be preserved
XML paper specification	.xps	Files with formatting that needs to be preserved and files that need to be shared
OpenDocument spreadsheet	.ods	Files created with OpenOffice

Understanding Excel file formats

The default file format for Excel 2013 files is the Office Open XML format, which supports all Excel features. This has been the default file format of Office files since Microsoft Office 2007. This format stores Excel files in small XML components that are zipped for compression, making the files smaller. The most often used format, .xlsx, does not support macros. **Macros**, programmed instructions that perform tasks, can be a security risk. If your worksheet contains macros, you need to save it with an extension of .xlsm so the macros can function in the workbook. If you use a workbook's text and formats repeatedly, you might want to save it as a template with the extension .xltx. If your template contains macros, you need to save it with the .xltm extension.

Group Worksheets

Learning Outcomes
- Group worksheets
- Edit grouped worksheets
- Add custom margins to worksheets

You can group worksheets to work on them as a collection. When you enter data into one grouped worksheet, that data is also automatically entered into all of the worksheets in the group. This is useful for data that is common to every sheet of a workbook, such as headers and footers, or for column headings that will apply to all monthly worksheets in a yearly summary. Grouping worksheets can also be used to print multiple worksheets at one time. **CASE** *Kate asks you to add the text "Quest" to the footer of both the Toronto and Vancouver worksheets. You will also add half-inch margins to the top of both worksheets.*

STEPS

1. **Open the EX F-Store Sales.xlsx file from the location where you store your Data Files**
2. **With the Toronto sheet active, press and hold [Shift], click the Vancouver sheet, then release [Shift]**
   Both sheet tabs are selected, and the title bar now contains "[Group]", indicating that the worksheets are grouped together. Now any changes you make to the Toronto sheet will also be made to the Vancouver sheet.
3. **Click the INSERT tab, then click the Header & Footer button in the Text group**
4. **On the HEADER & FOOTER TOOLS DESIGN tab, click the Go to Footer button in the Navigation group, type Quest in the center section of the footer, enter your name in the left section of the footer, click cell A1, then click the Normal button on the Status Bar**
   You decide to check the footers in Print Preview.
5. **With the worksheets still grouped, click the FILE tab, click Print, preview the first page, then click the Next Page button to preview the second page**
   Because the worksheets are grouped, both pages contain the footer with "Quest" and your name. The worksheets would look better with a smaller top margin.
6. **Click the Normal Margins list arrow, click Custom Margins, in the Top text box on the Margins tab of the Page Setup dialog box type .5, then click OK**
   You decide to ungroup the worksheets.
7. **Return to the worksheet, right-click the Toronto worksheet sheet tab, then click Ungroup Sheets**
8. **Save and close the workbook, exit Excel, then submit the workbook to your instructor**
   The completed worksheets are shown in **FIGURES F-18** and **F-19**.

QUICK TIP
You can group noncontiguous worksheets by pressing and holding [Ctrl] while clicking the sheet tabs that you want to group.

Adding a digital signature to a workbook

You can digitally sign a workbook to establish its validity and prevent it from being changed. You can obtain a valid certificate from a certificate authority to authenticate the workbook or you can create your own digital signature. To add a signature line in a workbook, click the INSERT tab, then click the Signature Line button in the Text group. In the Signature Setup dialog box, enter information about the signer of the worksheet and then click OK. A signature line with your name under it appears on the worksheet. To add a signature, double-click the signature line, click Yes; if you want to get a digital ID from a Microsoft partner and your browser will open with providers of digital IDs.

FIGURE F-18: Toronto worksheet

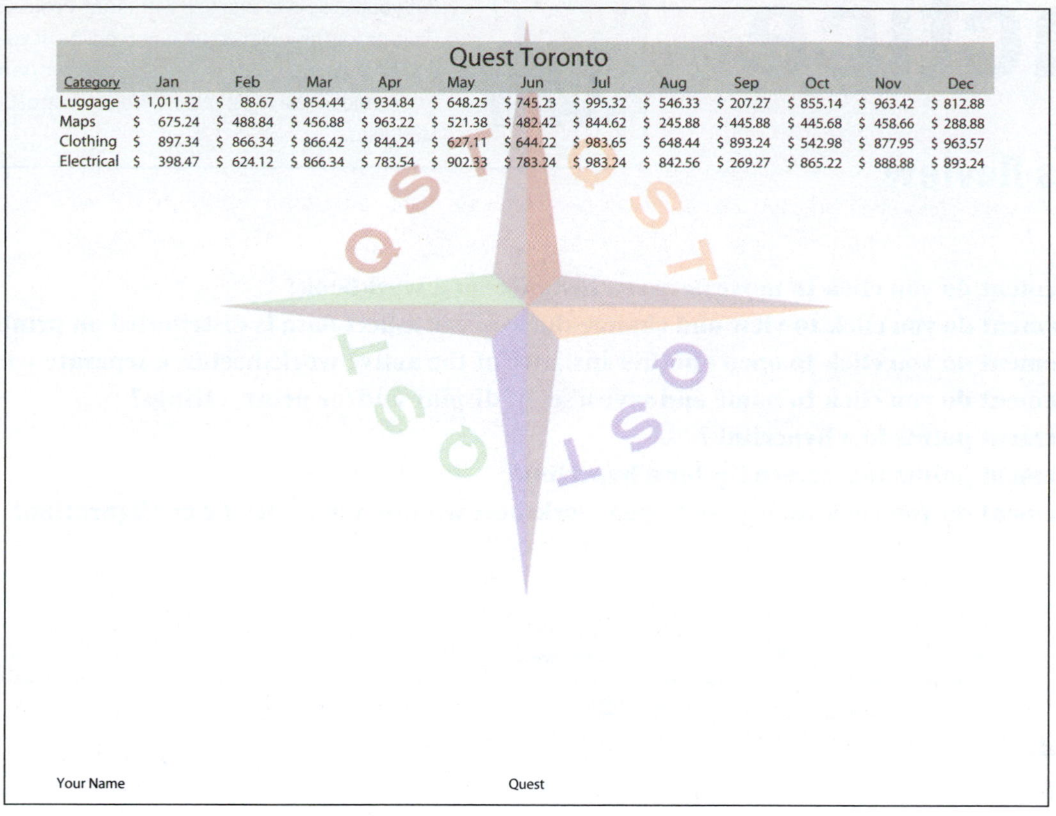

Quest Toronto

Category	Jan	Feb	Mar	Apr	May	Jun	Jul	Aug	Sep	Oct	Nov	Dec
Luggage	$ 1,011.32	$ 88.67	$ 854.44	$ 934.84	$ 648.25	$ 745.23	$ 995.32	$ 546.33	$ 207.27	$ 855.14	$ 963.42	$ 812.88
Maps	$ 675.24	$ 488.84	$ 456.88	$ 963.22	$ 521.38	$ 482.42	$ 844.62	$ 245.88	$ 445.88	$ 445.68	$ 458.66	$ 288.88
Clothing	$ 897.34	$ 866.34	$ 866.42	$ 844.24	$ 627.11	$ 644.22	$ 983.65	$ 648.44	$ 893.24	$ 542.98	$ 877.95	$ 963.57
Electrical	$ 398.47	$ 624.12	$ 866.34	$ 783.54	$ 902.33	$ 783.24	$ 983.24	$ 842.56	$ 269.27	$ 865.22	$ 888.88	$ 893.24

Your Name Quest

FIGURE F-19: Vancouver worksheet

Quest Vancouver

Category	Jan	Feb	Mar	Apr	May	Jun	Jul	Aug	Sep	Oct	Nov	Dec
Luggage	$ 912.68	$ 869.54	$ 844.32	$ 951.55	$ 877.34	$ 865.32	$ 951.53	$ 782.54	$ 445.32	$ 951.55	$ 963.54	$ 511.37
Maps	$ 782.51	$ 863.54	$ 458.35	$ 874.21	$ 125.68	$ 799.39	$ 117.36	$ 185.67	$ 136.24	$ 536.54	$ 959.77	$ 999.99
Clothing	$ 899.30	$ 951.35	$ 752.21	$ 453.21	$ 933.35	$ 231.55	$ 745.21	$ 526.68	$ 158.69	$ 752.36	$ 422.31	$ 231.58
Electrical	$ 793.21	$ 532.54	$ 785.34	$ 423.36	$ 744.35	$ 401.23	$ 455.62	$ 953.57	$ 855.47	$ 975.11	$ 999.99	$ 963.24

Your Name Quest

Practice

Put your skills into practice with **SAM Projects**! SAM Projects for this unit can be found online. If you have a SAM account, go to www.cengage.com/sam2013 to download the most recent Project Instruction and Start Files.

Concepts Review

1. **Which element do you click to move between instances of a workbook?**
2. **Which element do you click to view and change the way worksheet data is distributed on printed pages?**
3. **Which element do you click to open another instance of the active worksheet in a separate window?**
4. **Which element do you click to name and save a set of display and/or print settings?**
5. **Which element points to a hyperlink?**
6. **Which element points to a ScreenTip for a hyperlink?**
7. **Which element do you click to organize open worksheet windows in a specific configuration?**

FIGURE F-20

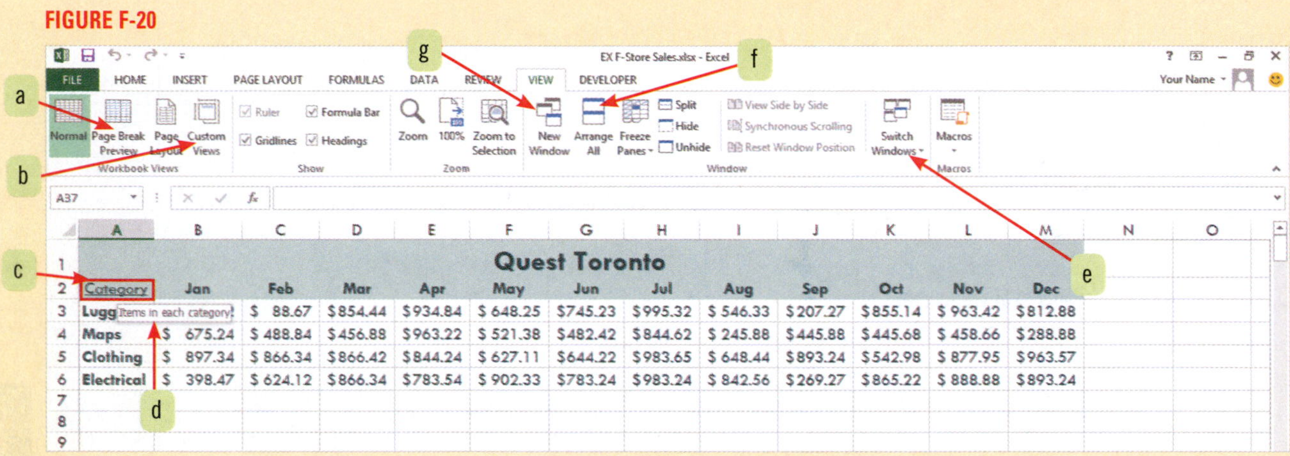

Match each term with the statement that best describes it.

8. **HTML**
9. **Dynamic page breaks**
10. **Hyperlink**
11. **Watermark**
12. **Data entry area**

a. Web page format
b. Portion of a worksheet that can be changed
c. Translucent background design on a printed worksheet
d. An object that when clicked displays another worksheet or a Web page
e. Adjusted automatically when rows and columns are inserted or deleted

Select the best answer from the list of choices.

13. You can establish the validity of a workbook by adding a:

- **a.** Digital signature.
- **b.** Template.
- **c.** Custom View.
- **d.** Keyword.

14. Which of the following formats means that users can view but not change data in a workbook?

- **a.** Macro
- **b.** Read-only
- **c.** Web page
- **d.** Template

15. You can group contiguous worksheets by clicking the first sheet, and then pressing and holding __________ while clicking the last sheet tab that you want to group.

- **a.** [Alt]
- **b.** [Spacebar]
- **c.** [Shift]
- **d.** [F6]

Skills Review

1. View and arrange worksheets.

- **a.** Start Excel, open the file EX F-2.xlsx from the location where you store your Data Files, then save it as **EX F-Coffee**.
- **b.** Open another instance of the workbook in a new window.
- **c.** Activate the East sheet in the EX F-Coffee.xlsx:1 workbook. Activate the West sheet in the EX F-Coffee.xlsx:2 workbook.
- **d.** View the EX F-Coffee.xlsx:1 and EX F-Coffee.xlsx:2 workbooks tiled horizontally. View the workbooks in a vertical arrangement.
- **e.** Hide the EX F-Coffee.xlsx:2 instance, then unhide the instance. Close the EX F-Coffee.xlsx:2 instance, and maximize the EX F-Coffee.xlsx workbook.

2. Protect worksheets and workbooks.

- **a.** On the East sheet, unlock the expense data in the range B12:F19.
- **b.** Protect the sheet without using a password.
- **c.** To make sure the other cells are locked, attempt to make an entry in cell D4 and verify that you receive an error message.
- **d.** Change the first-quarter mortgage expense in cell B12 to 5500.
- **e.** Protect the workbook's structure without applying a password. Right-click the East and West sheet tabs to verify that you cannot insert, delete, rename, move, copy, hide, or unhide the sheets, or change their tab color.
- **f.** Unprotect the workbook. Unprotect the East worksheet.
- **g.** Save the workbook.

3. Save custom views of a worksheet.

- **a.** Using the East sheet, create a custom view of the entire worksheet called **Entire East Budget**.
- **b.** Hide rows 10 through 23, then create a new view called **Income** showing only the income data.
- **c.** Use the Custom Views dialog box to display all of the data on the East worksheet.
- **d.** Use the Custom Views dialog box to display only the income data on the East worksheet.
- **e.** Use the Custom Views dialog box to return to the Entire East Budget view.
- **f.** Save the workbook.

Skills Review (continued)

4. **Add a worksheet background.**
   a. Use EX F-3.jpg as a worksheet background for the East sheet, then delete it.
   b. Add EX F-3.jpg to the East header, then preview the sheet to verify that the background will print.
   c. Add your name to the center section of the East worksheet footer, then save the workbook.
5. **Prepare a workbook for distribution.**
   a. Inspect the workbook and remove any properties, personal data, and header and footer information.
   b. Use the Document Properties Panel to add a title of **Quarterly Budget**, the keyword **campus** and the category **coffee**.
   c. Mark the workbook as final and verify that "[Read-Only]" is in the title bar.
   d. Remove the final status, then save the workbook.
6. **Insert hyperlinks.**
   a. On the East worksheet, make cell A11 a hyperlink to the file **EX F-Expenses.xlsx** in your Data Files folder.
   b. Test the link and verify that Sheet1 of the target file displays expense details.
   c. Return to the EX F-Coffee.xlsx workbook, edit the hyperlink in cell A11, adding a ScreenTip that reads **Expense Details**, then verify that the ScreenTip appears.
   d. On the West worksheet, enter the text **East Campus Budget** in cell A25.
   e. Make the text in cell A25 a hyperlink to cell A1 in the East worksheet. (*Hint*: Use the Place in This Document button and note the cell reference in the Type the cell reference text box.)
   f. Test the hyperlink. Remove the hyperlink in cell A25 of the West worksheet, remove the text in the cell, then save the workbook.
7. **Save a workbook for distribution.**
   a. Save the EX F-Coffee.xlsx workbook as a single file Web page with the name **coffee.mht**.
   b. Close the coffee.mht file that is open in Excel, then open the coffee.mht file in your Web browser. (If you see an Information bar at the top of the Web page notifying you about blocked content, you can ignore it because your Web page doesn't contain any scripts that need to run.)
   c. Close your browser window, and reopen EX F-Coffee.xlsx.
   d. Save the EX F-Coffee.xlsx workbook as an Excel 97-2003 workbook, and review the results of the Compatibility Checker.
   e. Close the EX F-Coffee.xls file, and reopen the EX F-Coffee.xls file in Compatibility Mode.
   f. Convert the .xls file to .xlsx format, resaving the file with the same name and replacing the previously saved file. This allows the workbook to be closed and reopened.
   g. Save the workbook.
8. **Grouping worksheets.**
   a. Group the East and West worksheet.
   b. Add your name to the center footer section of the worksheets. Add 1.5" custom margins to the top of both worksheets.
   c. Preview both sheets, verify the coffee cup will not print (it was removed when the file was inspected), then ungroup the sheets.
   d. Save the workbook, comparing your worksheets to **FIGURE F-21**.
   e. Submit your EX F-Coffee.xlsx, coffee.mht, and EX F-Expenses (the linked file) files to your instructor, close all open files, and exit Excel.

FIGURE F-21

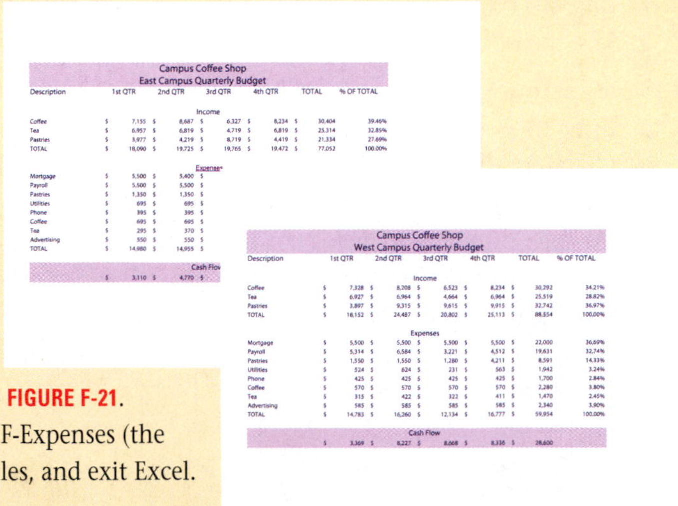

Independent Challenge 1

You manage Cove Road Rugs, a wholesale supplier to retail stores. You are organizing your first-quarter sales in an Excel worksheet. Because the sheet for the month of January includes the same type of information you need for February and March, you decide to enter the headings for all of the first-quarter months at the same time. You use a separate worksheet for each month and create data for 3 months.

a. Start Excel, then save a new workbook as **EX F-Rug Sales.xlsx** in the location where you store your Data Files.

b. Name the first sheet **January**, name the second sheet **February**, and name the third sheet **March**.

c. Group the worksheets.

d. With the worksheets grouped, add the title **Cove Road Rugs** centered across cells A1 and B1. Enter the labels **Type** in cell A2 and **Sales** in cell B2. Enter rug labels in column A beginning in cell A3 and ending in cell A9. Use the following rug types in the range A3:A9: **Wool**, **Custom**, **Antique**, **Commercial**, **Cotton**, **Outdoor**, and **Contemporary**. Add the label **TOTAL** in cell A10. Enter the formula to sum the Sales column in cell B10.

e. Ungroup the worksheets, and enter your own sales data for each of the sales categories in the range B3:B9 in the January, February, and March sheets.

f. Display each worksheet in its own window, then arrange the three sheets vertically.

g. Hide the window displaying the March sheet. Unhide the March sheet window.

h. Split the March window into two panes: the upper pane displaying rows 1 through 5, and the lower pane displaying rows 6 through 10. Scroll through the data in each pane, then remove the split. (*Hint*: Select row 6, click the VIEW tab, then click Split in the Window group Clicking Split again will remove the split.)

i. Close the windows displaying EX F-Rug Sales.xlsx:2 and EX F-Rug Sales.xlsx:3, then maximize the EX F-Rug Sales.xlsx workbook.

j. Add the keywords **rugs custom** to your workbook, using the Document Properties Panel.

k. Group the worksheets again.

l. Add headers to all three worksheets that include your name in the left section and the sheet name in the center section. (*Hint*: You can add the sheet name to a header by clicking the Sheet Name button in the Header and Footer Elements group of the HEADER & FOOTER TOOLS DESIGN tab.)

m. With the worksheets still grouped, format the worksheets using the fill and color buttons on the Home tab appropriately.

n. Ungroup the worksheets, then mark the workbook status as final. Close the workbook, reopen the workbook, and enable editing.

o. Save the workbook, submit the workbook to your instructor, then exit Excel.

Independent Challenge 2

As the payroll manager at Digital Solutions, a Web Development firm, you decide to organize the weekly timecard data using Excel worksheets. You use a separate worksheet for each week and track the hours for employees with different job classifications. A hyperlink in the worksheet provides pay rates for each classification, and custom views limit the information that is displayed.

a. Start Excel, open the file EX F-4.xlsx from the location where you store your Data Files, then save it as **EX F-Timesheets**.

b. Compare the data in the workbook by arranging the Week 1, Week 2, and Week 3 sheets horizontally.

c. Maximize the Week 1 window. Unlock the hours data in the Week 1 sheet and protect the worksheet. Verify that the employee names, numbers, and classifications cannot be changed. Verify that the total hours data can be changed, but do not change the data.

d. Unprotect the Week 1 sheet, and create a custom view called **Complete Worksheet** that displays all the data.

Independent Challenge 2 (continued)

e. Hide column E and create a custom view of the data in the range A1:D22. Name the view **Employee Classifications**. Display each view, then return to the Complete Worksheet view.

f. Add a page break between columns D and E so that the Total Hours data prints on a second page. Preview the worksheet, then remove the page break. (*Hint*: Use the Breaks button on the PAGE LAYOUT tab.)

g. Add a hyperlink to the Classification heading in cell D1 that links to the file EX F-Classifications.xlsx. Add a ScreenTip that reads Pay Rates, then test the hyperlink. Compare your screen to FIGURE F-22.

h. Save the EX F-Classifications workbook as an Excel 97-2003 workbook, reviewing the Compatibility Checker information. Close the EX F-Classifications.xls file.

i. Group the three worksheets in the EX F-Timesheets.xlsx workbook, and add your name to the center footer section.

j. Save the workbook, then preview the grouped worksheets.

k. Ungroup the worksheets, and add 2-inch top and left margins to the Week 1 worksheet.

l. Hide the Week 2 and Week 3 worksheets, inspect the file and remove all document properties, personal information, and hidden worksheets. Do not remove header and footer information.

m. Add the keyword **hours** to the workbook, save the workbook, then mark it as final.

n. Close the workbook, submit the workbook to your instructor, then exit Excel.

FIGURE F-22

	A	B
1	Digital Solutions	
2	Classifications	Pay Rate
3	Developer	$65
4	Senior Developer	$85
5	Designer	$60
6	Senior Designer	$80
7		

Independent Challenge 3

One of your responsibilities as the office manager at North Shore Management Consultants is to track supplies for the home office. You decide to create a spreadsheet to track these orders, placing each month's orders on its own sheet. You create custom views that will focus on the categories of supplies. A hyperlink will provide the supplier's contact information.

a. Start Excel, open the file EX F-5.xlsx from the location where you store your Data Files, then save it as **EX F-Supplies**.

b. Arrange the sheets for the 3 months horizontally to compare expenses, then close the extra workbook windows and maximize the remaining window. (*Hint*: If you want to hide the Ribbon to see more of the worksheet, double-click a Ribbon tab. To display the Ribbon later, double-click a tab again.)

c. Create a custom view of the entire January worksheet named **All Supplies**. Hide the paper, pens, and miscellaneous supply data, and create a custom view displaying only the hardware supplies. Call the view **Hardware**.

d. Display the All Supplies view, group the worksheets, and create a total for the total costs in cell D32 on each month's sheet. If necessary, use the Format Painter to copy the format from cell D31 to cell D32.

e. With the sheets grouped, add the sheet name to the center section of all the sheets' headers and your name to the center section of all the sheets' footers.

f. Ungroup the sheets and use the Compatibility Checker to view the features that are unsupported in earlier Excel formats. (*Hint*: Click the File tab, click Info, click the Check for Issues button, then click Check Compatibility.)

g. Add a hyperlink in cell A1 of the January sheet that opens the file EX F-Hardware.xlsx. Add a ScreenTip of **Hardware Supplier**. Test the link, viewing the ScreenTip, then return to the EX F-Supplies.xlsx workbook without closing the EX F-Hardware.xlsx workbook. Save the EX F-Supplies.xlsx workbook.

h. Hide the EX F-Hardware.xlsx workbook, then unhide it.

Independent Challenge 3 (continued)

i. Freeze worksheet rows one through three on the January Sheet of the EX F-Suppliers.xlsx workbook. (*Hint*: Select row 4, click the VIEW tab, click the Freeze Panes button in the Window group, then click Freeze Panes.) Scroll down in the worksheet to verify the top three rows remain visible.

j. Unfreeze rows one through three. (*Hint*: Click the VIEW tab, click Freeze panes, then click Unfreeze Panes.)

k. Close both the EX F-Hardware.xlsx and the EX F-Supplies.xlsx workbooks.

l. Submit the workbooks to your instructor, then exit Excel.

Independent Challenge 4: Explore

As the assistant to the director of contracting services at a nonprofit educational consulting firm, you review the non-payroll expense sheets submitted by employees for each contract. You decide to create a spreadsheet to track these contract expenses.

a. Start Excel, open the file EX F-6.xlsx from the location where you store your Data Files, then save it as **EX F-Invoice** in the location where you store your Data Files.

b. Freeze rows 1 through 5 in the worksheet. Scroll vertically to verify rows 1 through 5 are visible at the top of the worksheet.

c. Research the steps necessary to hide a formula in the Formula Bar of a worksheet. Record these steps in cell A1 on Sheet2 of the workbook, then hide the display of the formula for cell B38 on Sheet1. Check the Formula Bar to verify the formula is hidden.
Compare your worksheet to FIGURE F-23.

d. Save your workbook. If you don't have a Microsoft account, research the steps for creating an account and create your Microsoft ID. Use your Microsoft ID to log into your SkyDrive, then save your file on your SkyDrive.

e. Share your workbook with a classmate.

f. Unprotect Sheet1. (Your formula will be displayed.) Add a header that includes your name on the left side of the worksheet (this will unfreeze rows 1 through 5). Using the PAGE LAYOUT tab, scale Sheet1 to fit vertically on one page. Save the workbook, then preview the worksheet.

g. If you are able to create a folder on the computer you are working on, create a folder named Templates in the location where you store your Data Files. Use the Excel Options menu to change the location where templates are saved to the path of your new template folder. (*Hint*: Click the File menu, click Options, click Save, then enter the path in the Default Personal Templates location text box. You may want to copy the path from the Address bar of a File Explorer window.)

h. Delete the amount values in column B, and save the workbook as an Excel template in the Templates folder you created in the step above.

i. Open a new workbook based on the template. (*Hint*: Click File, click New, then click Personal, then click the template name.)

j. Submit the workbook and template to your instructor, then exit Excel.

FIGURE F-23

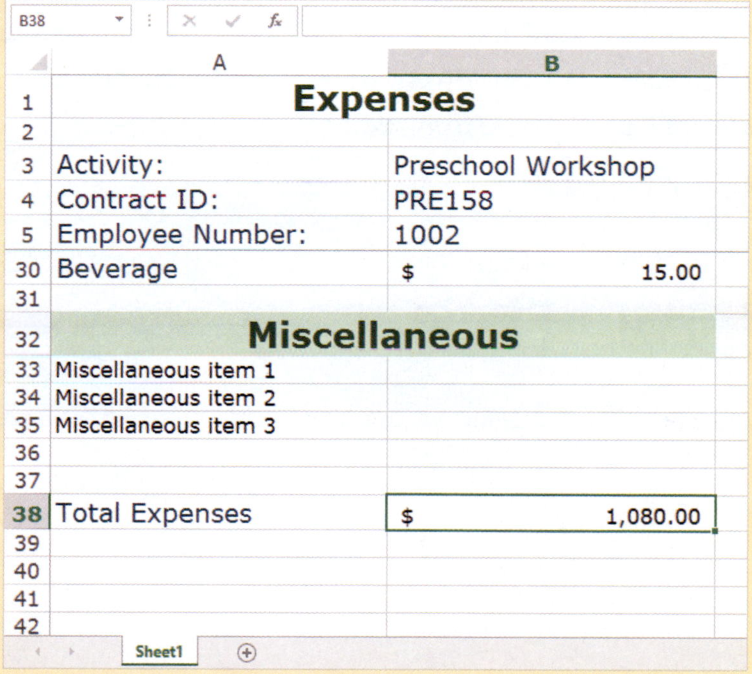

B38

	A	B
1	Expenses	
2		
3	Activity:	Preschool Workshop
4	Contract ID:	PRE158
5	Employee Number:	1002
30	Beverage	$ 15.00
31		
32	Miscellaneous	
33	Miscellaneous item 1	
34	Miscellaneous item 2	
35	Miscellaneous item 3	
36		
37		
38	Total Expenses	$ 1,080.00
39		
40		
41		
42		

Sheet1

Visual Workshop

Start Excel, open the file EX F-7.xlsx from the location where you store your Data Files, then save it as **EX F-Rentals**. Make your worksheet look like the one shown in **FIGURE F-24**. The text in cell A4 is a hyperlink to the EX F-Price Information workbook. The worksheet background is the Data File EX F-8.jpg. Enter your name in the footer, save the workbook, submit the workbook to your instructor, close the workbook, then exit Excel.

FIGURE F-24

1	Lake Side Realty					
2	Seasonal Rentals					
3	Listing Number	Location	Type	Bed	Bath	Pets
4	1011	Waterfront	House	3	2	No
5	1551	Village	Condominium	2	2	No
6	1987	1 block from water	House	4	2	Yes
7	1440	1 mile from water	House	5	3	No
8	1321	Waterfront	Condominium	4	2	No
9	1522	Village	House	2	1	No
10	1330	Waterfront	House	3	1	Yes
11	1563	Village	Condominium	3	2	No
12	1966	1 block from water	House	4	2	Yes
13	1458	1 mile from water	Condominium	2	2	No
14	1221	Waterfront	House	4	2	No
15	1469	Village	House	2	1	No
16	1887	Village	Condominium	2	1	No
17	1964	1 block from water	House	2	2	Yes
18						
19						

Carsten Ranke Photography www.carstenranke.com/Getty Images

Managing Data Using Tables

CASE Quest uses tables to analyze tour data. The vice president of sales, Kate Morgan, asks you to help her build and manage a table of 2016 tour information. You will help by planning and creating a table; adding, changing, finding, and deleting table information; sorting table data, and performing calculations with table data.

Unit Objectives

After completing this unit, you will be able to:

- Plan a table
- Create and format a table
- Add table data
- Find and replace table data
- Delete table data
- Sort table data
- Use formulas in a table
- Print a table

Files You Will Need

EX G-1.xlsx
EX G-2.xlsx
EX G-3.xlsx
EX G-4.xlsx
EX G-5.xlsx
EX G-6.xlsx

Plan a Table

Learning Outcomes
- Plan the data organization for a table
- Plan the data elements for a table

In addition to using Excel spreadsheet features, you can analyze and manipulate data in a table structure. An Excel **table** is an organized collection of rows and columns of similarly structured worksheet data. Tables are a convenient way to understand and manage large amounts of information. When planning a table, consider what information you want your table to contain and how you want to work with the data, now and in the future. As you plan a table, you should understand its most important components. A table is organized into rows called records. A **record** is a table row that contains data about an object, person, or other item. Records are composed of fields. **Fields** are columns in the table; each field describes a characteristic of the record, such as a customer's last name or street address. Each field has a **field name**, which is a column label, such as "Address," that describes its contents. Tables usually have a **header row** as the first row, which contains the field names. To plan your table, use the guidelines below. **CASE** *Kate asks you to compile a table of the 2016 tours. Before entering the tour data into an Excel worksheet, you plan the table contents.*

DETAILS

As you plan your table, use the following guidelines:

- **Identify the purpose of the table**
  The purpose of the table determines the kind of information the table should contain. You want to use the tours table to find all departure dates for a particular tour and to display the tours in order of departure date. You also want to quickly calculate the number of available seats for a tour.

- **Plan the structure of the table**
  In designing your table's structure, determine the fields (the table columns) you need to achieve the table's purpose. You have worked with the sales department to learn the type of information they need for each tour. FIGURE G-1 shows a layout sketch for the table. Each row will contain one tour record. The columns represent fields that contain pieces of descriptive information you will enter for each tour, such as the name, departure date, and duration.

- **Plan your row and column structure**
  You can create a table from any contiguous range of cells on your worksheet. Plan and design your table so that all rows have similar types of information in the same column. A table should not have any blank rows or columns. Instead of using blank rows to separate table headings from data, use a table style, which will use formatting to make column labels stand out from your table data. FIGURE G-2 shows a table, populated with data that has been formatted using a table style.

- **Document the table design**
  In addition to your table sketch, you should make a list of the field names to document the type of data and any special number formatting required for each field. Field names should be as short as possible while still accurately describing the column information. When naming fields it is important to use text rather than numbers because Excel could interpret numbers as parts of formulas. Your field names should be unique and not easily confused with cell addresses, such as the name D2. You want your tours table to contain eight field names, each one corresponding to the major characteristics of the 2016 tours. TABLE G-1 shows the documentation of the field names in your table.

FIGURE G-1: Table layout sketch

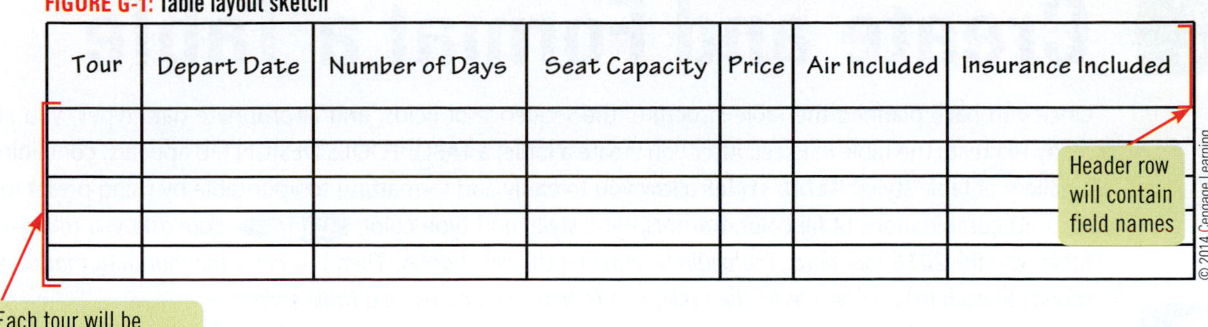

FIGURE G-2: Formatted table with data

Header row contains field names

Records for each tour, organized by field name

	A	B	C	D	E	F	G	H
1	Tour	Depart Date	Number of Days	Seat Capacity	Seats Reserved	Price	Air Included	Insurance Included
2	Pacific Odyssey	1/12/2016	14	50	50	$ 2,255	Yes	No
3	Old Japan	1/13/2016	21	47	42	$ 1,984	Yes	No
4	Costa Rica	1/19/2016	10	31	28	$ 1,966	Yes	Yes
5	Yellowstone	1/21/2016	18	51	40	$ 1,850	Yes	Yes
6	Amazing Amazon	2/22/2016	14	43	39	$ 2,134	No	No
7	Hiking Patagonia	2/28/2016	7	20	15	$ 2,812	Yes	No
8	Pearls of the Orient	3/13/2016	14	45	15	$ 2,350	Yes	No
9	Silk Road Travels	3/19/2016	18	23	19	$ 2,110	Yes	Yes
10	Photographing France	3/20/2016	7	20	20	$ 1,755	Yes	Yes
11	Green Adventures in Ecuado	3/23/2016	18	25	22	$ 2,450	No	No
12	African National Parks	4/8/2016	30	12	10	$ 3,115	Yes	Yes
13	Experience Cambodia	4/11/2016	12	35	21	$ 2,441	Yes	No
14	Old Japan	4/15/2016	21	47	30	$ 1,900	Yes	No
15	Costa Rica	4/18/2016	10	30	20	$ 2,800	Yes	Yes
16	Yellowstone	4/20/2016	18	51	31	$ 1,652	Yes	Yes

TABLE G-1: Table documentation

field name	type of data	description of data
Tour	Text	Name of tour
Depart Date	Date	Date tour departs
Number of Days	Number with 0 decimal places	Duration of the tour
Seat Capacity	Number with 0 decimal places	Maximum number of people the tour can accommodate
Seats Reserved	Number with 0 decimal places	Number of reservations for the tour
Price	Accounting with 0 decimal places and $ symbol	Tour price (This price is not guaranteed until a 30% deposit is received)
Air Included	Text	Yes: Airfare is included in the price No: Airfare is not included in the price
Insurance Included	Text	Yes: Insurance is included in the price No: Insurance is not included in the price

Excel 2013
UNIT G

Create and Format a Table

Learning Outcomes
- Create a table
- Format a table

Once you have planned the table structure, the sequence of fields, and appropriate data types, you are ready to create the table in Excel. After you create a table, a TABLE TOOLS DESIGN tab appears, containing a gallery of table styles. **Table styles** allow you to easily add formatting to your table by using preset formatting combinations of fill color, borders, type style, and type color. **CASE** *Kate asks you to build a table with the 2016 tour data. You begin by entering the field names. Then you enter the tour data that corresponds to each field name, create the table, and format the data using a table style.*

STEPS

TROUBLE
Don't worry if your field names are wider than the cells; you will fix this later.

QUICK TIP
Do not insert extra spaces at the beginning of a cell because it can affect sorting and finding data in a table.

QUICK TIP
You can also create a table using the shortcut key combination [Ctrl][T].

1. **Start Excel, open the file EX G-1.xlsx from the location where you store your Data Files, then save it as EX G-2016 Tours**
2. **Beginning in cell A1 of the Practice sheet, enter each field name in a separate column, as shown in FIGURE G-3**
   Field names are usually in the first row of the table.
3. **Enter the information from FIGURE G-4 in the rows immediately below the field names, leaving no blank rows**
   The data appears in columns organized by field name.
4. **Select the range A1:H4, click the Format button in the Cells group, click AutoFit Column Width, then click cell A1**
   Resizing the column widths this way is faster than double-clicking the column divider lines.
5. **With cell A1 selected, click the INSERT tab, click the Table button in the Tables group, in the Create Table dialog box verify that your table data is in the range $A$1:$H$4, and make sure My table has headers is checked as shown in FIGURE G-5, then click OK**
   The data range is now defined as a table. **Filter list arrows**, which let you display portions of your data, now appear next to each column header. When you create a table, Excel automatically applies a table style. The default table style has a dark blue header row and alternating gray and blue data rows. The TABLE TOOLS DESIGN tab appears, and the Table Styles group displays a gallery of table formatting options. You decide to choose a different table style from the gallery.
6. **Click the Table Styles More button, scroll to view all of the table styles, then move the mouse pointer over several styles without clicking**
   The Table Styles gallery on the TABLE TOOLS DESIGN tab has three style categories: Light, Medium, and Dark. Each category has numerous design types; for example, in some of the designs, the header row and total row are darker and the rows alternate colors. The available table designs use the current workbook theme colors so the table coordinates with your existing workbook content. If you select a different workbook theme and color scheme in the Themes group on the PAGE LAYOUT tab, the Table Styles gallery uses those colors. As you point to each table style, Live Preview shows you what your table will look like with the style applied. However, you only see a preview of each style; you need to click a style to apply it.
7. **Click Table Style Medium 24 to apply it to your table, then click cell A1**
   Compare your table to FIGURE G-6.

FIGURE G-3: Field names entered in row 1

	A	B	C	D	E	F	G	H
1	Tour	Depart Date	Number of Days	Seat Capacity	Seats Reserved	Price	Air Included	Insurance Included

FIGURE G-4: Three records entered in the worksheet

	A	B	C	D	E	F	G	H
1	Tour	Depart Date	Number of Days	Seat Capacity	Seats Reserved	Price	Air Included	Insurance Included
2	Pacific Odyssey	1/12/2016	14	50	40	2255	Yes	No
3	Old Japan	1/13/2016	21	47	42	1964	Yes	No
4	Costa Rica	1/19/2016	10	31	28	1833	Yes	Yes
5								

FIGURE G-5: Create Table dialog box

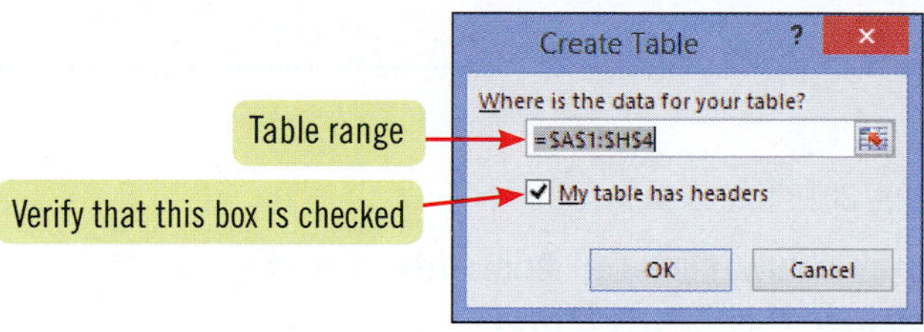

FIGURE G-6: Formatted table with three records

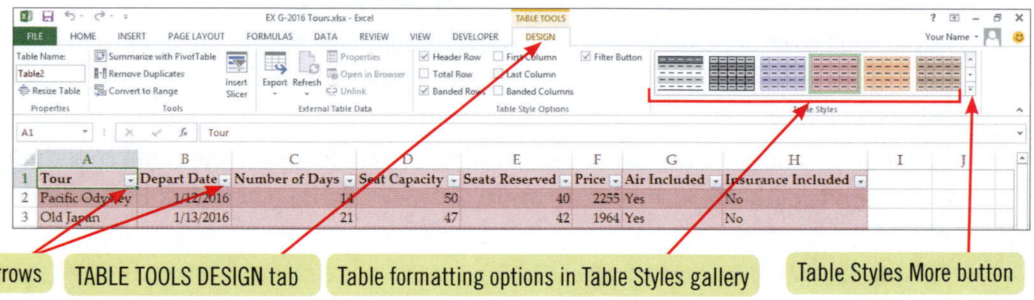

Changing table style options

You can change a table's appearance by using the check boxes in the Table Styles Options group on the TABLE TOOLS DESIGN tab, shown in **FIGURE G-7**. For example, you can turn on or turn off the following options: Header Row, which displays or hides the header row; Total Row, which calculates totals for each column; **banding**, which creates different formatting for adjacent rows and columns; and special formatting for first and last columns. Use these options to modify a table's appearance either before or after applying a table style. For example, if your table has banded rows, you can select the Banded Columns check box to change the table to be displayed with banded columns as well. Also, you may want to deselect the Header Row check box to hide a table's header row if a table will be included in a presentation where the header row repeats slide labels.

You can also create your own table style by clicking the Table Styles More button, then at the bottom of the Table Styles Gallery, clicking New Table Style. In the New Table Style dialog box, name the style in the Name text box, click a table element, then format selected table elements by clicking Format. You can also set a custom style as the default style for your tables by checking the Set as default table quick style for this document check box. You can click Clear at the bottom of the Table Styles gallery if you want to delete a table style from the currently selected table.

FIGURE G-7: Table Styles Options

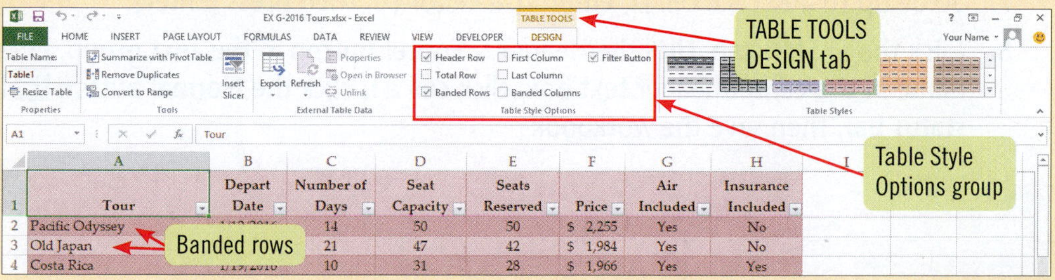

Add Table Data

Learning Outcomes
- Add fields to a table
- Add records to a table

You can add records to a table by typing data directly below the last row of the table. After you press [Enter], the new row becomes part of the table and the table formatting extends to the new data. When the active cell is the last cell of a table, you can add a new row by pressing [Tab]. You can also insert rows in any table location. If you decide you need additional data fields, you can add new columns to a table. You can also expand a table by dragging the sizing handle in a table's lower-right corner; drag down to add rows and drag to the right to add columns. **CASE** *After entering all of the 2016 tour data, Kate decides to offer two additional tours. She also wants the table to display the number of available seats for each tour and whether visas are required for the destination.*

STEPS

1. **Click the 2016 Tours sheet tab**
   The 2016 sheet containing the 2016 tour data becomes active.

2. **Scroll down to the last table row, click cell A65, enter the data for the new Pearls of the Orient tour, as shown below, then press [Enter]**

Pearls of the Orient	7/25/2016	14	50	0	$ 2,400	Yes	No

   As you scroll down, the table headers are visible at the top of the table as long as the active cell is inside the table. The new Pearls of the Orient tour is now part of the table. You want to enter a record about a new January tour above row 6.

3. **Scroll up to and click the inside left edge of cell A6 to select the table row data as shown in FIGURE G-8, click the Insert list arrow in the Cells group, then click Insert Table Rows Above**
   Clicking the left edge of the first cell in a table row selects the entire table row, rather than the entire worksheet row. A new blank row 6 is available for the new record.

4. **Click cell A6, then enter the Yellowstone record shown below**

Yellowstone	1/28/2016	18	51	0	$ 1,850	Yes	Yes

   The new Yellowstone tour is part of the table. You want to add a new field that displays the number of available seats for each tour.

5. **Click cell I1, enter the field name Seats Available, then press [Enter]**
   The new field becomes part of the table, and the header formatting extends to the new field as shown in FIGURE G-9. The AutoCorrect menu allows you to undo or stop the automatic table expansion, but in this case you decide to leave this feature on. You want to add another new field to the table to display tours that require visas, but this time you will add the new field by resizing the table.

QUICK TIP
You can also resize a table by clicking the TABLE TOOLS DESIGN tab, clicking the Resize Table button in the Properties group, selecting the new data range for the table, then clicking OK.

6. **Scroll down until cell I66 is visible, drag the sizing handle in the table's lower-right corner one column to the right to add column J to the table, as shown in FIGURE G-10**
   The table range is now A1:J66, and the new field name is Column1.

7. **Scroll up to and click cell J1, enter Visa Required, then press [Enter]**

8. **Click the INSERT tab, click the Header & Footer button in the Text group, enter your name in the center header text box, click cell A1, click the Normal button in the status bar, then save the workbook**

FIGURE G-8: Table row 6 selected

	Tour	Depart Date	Number of Days	Seat Capacity	Seats Reserved	Price	Air Included	Insurance Included
2	Pacific Odyssey	1/12/2016	14	50	50	$ 2,255	Yes	No
3	Old Japan	1/13/2016	21	47	42	$ 1,984	Yes	No
4	Costa Rica	1/19/2016	10	31	28	$ 1,966	Yes	Yes
5	Yellowstone	1/21/2016	18	51	40	$ 1,850	Yes	Yes
6	Amazing Amazon	2/22/2016	14	43	39	$ 2,134	No	No
7	Hiking Patagonia	2/28/2016	7	20	15	$ 2,812	Yes	No
8	Pearls of the Orient	3/13/2016	14	45	15	$ 2,350	Yes	No
9	Silk Road Travels	3/19/2016	18	23	19	$ 2,110	Yes	Yes
10	Photographing France	3/20/2016	7	20	20	$ 1,755	Yes	Yes
11	Green Adventures in Ecuado	3/23/2016	18	25	22	$ 2,450	No	No
12	African National Parks	4/8/2016	30	12	10	$ 3,115	Yes	Yes

Row 6 selected

Place the pointer over the inside left edge of cell to select only the table row

FIGURE G-9: New table column

	A	B	C	D	E	F	G	H	I
1	Tour	Depart Date	Number of Days	Seat Capacity	Seats Reserved	Price	Air Included	Insurance Included	Seats Available
2	Pacific Odyssey	1/12/2016	14	50	50	$ 2,255	Yes	No	
3	Old Japan	1/13/2016	21	47	42	$ 1,984	Yes	No	
4	Costa Rica	1/19/2016	10	31	28	$ 1,966	Yes	Yes	
5	Yellowstone	1/21/2016	18	51	40	$ 1,850	Yes	Yes	
6	Yellowstone	1/28/2016	18	51	0	$ 1,850	Yes	Yes	
7	Amazing Amazon	2/22/2016	14	43	39	$ 2,134	No	No	
8	Hiking Patagonia	2/28/2016	7	20	15	$ 2,812	Yes	No	

New table column will show available seats for each tour

New record in row 6

FIGURE G-10: Resizing a table using the resizing handle

	Depart Da	Number of	Seat Capacit	Seats Reserv	Price	Air Include	Insurance In	Seats Avail	J	K
55	10/29/2016	14	18	8	$ 4,200	Yes	Yes			
56	10/31/2016	7	38	15	$ 1,900	Yes	No			
57	10/31/2016	12	40	2	$ 2,908	Yes	No			
58	11/18/2016	10	41	12	$ 2,200	Yes	Yes			
59	12/18/2016	10	50	21	$ 2,204	Yes	Yes			
60	12/18/2016	10	50	21	$ 2,204	Yes	Yes			
61	12/20/2016	14	15	1	$ 2,100	Yes	Yes			
62	12/20/2016	14	15	1	$ 2,100	Yes	Yes			
63	12/21/2016	14	50	10	$ 2,105	Yes	No			
64	12/30/2016	18	51	15	$ 2,922	Yes	Yes			
65	12/31/2016	21	47	4	$ 2,100	Yes	No			
66	7/25/2016	14	50	0	$ 2,400	Yes	No			

Drag sizing handle to add column J to table

Selecting table elements

When working with tables you often need to select rows, columns, and even the entire table. Clicking to the right of a row number, inside column A, selects the entire table row. You can select a table column by clicking the top edge of the header. Be careful not to click a column letter or row number, however, because this selects the entire worksheet row or column. You can select the table data by clicking the upper-left corner of the first table cell. When selecting a column or a table, the first click selects only the data in the column or table. If you click a second time, you add the headers to the selection.

Find and Replace Table Data

Learning Outcomes
- Find data in a table
- Replace data in a table

From time to time, you need to locate specific records in your table. You can use the Excel Find feature to search your table for the information you need. You can also use the Replace feature to locate and replace existing entries or portions of entries with information you specify. If you don't know the exact spelling of the text you are searching for, you can use wildcards to help locate the records. **Wildcards** are special symbols that substitute for unknown characters. **CASE** *In response to a change in the bike trip from Ireland to Scotland, Kate needs to replace "Ireland" with "Scotland" in all of the tour names. She also wants to know how many Pacific Odyssey tours are scheduled for the year. You begin by searching for records with the text "Pacific Odyssey".*

STEPS

1. **Click cell A1 if necessary, click the HOME tab, click the Find & Select button in the Editing group, then click Find**
   The Find and Replace dialog box opens, as shown in FIGURE G-11. In the Find what text box, you enter criteria that specify the records you want to find. You want to search for records whose Tour field contains the label "Old Japan".
2. **Type Old Japan in the Find what text box, then click Find Next**
   A3 is the active cell because it is the first instance of Old Japan in the table.
3. **Click Find Next and examine the record for each Old Japan tour found until no more matching cells are found in the table and the active cell is A3 again, then click Close**
   There are four Old Japan tours.
4. **Return to cell A1, click the Find & Select button in the Editing group, then click Replace**
   The Find and Replace dialog box opens with the Replace tab selected and "Old Japan" in the Find what text box, as shown in FIGURE G-12. You will search for entries containing "Ireland" and replace them with "Scotland". To save time, you will use the asterisk (*) wildcard to help you locate the records containing Ireland.

QUICK TIP
You can also use the question mark (?) wildcard to represent any single character. For example, using "to?" as your search text would only find 3-letter words beginning with "to", such as "top" and "tot"; it would not find "tone" or "topography".

5. **Delete the text in the Find what text box, type Ir* in the Find what text box, click the Replace with text box, then type Scotland**
   The asterisk (*) wildcard stands for one or more characters, meaning that the search text "Ir*" will find words such as "iron", "hair", and "bird". Because you notice that there are other table entries containing the text "ir" with a lowercase "i" (in the Air Included column heading), you need to make sure that only capitalized instances of the letter "I" are replaced.
6. **Click Options >>, click the Match case check box to select it, click Options <<, then click Find Next**
   Excel moves the cell pointer to the cell containing the first occurrence of "Ireland".
7. **Click Replace All, click OK, then click Close**
   The dialog box closes. Excel made three replacements, in cells A27, A36, and A40. The Air Included field heading remains unchanged because the "ir" in "Air" is lowercase.
8. **Save the workbook**

FIGURE G-11: Find and Replace dialog box

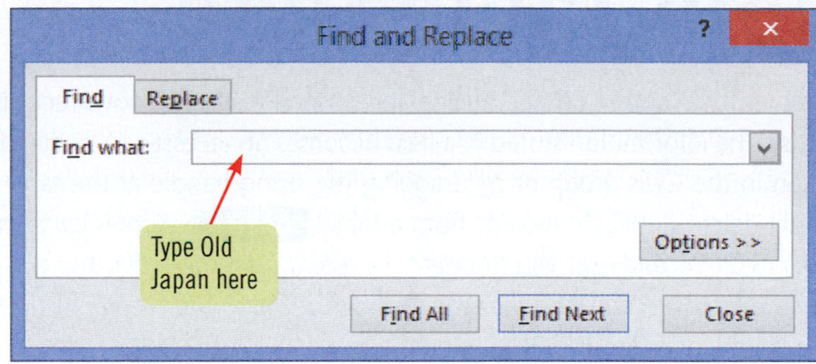

FIGURE G-12: The Replace tab in the Find and Replace dialog box

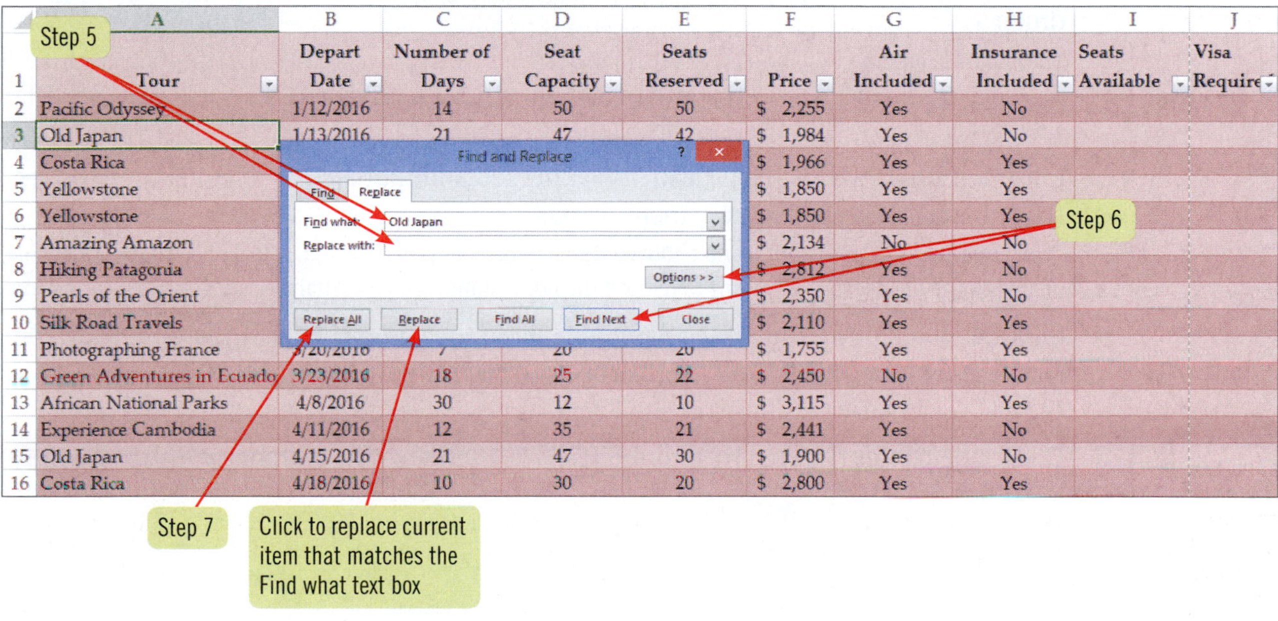

Using Find and Select features

You can also use the Find feature to navigate to a specific place in a workbook by clicking the Find & Select button in the Editing group, clicking Go To, typing a cell address, then clicking OK. Clicking the Find & Select button also allows you to find comments and conditional formatting in a worksheet. You can use the Go to Special dialog box to select cells that contain different types of formulas or objects. Some Go to Special commands also appear on the Find & Select menu. Using this menu, you can also change the mouse pointer shape to the Select Objects pointer so you can quickly select drawing objects when necessary. To return to the standard Excel pointer, press [Esc].

Excel 2013
UNIT G

Delete Table Data

Learning Outcomes
- Delete a table field
- Delete a table row
- Remove duplicate data from a table

To keep a table up to date, you need to be able to periodically remove records. You may even need to remove fields if the information stored in a field becomes unnecessary. You can delete table data using the Delete button in the Cells group or by dragging the sizing handle at the table's lower-right corner. You can also easily delete duplicate records from a table. **CASE** *Kate is canceling the Old Japan tour that departs on 1/13/2016 and asks you to delete the record from the table. You will also remove any duplicate records from the table. Because the visa requirements are difficult to keep up with, Kate asks you to delete the field with visa information.*

STEPS

1. **Click the left edge of cell A3 to select the table row data, click the Delete list arrow in the Cells group, then click Delete Table Rows**

   The Old Japan tour is deleted, and the Costa Rica tour moves up to row 3, as shown in FIGURE G-13. You can also delete a table row or a column using the Resize Table button in the Properties group of the TABLE TOOLS DESGIN tab, or by right-clicking the row or column, pointing to Delete on the shortcut menu, then clicking Table Columns or Table Rows. You decide to check the table for duplicate records.

QUICK TIP
You can also remove duplicates from worksheet data by clicking the DATA tab, then clicking the Remove Duplicates button in the Data Tools group.

2. **Click the TABLE TOOLS DESIGN tab, then click the Remove Duplicates button in the Tools group**

   The Remove Duplicates dialog box opens, as shown in FIGURE G-14. You need to select the columns that will be used to evaluate duplicates. Because you don't want to delete tours with the same destination but different departure dates, you will look for duplicate data in all of the columns.

3. **Make sure that "My data has headers" is checked and that all the Columns check boxes (column headers) are checked, then click OK**

   Two duplicate records are found and removed, leaving 62 records of data and a total of 63 rows in the table, including the header row. You want to remove the last column, which contains space for visa information.

4. **Click OK, scroll down until cell J63 is visible, drag the sizing handle of the table's lower-right corner one column to the left to remove column J from the table**

   The table range is now A1:I63, and the Visa Required field no longer appears in the table.

5. **Delete the contents of cell J1, return to cell A1, then save the workbook**

FIGURE G-13: Table with row deleted

	A	B	C	D	E	F	G	H	I	J
1	Tour	Depart Date	Number of Days	Seat Capacity	Seats Reserved	Price	Air Included	Insurance Included	Seats Available	Visa Require
2	Pacific Odyssey	1/12/2016	14	50	50	$ 2,255	Yes	No		
3	Costa Rica	1/19/2016	10	31	28	$ 1,966	Yes	Yes		
4	Yellowstone	1/21/2016	18	51	40	$ 1,850	Yes	Yes		
5	Yellowstone	1/28/2016	18	51	0	$ 1,850	Yes	Yes		
6	Amazing Amazon	2/22/2016	14	43	39	$ 2,134	No	No		
7	Hiking Patagonia	2/28/2016	7	20	15	$ 2,812	Yes	No		
8	Pearls of the Orient	3/13/2016	14	45	15	$ 2,350	Yes	No		
9	Silk Road Travels	3/19/2016	18	23	19	$ 2,110	Yes	Yes		
10	Photographing France	3/20/2016	7	20	20	$ 1,755	Yes	Yes		
11	Green Adventures in Ecuado	3/23/2016	18	25	22	$ 2,450	No	No		
12	African National Parks	4/8/2016	30	12	10	$ 3,115	Yes	Yes		
13	Experience Cambodia	4/11/2016	12	35	21	$ 2,441	Yes	No		
14	Old Japan	4/15/2016	21	47	30	$ 1,900	Yes	No		
15	Costa Rica	4/18/2016	10	30	20	$ 2,800	Yes	Yes		
16	Yellowstone	4/20/2016	18	51	31	$ 1,652	Yes	Yes		

Row is deleted and tours move up one row

FIGURE G-14: Remove Duplicates dialog box

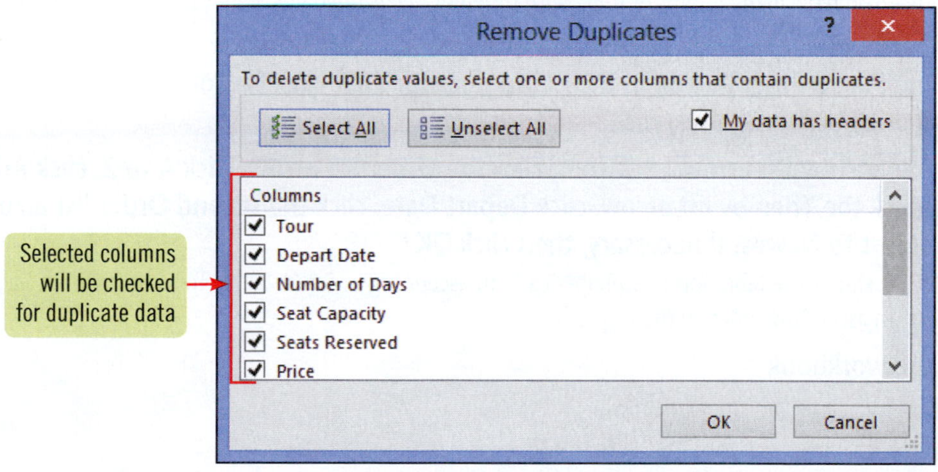

Excel 2013

Sort Table Data

Learning Outcomes
- Sort a table in ascending order
- Sort a table in descending order
- Sort a table using custom sort options

Usually, you enter table records in the order in which you receive information, rather than in alphabetical or numerical order. When you add records to a table, you usually enter them at the end of the table. You can change the order of the records any time using the Excel **sort** feature. Because the data is structured as a table, Excel changes the order of the records while keeping each record, or row of information, together. You can sort a table in ascending or descending order on one field using the filter list arrows next to the field name. In **ascending order**, the lowest value (the beginning of the alphabet or the earliest date) appears at the top of the table. In a field containing labels and numbers, numbers appear first in the sorted list. In **descending order**, the highest value (the end of the alphabet or the latest date) appears at the top of the table. In a field containing labels and numbers, labels appear first. TABLE G-2 provides examples of ascending and descending sorts. CASE *Kate wants the tour data sorted by departure date, displaying tours that depart the soonest at the top of the table.*

STEPS

1. **Click the Depart Date filter list arrow, then click Sort Oldest to Newest**
   Excel rearranges the records in ascending order by departure date, as shown in FIGURE G-15. The Depart Date filter list arrow has an upward pointing arrow indicating the ascending sort in the field. You can also sort the table on one field using the Sort & Filter button.

> **QUICK TIP**
> Before you sort records, consider making a backup copy of your table or create a field that numbers the records so you can return them to their original order, if necessary.

2. **Click the HOME tab, click any cell in the Price column, click the Sort & Filter button in the Editing group, then click Sort Largest to Smallest**
   Excel sorts the table, placing those records with the higher price at the top. The Price filter list arrow now has a downward pointing arrow next to the filter list arrow, indicating the descending sort order. You can also rearrange the table data using a **multilevel sort**. This type of sort rearranges the table data using more than one field, where each field is a different level, based on its importance in the sort. If you use two sort levels, the data is sorted by the first field, and the second field is sorted within each grouping of the first field. Since you have many groups of tours with different departure dates, you want to use a multilevel sort to arrange the table data by tours and then by departure dates within each tour.

> **QUICK TIP**
> You can also add a multilevel sort by clicking the DATA tab and then clicking the Sort button in the Sort & Filter group.

3. **Click the Sort & Filter button in the Editing group, then click Custom Sort**
   The Sort dialog box opens, as shown in FIGURE G-16.

> **QUICK TIP**
> You can include capitalization as a sort criterion by clicking Options in the Sort dialog box, then selecting the Case sensitive check box. When you choose this option, lowercase entries precede uppercase entries in an ascending order.

4. **Click the Sort by list arrow, click Tour, click the Order list arrow, click A to Z, click Add Level, click the Then by list arrow, click Depart Date, click the second Order list arrow, click Oldest to Newest if necessary, then click OK**
   FIGURE G-17 shows the table sorted alphabetically in ascending order (A–Z) by Tour and, within each tour grouping, in ascending order by the Depart Date.

5. **Save the workbook**

Sorting conditionally formatted data

If conditional formats have been applied to a table, you can sort the table using conditional formatting to arrange the rows. For example, if cells are conditionally formatted with color, you can sort a field on Cell Color, using the color with the order of On Top or On Bottom in the Sort dialog box. If the data is not in a table, you can select a cell in the column of conditionally formatted data you want to sort by, or select the range of cells to be sorted, right-click the selection, point to Sort, then select the font color, highlighted color, or icon that you want to appear on top.

FIGURE G-15: Table sorted by departure date

	A	B	C	D	E	F	G	H	I
1	Tour	Depart Date	Number of Days	Seat Capacity	Seats Reserved	Price	Air Included	Insurance Included	Seats Available
2	Pacific Odyssey	1/12/2016	14	50		255	Yes	No	
3	Costa Rica	1/19/2016	10	31		966	Yes	Yes	
4	Yellowstone	1/21/2016	18	51		350	Yes	Yes	
5	Yellowstone	1/28/2016	18	51		350	Yes	Yes	
6	Amazing Amazon	2/22/2016	14	43		,134	No	No	
	ng Patagonia	2/28/2016	7	20	15	$ 2,812	Yes	No	
	ls of the Orient	3/13/2016	14	45	15	$ 2,350	Yes	No	
	Road Travels	3/19/2016	18	23	19	$ 2,110	Yes	Yes	
	ographing France	3/20/2016	7	20	20	$ 1,755	Yes	Yes	
	en Adventures in Ecuado	3/23/2016	18	25	22	$ 2,450	No	No	
12	African National Parks	4/8/2016	30	12	10	$ 3,115	Yes	Yes	
13	Experience Cambodia	4/11/2016	12	35	21	$ 2,441	Yes	No	
14	Old Japan	4/15/2016	21	47	30	$ 1,900	Yes	No	
15	Costa Rica	4/18/2016	10	30	20	$ 2,800	Yes	Yes	
16	Yellowstone	4/20/2016	18	51	31	$ 1,652	Yes	Yes	

Up arrow indicates ascending sort in the field

Records are sorted by departure date in ascending order

FIGURE G-16: Sort dialog box

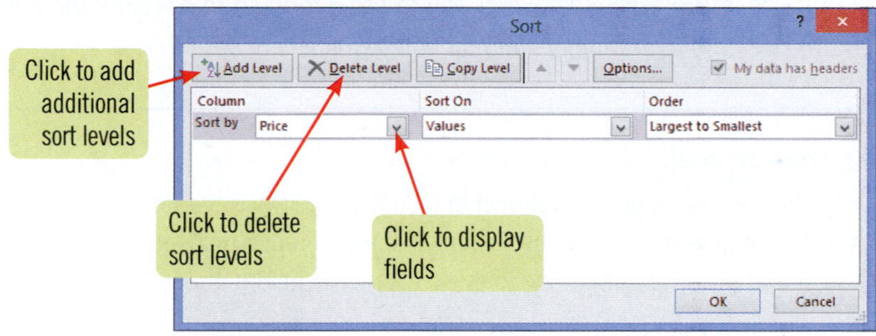

FIGURE G-17: Table sorted using two levels

	A	B	C	D	E	F	G	H	I
1	Tour	Depart Date	Number of Days	Seat Capacity	Seats Reserved	Price	Air Included	Insurance Included	Seats Available
2	African National Parks	4/8/2016	30	12	10	$ 3,115	Yes	Yes	
3	African National Parks	10/27/2016	30	12	8	$ 4,870	Yes	Yes	
4	Amazing Amazon	2/22/2016	14	43	39	$ 2,134	No	No	
5	Amazing Amazon	4/23/2016	14	43	30	$ 2,133	No	No	
6	Amazing Amazon	8/23/2016	14	43	18	$ 2,877	No	No	
7	Biking in France	5/23/2016	7	12	10	$ 1,635	No	No	
8	Biking in France	9/23/2016	7	12	7	$ 2,110	No	No	
9	Biking in Scotland	6/11/2016	10	15	10	$ 2,600	Yes	No	
10	Biking in Scotland	7/11/2			9	$ 2,600	Yes	No	
11	Biking in Scotland	8/11/2			6	$ 2,600	Yes	No	
12	Catalonia Adventure	5/9/2			30	$ 2,587	Yes	No	
13	Catalonia Adventure	6/9/2			15	$ 2,100	Yes	No	
14	Catalonia Adventure	10/9/2016	14	51	11	$ 2,100	Yes	No	
15	Corfu	10/2016	21	12	10	$ 2,190	Yes	No	
16	Corfu	9/2016	21	12	1	$ 2,190	Yes	No	

Second-level sort arranges records by departure date within each tour grouping

Top-level sort on Tour arranges records by tour name

TABLE G-2: Sort order options and examples

option	alphabetic	numeric	date	alphanumeric
Ascending	A, B, C	7, 8, 9	1/1, 2/1, 3/1	12A, 99B, DX8, QT7
Descending	C, B, A	9, 8, 7	3/1, 2/1, 1/1	QT7, DX8, 99B, 12A

Specifying a custom sort order

You can identify a custom sort order for the field selected in the Sort by box. Click the Order list arrow in the Sort dialog box, click Custom List, then click the desired custom order. Commonly used custom sort orders are days of the week (Sun, Mon, Tues, Wed, etc.) and months (Jan, Feb, Mar, etc.); alphabetic sorts do not sort these items properly.

Use Formulas in a Table

Learning Outcomes
- Build a table formula
- Use calculated columns to display formula results
- Use the table style options to add summary information to a table

Many tables are large, making it difficult to know from viewing them the "story" the table tells. The Excel table calculation features help you summarize table data so you can see important trends. After you enter a single formula into a table cell, the **calculated columns** feature fills in the remaining cells with the formula's results. The column continues to fill with the formula results as you enter rows in the table. This makes it easy to update your formulas because you only need to edit the formula once, and the change will fill in to the other column cells. The **structured reference** feature allows your formulas to refer to table columns by names that are automatically generated when you create the table. These names adjust as you add or delete table fields. An example of a table reference is =[Sales]–[Costs], where Sales and Costs are field names in the table. Tables also have a specific area at the bottom called the **table total row** for calculations using the data in the table columns. The cells in this row contain a dropdown list of functions that can be used for the column calculation. The table total row adapts to any changes in the table size. **CASE** *Kate wants you to use a formula to calculate the number of available seats for each tour. You will also add summary information to the end of the table.*

STEPS

1. **Click cell I2, then type =[**
   A list of the table field names appears, as shown in **FIGURE G-18**. Structured referencing allows you to use the names that Excel created when you defined your table to reference fields in a formula. You can choose a field by clicking it and pressing [Tab] or by double-clicking the field name.
2. **Click [Seat Capacity], press [Tab], then type]**
   Excel begins the formula, placing [Seat Capacity] in the cell in blue and framing the Seat Capacity data in a blue border.
3. **Type -[, double-click [Seats Reserved], then type]**
   Excel places [Seats Reserved] in the cell in red and outlines the Seats Reserved data in a red border.
4. **Press [Enter]**
   The formula result, 2, is displayed in cell I2. The table column also fills with the formula displaying the number of available seats for each tour.
5. **Click the AutoCorrect Options list arrow to view options for the column**
   Because the calculated columns option saves time, you decide to leave the feature on. You want to display the total number of available seats on all of the tours.
6. **Click any cell inside the table to close the menu, click the TABLE TOOLS DESIGN tab, then click the Total Row check box in the Table Style Options group to select it**
   A total row appears at the bottom of the table, and the sum of the available seats, 1088, is displayed in cell I64. You can select other formulas in the total row.
7. **Click cell C64, then click the cell list arrow on the right side of the cell**
   The list of available functions appears, as shown in **FIGURE G-19**. You want to find the average tour length.
8. **Click Average, then save your workbook**
   The average tour length, 13 days, appears in cell C64.

QUICK TIP
You can undo the calculated column results by clicking Undo Calculated Column in the AutoCorrect Options list. You can turn off the Calculated Columns feature by clicking Stop Automatically Creating Calculated Columns in the AutoCorrect Options list.

FIGURE G-18: Table field names

	A	B	C	D	E	F	G	H	I	J
1	Tour	Depart Date	Number of Days	Seat Capacity	Seats Reserved	Price	Air Included	Insurance Included	Seats Available	
2	African National Parks	4/8/2016	30	12	10	$ 3,115	Yes	Yes	=[	
3	African National Parks	10/27/2016	30	12	8	$ 4,870	Yes	Yes		
4	Amazing Amazon	2/22/2016	14	43	39	$ 2,134	No	No		
5	Amazing Amazon	4/23/2016	14	43	30	$ 2,133	No	No		
6	Amazing Amazon	8/23/2016	14	43	18	$ 2,877	No	No		
7	Biking in France	5/23/2016	7	12	10	$ 1,635	No	No		
8	Biking in France	9/23/2016	7	12	7	$ 2,110	No	No		
9	Biking in Scotland	6/11/2016	10	15	10	$ 2,600	Yes	No		
10	Biking in Scotland	7/11/2016	10	15	9	$ 2,600	Yes	No		
11	Biking in Scotland	8/11/2016	10	15	6	$ 2,600	Yes	No		
12	Catalonia Adventure	5/9/2016	14	51	30	$ 2,587	Yes	No		
13	Catalonia Adventure	6/9/2016	14	51	15	$ 2,100	Yes	No		
14	Catalonia Adventure	10/9/2016	14	51	11	$ 2,100	Yes	No		
15	Corfu Sailing Voyage	6/10/2016	21	12	10	$ 2,190	Yes	No		
16	Corfu Sailing Voyage	7/9/2016	21	12	1	$ 2,190	Yes	No		

Tour
Depart Date
Number of Days
Seat Capacity
Seats Reserved
Price
Air Included
Insurance Included
Seats Available

Field names list appears

FIGURE G-19: Functions in the Total Row

	Tour	Depart Da	Number of	Seat Capacit	Seats Reserv	Price	Air Include	Insurance In	Seats Avail
56	Wild River Escape	6/27/2016	10	21	21	$ 1,944	No	No	0
57	Wild River Escape	8/27/2016	10	21	11	$ 1,944	No	No	10
58	Yellowstone	1/21/2016	18	51	40	$ 1,850	Yes	Yes	11
59	Yellowstone	1/28/2016	18	51	0	$ 1,850	Yes	Yes	51
60	Yellowstone	4/20/2016	18	51	31	$ 1,652	Yes	Yes	20
61	Yellowstone	8/20/2016	18	51	20	$ 2,922	Yes	Yes	31
62	Yellowstone	9/11/2016	18	51	20	$ 2,922	Yes	Yes	31
63	Yellowstone	12/30/2016	18	51	15	$ 2,922	Yes	Yes	36
64	Total								1088
65									
66									
67									
68									
69									
70									
71									

None
Average
Count
Count Numbers
Max
Min
Sum
StdDev
Var
More Functions...

Functions available in the Total Row

Using structured references

When you create a table from worksheet data, Excel creates a default table name such as Table1. This table name appears in structured references. Structured references make it easier to work with formulas that use table data. You can reference the entire table, columns in the table, or specific data. Structured references are especially helpful to use in formulas because they automatically adjust as data ranges change in a table, so you don't need to edit formulas.

Excel 2013

Print a Table

Learning Outcomes
- Preview a table
- Add print titles to a table

You can determine the way a table will print using the PAGE LAYOUT tab. Because tables often have more rows than can fit on a page, you can define the first row of the table (containing the field names) as the **print title**, which prints at the top of every page. Most tables do not have any descriptive information above the field names on the worksheet, so to augment the field name information, you can use headers and footers to add identifying text, such as the table title or the report date. CASE *Kate asks you for a printout of the tour information. You begin by previewing the table.*

STEPS

1. **Click the FILE tab, click Print, then view the table preview**
   Below the table you see 1 of 3.
2. **In the Preview window, click the Next Page button ▶ in the Preview area to view the second page, then click ▶ again to view the third page**
   All of the field names in the table fit across the width of page 1. Because the records on pages 2 and 3 appear without column headings, you want to set up the first row of the table, which contains the field names, as a repeating print title.
3. **Return to the worksheet, click the PAGE LAYOUT tab, click the Print Titles button in the Page Setup group, click inside the Rows to repeat at top text box under Print titles, in the worksheet scroll up to row 1 if necessary, click any cell in row 1 on the table, then compare your Page Setup dialog box to FIGURE G-20**
   When you select row 1 as a print title, Excel automatically inserts an absolute reference to the row that will repeat at the top of each page.
4. **Click the Print Preview button in the Page Setup dialog box, click ▶ in the preview window to view the second page, then click ▶ again to view the third page**
   Setting up a print title to repeat row 1 causes the field names to appear at the top of each printed page. The printout would be more informative with a header to identify the table information.
5. **Return to the worksheet, click the INSERT tab, click the Header & Footer button in the Text group, click the left header section text box, then type 2016 Tours**
6. **Select the left header section information, click the HOME tab, click the Increase Font Size button A in the Font group twice to change the font size to 14, click the Bold button B in the Font group, click any cell in the table, then click the Normal button in the status bar**
7. **Save the table, preview it, close the workbook, exit Excel, then submit the workbook to your instructor**
   Compare your printed table with FIGURE G-21.

QUICK TIP
You can hide or print headings and gridlines using the check boxes in the Sheet Options group on the PAGE LAYOUT tab.

QUICK TIP
You can also add a header or a footer by clicking the Page Layout button in the status bar and clicking in the header or footer area.

FIGURE G-20: Page Setup dialog box

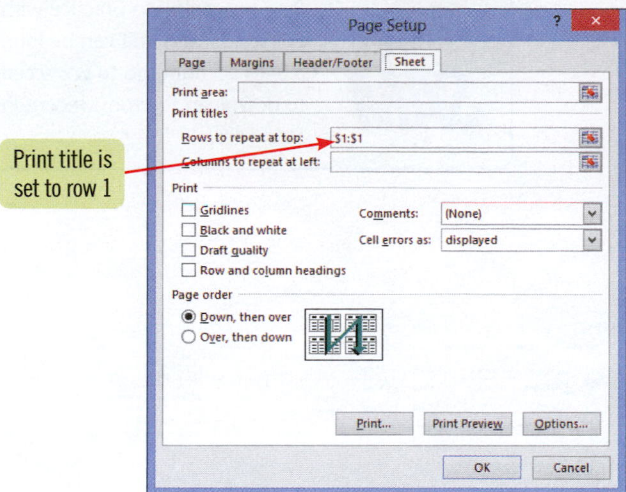

FIGURE G-21: Printed table

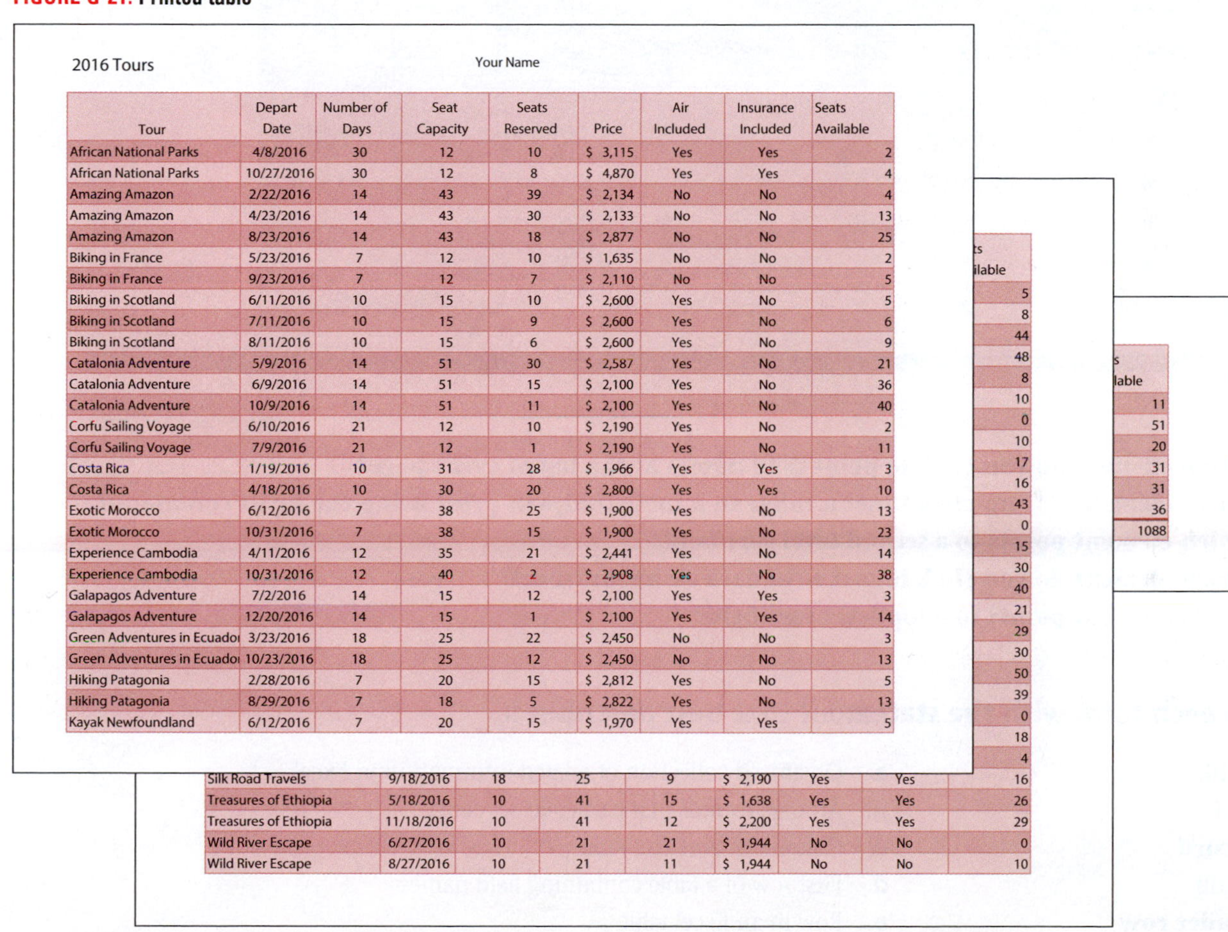

2016 Tours   Your Name

Tour	Depart Date	Number of Days	Seat Capacity	Seats Reserved	Price	Air Included	Insurance Included	Seats Available
African National Parks	4/8/2016	30	12	10	$ 3,115	Yes	Yes	2
African National Parks	10/27/2016	30	12	8	$ 4,870	Yes	Yes	4
Amazing Amazon	2/22/2016	14	43	39	$ 2,134	No	No	4
Amazing Amazon	4/23/2016	14	43	30	$ 2,133	No	No	13
Amazing Amazon	8/23/2016	14	43	18	$ 2,877	No	No	25
Biking in France	5/23/2016	7	12	10	$ 1,635	No	No	2
Biking in France	9/23/2016	7	12	7	$ 2,110	No	No	5
Biking in Scotland	6/11/2016	10	15	10	$ 2,600	Yes	No	5
Biking in Scotland	7/11/2016	10	15	9	$ 2,600	Yes	No	6
Biking in Scotland	8/11/2016	10	15	6	$ 2,600	Yes	No	9
Catalonia Adventure	5/9/2016	14	51	30	$ 2,587	Yes	No	21
Catalonia Adventure	6/9/2016	14	51	15	$ 2,100	Yes	No	36
Catalonia Adventure	10/9/2016	14	51	11	$ 2,100	Yes	No	40
Corfu Sailing Voyage	6/10/2016	21	12	10	$ 2,190	Yes	No	2
Corfu Sailing Voyage	7/9/2016	21	12	1	$ 2,190	Yes	No	11
Costa Rica	1/19/2016	10	31	28	$ 1,966	Yes	Yes	3
Costa Rica	4/18/2016	10	30	20	$ 2,800	Yes	Yes	10
Exotic Morocco	6/12/2016	7	38	25	$ 1,900	Yes	No	13
Exotic Morocco	10/31/2016	7	38	15	$ 1,900	Yes	No	23
Experience Cambodia	4/11/2016	12	35	21	$ 2,441	Yes	No	14
Experience Cambodia	10/31/2016	12	40	2	$ 2,908	Yes	No	38
Galapagos Adventure	7/2/2016	14	15	12	$ 2,100	Yes	Yes	3
Galapagos Adventure	12/20/2016	14	15	1	$ 2,100	Yes	Yes	14
Green Adventures in Ecuado	3/23/2016	18	25	22	$ 2,450	No	No	3
Green Adventures in Ecuado	10/23/2016	18	25	12	$ 2,450	No	No	13
Hiking Patagonia	2/28/2016	7	20	15	$ 2,812	Yes	No	5
Hiking Patagonia	8/29/2016	7	18	5	$ 2,822	Yes	No	13
Kayak Newfoundland	6/12/2016	7	20	15	$ 1,970	Yes	Yes	5

Silk Road Travels	9/18/2016	18	25	9	$ 2,190	Yes	Yes	16
Treasures of Ethiopia	5/18/2016	10	41	15	$ 1,638	Yes	Yes	26
Treasures of Ethiopia	11/18/2016	10	41	12	$ 2,200	Yes	Yes	29
Wild River Escape	6/27/2016	10	21	21	$ 1,944	No	No	0
Wild River Escape	8/27/2016	10	21	11	$ 1,944	No	No	10

Setting a print area

Sometimes you will want to print only part of a worksheet. To do this, select any worksheet range, click the FILE tab, click Print, click the Print Active Sheets list arrow, then click Print Selection. If you want to print a selected area repeatedly, it's best to define a **print area**, the area of the worksheet that previews and prints when you use the Print command in Backstage view. To set a print area, select the range of data on the worksheet that you want to print, click the PAGE LAYOUT tab, click the Print Area button in the Page Setup group, then click Set Print Area. You can add to the print area by selecting a range, clicking the Print Area button, then clicking Add to Print Area. A print area can consist of one contiguous range of cells, or multiple areas in different parts of a worksheet.

Practice

Put your skills into practice with **SAM Projects!** SAM Projects for this unit can be found online. If you have a SAM account, go to www.cengage.com/sam2013 to download the most recent Project Instruction and Start Files.

Concepts Review

FIGURE G-22

	A	B	C	D	E	F	G	H	I
1	Tour	Depart Date	Number of Days	Seat Capacity	Seats Reserved	Price	Air Included	Insurance Included	Seats Available
2	African National Parks	4/8/2016	30	12	10	$ 3,115	Yes	Yes	2
3	African National Parks	10/27/2016	30	12	8	$ 4,870	Yes	Yes	4
4	Amazing Amazon	2/22/2016	14	43	39	$ 2,134	No	No	4
5	Amazing Amazon	4/23/2016	14	43	30	$ 2,133	No	No	13
6	Amazing Amazon	8/23/2016	14	43	18	$ 2,877	No	No	25
7	Biking in France	5/23/2016	7	12	10	$ 1,635	No	No	2
8	Biking in France	9/23/2016	7	12	7	$ 2,110	No	No	5
9	Biking in Scotland	6/11/2016	10	15	10	$ 2,600	Yes	No	5
10	Biking in Scotland	7/11/2016	10	15	9	$ 2,600	Yes	No	6
11	Biking in Scotland	8/11/2016	10	15	6	$ 2,600	Yes	No	9
12	Catalonia Adventure	5/9/2016	14	51	30	$ 2,587	Yes	No	21
13	Catalonia Adventure	6/9/2016	14	51	15	$ 2,100	Yes	No	36
14	Catalonia Adventure	10/9/2016	14	51	11	$ 2,100	Yes	No	40
15	Corfu Sailing Voyage	6/10/2016	21	12	10	$ 2,190	Yes	No	2
16	Corfu Sailing Voyage	7/9/2016	21	12	1	$ 2,190	Yes	No	11

1. **Which element do you click to print field names at the top of every page?**
2. **Which element do you click to set a range in a table that will print using the Print command?**
3. **Which element points to a second-level sort field?**
4. **Which element do you click to sort field data on a worksheet?**
5. **Which element points to a top-level sort field?**

Match each term with the statement that best describes it.

6. Field	**a.** Organized collection of related information in Excel
7. Sort	**b.** Arrange records in a particular sequence
8. Record	**c.** Column in an Excel table
9. Table	**d.** First row of a table containing field names
10. Header row	**e.** Row in an Excel table

Select the best answer from the list of choices.

11. **Which of the following Excel sorting options do you use to sort a table of employee names in order from Z to A?**
    - **a.** Ascending
    - **b.** Absolute
    - **c.** Alphabetic
    - **d.** Descending

12. **Which of the following series appears in descending order?**
   - **a.** 8, 6, 4, C, B, A
   - **b.** 4, 5, 6, A, B, C
   - **c.** 8, 7, 6, 5, 6, 7
   - **d.** C, B, A, 6, 5, 4
13. **You can easily add formatting to a table by using:**
   - **a.** Table styles.
   - **b.** Print titles.
   - **c.** Print areas.
   - **d.** Calculated columns.
14. **When printing a table on multiple pages, you can define a print title to:**
   - **a.** Include the sheet name in table reports.
   - **b.** Include field names at the top of each printed page.
   - **c.** Exclude from the printout all rows under the first row.
   - **d.** Include gridlines in the printout.

Skills Review

1. **Create and format a table.**
   - **a.** Start Excel, open the file EX G-2.xlsx from the location where you store your Data Files, then save it as **EX G-Employees**.
   - **b.** Using the Practice sheet, enter the field names in the first row and the first two records in rows two and three, as shown in the table below, adjusting column widths as necessary to fit the text entries.

Last Name	First Name	Years Employed	Department	Full/Part Time	Training Completed
Diaz	Irina	3	Print Books	P	Y
Merril	Doreen	2	E-Books	F	N

   - **c.** Create a table using the data you entered.
   - **d.** On the Staff sheet, create a table with a header row. Adjust the column widths, if necessary, to display the field names. Enter your name in the center section of the worksheet footer, return to Normal view if necessary, then save the workbook.
   - **e.** Apply a table style of Light 16 to the table.
   - **f.** Enter your name in the center section of the worksheet footer, return to Normal view if necessary, then save the workbook.
2. **Add table data.**
   - **a.** Add a new record in row seven for **Heather Walker**, a 5-year employee in the Print Books department. Heather works part time and has completed training. Adjust the height of the new row to match the other table rows.
   - **b.** Insert a table row above Julie Kosby's record, and add a new record for **Sarah Allen**. Sarah works full time, has worked at the company for 2 years in E-Books, and has not completed training. Adjust the table formatting if necessary.
   - **c.** Insert a new data field in cell G1 with a label **Weeks Vacation**. Adjust the column width, and wrap the label in the cell to display the field name with **Weeks** above **Vacation**. (*Hint*: Use the Wrap Text button in the Alignment group on the HOME tab.)
   - **d.** Add a new column to the table by dragging the table's sizing handle, and give the new field a label of **Employee #**. Widen the column to fit the label.
   - **e.** Save the file.
3. **Find and replace table data.**
   - **a.** Return to cell A1.
   - **b.** Open the Find and Replace dialog box and if necessary uncheck the Match case option. Find the first record that contains the text **Print Books**.
   - **c.** Find the second and third records that contain the text **Print Books**.
   - **d.** Replace all **Print Books** text in the table with **Books**, then save the file.

Skills Review (continued)

4. **Delete table data.**
   a. Go to cell A1.
   b. Delete the record for Irina Diaz.
   c. Use the Remove Duplicates button to confirm that the table does not have any duplicate records.
   d. Delete the Employee # table column, then delete its column header, if necessary.
   e. Save the file.
5. **Sort table data.**
   a. Sort the table by years employed in largest to smallest order.
   b. Sort the table by last name in A to Z order.
   c. Perform a multilevel sort: Sort the table first by Full/Part Time in A to Z order and then by last name in A to Z order.
   d. Check the table to make sure the records appear in the correct order.
   e. Save the file.
6. **Use formulas in a table.**
   a. In cell G2, enter the formula that calculates an employee's vacation time; base the formula on the company policy that employees working at the company less than 3 years have 2 weeks of vacation. At 3 years of employment and longer, an employee has 3 weeks of vacation time. Use the table's field names where appropriate. (*Hint*: The formula is: **=IF([Years Employed]<3,2,3)**.)
   b. Check the table to make sure the formula filled into the cells in column G and that the correct vacation time is calculated for all cells in the column.
   c. Add a Total Row to display the total number of vacation weeks.
   d. Change the function in the Total Row to display the maximum number of vacation weeks. Change the entry in cell A8 from Total to **Maximum**.
   e. Compare your table to **FIGURE G-23**, then save the workbook.

FIGURE G-23

	A	B	C	D	E	F	G
1	Last Name	First Name	Years Employed	Department	Full/Part Time	Training Completed	Weeks Vacation
2	Allen	Sarah	2	E-Books	F	N	2
3	Green	Jane	1	Books	F	N	2
4	Kosby	Julie	4	E-Books	F	Y	3
5	Merril	Doreen	2	E-Books	F	N	2
6	Ropes	Mark	1	E-Books	P	Y	2
7	Walker	Heather	5	Books	P	Y	3
8	Maximum						3

7. **Print a table.**
   a. Add a header that reads **Employees** in the left section, then format the header in bold with a font size of 16.
   b. Add column A as a print title that repeats at the left of each printed page.
   c. Preview your table to check that the last names appear on both pages.
   d. Change the page orientation to landscape, preview the worksheet, then save the workbook.
   e. Submit your workbook to your instructor. Close the workbook, then exit Excel.

Independent Challenge 1

You are the marketing director for a fitness equipment sales firm. Your administrative assistant created an Excel worksheet with customer data including the results of an advertising survey. You will create a table using the customer data, and analyze the survey results to help focus the company's advertising expenses in the most successful areas.

   a. Start Excel, open the file EX G-3.xlsx from the location where you store your Data Files, then save it as **EX G-Customers**.
   b. Create a table from the worksheet data, and apply Table Style Light 18.

Independent Challenge 1 (continued)

c. Add the two records shown in the table below:

Last Name	First Name	Street Address	City	State	Zip	Area Code	Ad Source
Riley	Cate	81 Apple St.	San Francisco	CA	94177	415	Fitness Center
Jenkins	Sam	307 7th St.	Seattle	WA	98001	206	Newspaper

d. Find the record for Mike Rondo, then delete it.

e. Click cell A1 and replace all instances of **TV** with **Social Media**. Compare your table to **FIGURE G-24**.

FIGURE G-24

	A	B	C	D	E	F	G	H
1	Last Name	First Name	Street Address	City	State	Zip	Area Code	Ad Source
2	Kahil	Kathy	14 South St.	San Francisco	CA	94177	415	Social Media
3	Johnson	Mel	17 Henley St.	Reading	MA	03882	413	Newspaper
4	Malone	Kris	1 South St.	San Francisco	CA	94177	415	Fitness Center
5	Worthen	Sally	2120 Central St.	San Francisco	CA	93772	415	Fitness Center
6	Herbert	Greg	1192 Dome St.	San Diego	CA	93303	619	Newspaper
7	Chavez	Jane	11 Northern St.	San Diego	CA	92208	619	Social Media
8	Chelly	Yvonne	900 Sola St.	San Diego	CA	92106	619	Fitness Center
9	Smith	Carolyn	921 Lopez St.	San Diego	CA	92104	619	Newspaper
10	Oren	Scott	72 Yankee St.	Brookfield	CT	06830	203	Health Website
11	Warner	Salvatore	100 Westside St.	Chicago	IL	60620	312	Newspaper
12	Roberts	Bob	56 Water St.	Chicago	IL	60618	771	Fitness Center
13	Miller	Hope	111 Stratton St.	Chicago	IL	60614	773	Newspaper
14	Duran	Maria	Galvin St.	Chicago	IL	60614	773	Health Website
15	Roberts	Bob	56 Water St.	Chicago	IL	60614	312	Newspaper
16	Graham	Shelley	989 26th St.	Chicago	IL	60611	773	Education Website
17	Kelly	Janie	9 First St.	San Francisco	CA	94177	415	Newspaper
18	Kim	Janie	9 First St.	San Francisco	CA	94177	415	Health Website
19	Williams	Tasha	1 Spring St.	Reading	MA	03882	413	Newspaper
20	Juarez	Manuel	544 Cameo St.	Belmont	MA	02483	617	Newspaper
21	Masters	Latrice	88 Las Puntas Rd.	Boston	MA	02205	617	Education Website
22	Kooper	Peter	671 Main St.	Cambridge	MA	02138	617	Social Media
23	Kelly	Shawn	22 Kendall St.	Cambridge	MA	02138	617	Education Website
24	Rodriguez	Virginia	123 Main St.	Boston	MA	02007	617	Radio
25	Frei	Carol	123 Elm St.	Salem	MA	01970	978	Newspaper
26	Stevens	Crystal	14 Waterford St.	Salem	MA	01970	508	Radio
27	Ichikawa	Pam	232 Shore Rd.	Boston	MA	01801	617	Newspaper
28	Paxton	Gail	100 Main St.	Woburn	MA	01801	508	Newspaper
29	Spencer	Robin	293 Serenity Dr.	Concord	MA	01742	508	Radio
30	Lopez	Luis	1212 City St.	Kansas City	MO	64105	816	Social Media
31	Nelson	Michael	229 Rally Rd.	Kansas City	MO	64105	816	Education Website

f. Remove duplicate records where all fields are identical.

g. Sort the list by Last Name in A to Z order.

h. Sort the list again by Area Code in Smallest to Largest order.

i. Sort the table first by State in A to Z order, then within the state, by Zip in Smallest to Largest order.

j. Enter your name in the center section of the worksheet footer.

k. Add a centered header that reads **Ad Survey** in bold with a font size of 16.

l. Add print titles to repeat the first row at the top of each printed page.

m. Save the workbook, preview it, then submit the workbook to your instructor.

n. Close the workbook, then exit Excel.

Independent Challenge 2

You manage Green Living, a store that sells environmentally friendly cleaning supplies in bulk online. Your customers purchase items in quantities of 10 or more. You decide to plan and build a table of sales information with eight records using the items sold.

a. Prepare a plan for a table that states your goal, outlines the data you need, and identifies the table elements.

b. Sketch a sample table on a piece of paper, indicating how the table should be built. Create a table documenting the table design including the field names, type of data, and description of the data. Some examples of items are glass cleaner, tile cleaner, carpet cleaner, stone cleaner, and paper towels.

Independent Challenge 2 (continued)

c. Start Excel, create a new workbook, then save it as **EX G-Store Items** in the location where you store your Data Files. Enter the field names shown in the table below in the designated cells:

cell	field name
A1	Customer Last
B1	Customer First
C1	Item
D1	Quantity
E1	Cost

d. Enter eight data records using your own data.

e. Create a table using the data in the range A1:E9. Adjust the column widths as necessary.

f. Apply the Table Style Light 11 to the table.

g. Add a field named **Total** in cell F1.

h. Enter a formula in cell F2 that calculates the total by multiplying the Quantity field by the Cost field. Check that the formula was filled down in the column.

i. Format the Cost and Total columns using the Accounting number format. Adjust the column widths as necessary.

j. Add a new record to your table in row 10. Add another record above row 4.

k. Sort the table in ascending order by Item.

l. Enter your name in the worksheet footer, then save the workbook.

m. Preview the worksheet, then submit your workbook to your instructor.

n. Close the workbook, then exit Excel.

Independent Challenge 3

You are a property manager at a firm that manages condominiums and apartments. You are managing your accounts using an Excel worksheet and have decided that a table will provide additional features to help you keep track of the accounts. You will use the table sorting features and table formulas to analyze your account data.

a. Start Excel, open the file EX G-4.xlsx from the location where you store your Data Files, then save it as **EX G-Accounts**.

b. Create a table with the worksheet data, and apply a table style of your choice. Adjust the column widths as necessary.

c. Sort the table on the Budget field using the Smallest to Largest order.

d. Sort the table using two fields, by Contact in A to Z order, then by Budget in Smallest to Largest order. Compare your table to **FIGURE G-25**. (Your table style may differ.)

FIGURE G-25

	A	B	C	D	E	F
1	Property	Type	Code	Budget	Expenses	Contact
2	South End	Apartment	SE	$ 250,000	$ 225,000	Cindy Boil
3	Northfield	Apartment	NF	$ 275,000	$ 215,000	Cindy Boil
4	Warren	Condominium	WR	$ 375,000	$ 250,000	Cindy Boil
5	Langley Place	Condominium	LP	$ 650,000	$ 550,000	Cindy Boil
6	River Place	Condominium	RP	$ 175,000	$ 150,000	Jane Smith
7	Deer Run	Condominium	DR	$ 250,000	$ 210,000	Jane Smith
8	Green Ridge	Condominium	GR	$ 350,000	$ 210,000	Jane Smith
9	Rangeley	Condominium	RG	$ 410,000	$ 320,000	Jane Smith
10	Northridge	Apartment	NR	$ 550,000	$ 525,000	Kathy Jenkins
11	West End	Apartment	WE	$ 750,000	$ 600,000	Kathy Jenkins

Independent Challenge 3 (continued)

e. Add the new field label **Balance** in cell G1, and adjust the column width as necessary.
f. Enter a formula in cell G2 that uses structured references to table fields to calculate the balance on an account as the Budget minus the Expenses.
g. Add a new record for a property named **Riverside** with a type of **Condominium**, a code of **RS**, a budget of **$350,000**, expenses of **$250,000**, and a contact of **Cindy Boil**.
h. Verify that the formula accurately calculated the balance for the new record.
i. Replace all of the Jane Smith data with **Jane Atkins**.
j. Find the record for the Green Ridge property and delete it.
k. Delete the Type field from the table.
l. Add a total row to the table and display the totals for appropriate columns. Adjust the column widths as necessary.
m. Enter your name in the center section of the worksheet footer, add a center section header of **Accounts** using formatting of your choice, change the page orientation to landscape, then save the workbook.
n. Preview your workbook, submit the workbook to your instructor, close the workbook, then exit Excel.

Independent Challenge 4: Explore

As the Vice President of Marketing at a design firm, you track the expense accounts of the associates in the department using a table in Excel. You decide to highlight accounts that are over budget for the monthly meeting.

a. Start Excel, open the file EX G-5.xlsx from the location where you store your Data Files, then save it as **EX G-Associates**.
b. Create a table with the worksheet data, and apply the table style of your choice. Adjust the column widths as necessary.
c. Sort the table on the Balance field using the Smallest to Largest order.
d. Use conditional formatting to format the cells of the table containing negative balances with a green fill with dark green text.
e. Sort the table using the Balance field with the order of no cell color on top.
f. Format the table to emphasize the Balance column, and turn off the banded rows. (*Hint*: Use the Table Style Options on the TABLE TOOLS DESIGN tab.)
g. Research how to print nonadjacent areas on a single page. (Excel prints nonadjacent areas of a worksheet on separate pages by default.) Enter the result of your research on Sheet2 of the workbook.
h. Return to Sheet1 and create a print area that prints only the Account Number, Associate, and Balance columns of the table on one page.
i. Compare your table with FIGURE G-26. Save the workbook.
j. Preview your print area to make sure it will print on a single page.
k. Enter your name in the worksheet footers, then save the workbook.
l. Submit the workbook to your instructor, close the workbook, then exit Excel.

FIGURE G-26

	A	B	F
1	Account Number	Associate	Balance
2	96634	Kris Lowe	$ 5,000
3	32577	George Well	$ 10,000
4	15334	Janet Colby	$ 19,790
5	98661	Judy Makay	$ 25,000
6	84287	Joe Wood	$ 345,000
7	78441	Nancy Allen	$ 600,000
8	41557	Judy Makay	$ (15,000)
9	21889	Nancy Allen	$ (10,000)
10	57741	George Well	$ (10,000)
11	38997	Janet Colby	$ (5,000)

Visual Workshop

Start Excel, open the file EX G-6.xlsx from the location where you store your Data Files, then save it as **EX G-Products**. Create the table and sort the data as shown in **FIGURE G-27**. (*Hint*: The table is formatted using Table Style Medium 5.) Add a worksheet header with the sheet name in the center section that is formatted in bold with a size of 14. Enter your name in the center section of the worksheet footer. Save the workbook, preview the table, close the workbook, submit the workbook to your instructor, then exit Excel.

FIGURE G-27

1	Order Number	Department	Amount	Shipping	Sales Rep
2	1111	Shoes	$ 52.31	Air	Ellie Cranson
3	1032	Home	$ 157.22	Air	Ellie Cranson
4	2187	Home	$ 157.33	Air	Ellie Cranson
5	1251	Food	$ 255.47	Air	Ellie Cranson
6	2357	Food	$ 287.66	Ground	Ellie Cranson
7	2113	Home	$ 109.66	Ground	Gene Coburn
8	2257	Shoes	$ 179.65	Air	Gene Coburn
9	1587	Children	$ 200.52	Ground	Gene Coburn
10	2588	Shoes	$ 333.74	Ground	Gene Coburn
11	1533	Children	$ 327.88	Ground	Neil Boxer
12	2001	Children	$ 532.44	Air	Neil Boxer

Analyzing Table Data

CASE The vice president of sales, Kate Morgan, asks you to display information from a table of the 2016 scheduled tours to help the sales representatives with customer inquiries. She also asks you to prepare summaries of the tour sales for a presentation at the international sales meeting. You will prepare these using various filters, subtotals, and Excel functions.

Unit Objectives

After completing this unit, you will be able to:

- Filter a table
- Create a custom filter
- Filter a table with the Advanced Filter
- Extract table data
- Look up values in a table
- Summarize table data
- Validate table data
- Create subtotals

Files You Will Need

EX H-1.xlsx
EX H-2.xlsx
EX H-3.xlsx
EX H-4.xlsx
EX H-5.xlsx
EX H-6.xlsx
EX H-7.xlsx

Filter a Table

Learning Outcomes
- Filter records using AutoFilter
- Filter records using search criteria

An Excel table lets you easily manipulate large amounts of data to view only the data you want, using a feature called **AutoFilter**. When you create a table, arrows automatically appear next to each column header. These arrows are called **filter list arrows**, **AutoFilter list arrows**, or **list arrows**, and you can use them to **filter** a table to display only the records that meet criteria you specify, temporarily hiding records that do not meet those criteria. For example, you can use the filter list arrow next to the Tour field header to display only records that contain Nepal Trekking in the Tour field. Once you filter data, you can copy, chart, and print the displayed records. You can easily clear a filter to redisplay all the records. **CASE** *Kate asks you to display only the records for the Yellowstone tours. She also asks for information about the tours that sell the most seats and the tours that depart in March.*

STEPS

1. **Start Excel, open the file EX H-1.xlsx from the location where you save your Data Files, then save it as EX H-Tours**
2. **Click the Tour list arrow**

   Sort options appear at the top of the menu, advanced filtering options appear in the middle, and at the bottom is a list of the tour data from column A, as shown in FIGURE H-1. Because you want to display data for only the Yellowstone tours, your **search criterion** (the text you are searching for) is Yellowstone. You can select one of the Tour data options in the menu, which acts as your search criterion.

QUICK TIP
You can also filter the table to display only the Yellowstone tour information by clicking the Tour list arrow, entering "Yellowstone" in the Search text box on the menu options below Text Filters, then clicking OK.

3. **In the list of tours for the Tour field, click Select All to clear the check marks from the tours, scroll down the list of tours, click Yellowstone, then click OK**

   Only those records containing "Yellowstone" in the Tour field appear, as shown in FIGURE H-2. The row numbers for the matching records change to blue, and the list arrow for the filtered field has a filter icon. Both indicate that there is a filter in effect and that some of the records are temporarily hidden.
4. **Move the pointer over the Tour list arrow**

   The ScreenTip Tour: Equals "Yellowstone" describes the filter for the field, meaning that only the Yellowstone records appear. You decide to remove the filter to redisplay all of the table data.
5. **Click the Tour list arrow, then click Clear Filter From "Tour"**

   You have cleared the Yellowstone filter, and all the records reappear. You want to display the most popular tours, those that are in the top five percent of seats reserved.

QUICK TIP
You can also filter or sort a table by the color of the cells if conditional formatting has been applied.

6. **Click the Seats Reserved list arrow, point to Number Filters, click Top 10, select 10 in the middle box, type 5, click the Items list arrow, click Percent, then click OK**

   Excel displays the records for the top five percent in the number of Seats Reserved field, as shown in FIGURE H-3. You decide to clear the filter to redisplay all the records.
7. **On the HOME tab, click the Sort & Filter button in the Editing group, then click Clear**

   You have cleared the filter and all the records reappear. You can clear a filter using either the AutoFilter menu command or the Sort & Filter button on the HOME tab. The Sort & Filter button is convenient for clearing multiple filters at once. You want to find all of the tours that depart in March.
8. **Click the Depart Date list arrow, point to Date Filters, point to All Dates in the Period, then click March**

   Excel displays the records for only the tours that leave in March. You decide to clear the filter and display all of the records.

QUICK TIP
You can also clear a filter by clicking the Clear button in the Sort & Filter group on the DATA tab.

9. **Click the Sort & Filter button in the Editing group, click Clear, then save the workbook**

FIGURE H-1: Worksheet showing AutoFilter options

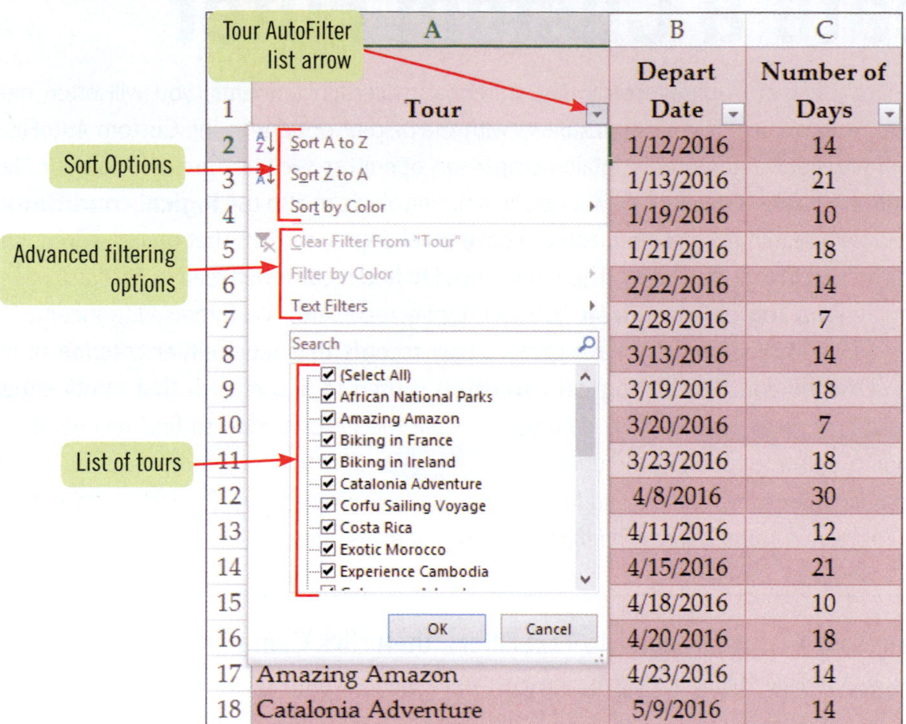

FIGURE H-2: Table filtered to show Yellowstone tours

	A	B	C	D	E	F	G	H
1	Tour	Depart Date	Number of Days	Seat Capacity	Seats Reserved	Price	Air Included	Insurance Included
5	Yellowstone	1/21/2016	18	51	40	$ 1,850	Yes	Yes
16	Yellowstone	4/20/2016	18	51	31	$ 1,652	Yes	Yes
41	Yellowstone	8/20/2016	18	51	20	$ 2,922	Yes	Yes
45	Yellowstone	9/11/2016	18	51	20	$ 2,922	Yes	Yes
63	Yellowstone	12/30/2016	18	51	15	$ 2,922	Yes	Yes
65								

List arrow changed to filter icon

Matching row numbers are blue and sequence indicates that not all rows appear

Filter displays only Yellowstone tours

FIGURE H-3: Table filtered with top 5% of Seats Reserved

	A	B	C	D	E	F	G	H
1	Tour	Depart Date	Number of Days	Seat Capacity	Seats Reserved	Price	Air Included	Insurance Included
2	Pacific Odyssey	1/12/2016	14	50	50	$ 2,255	Yes	No
3	Old Japan	1/13/2016	21	47	42	$ 1,984	Yes	No
5	Yellowstone	1/21/2016	18	51	40	$ 1,850	Yes	Yes
65								

Table filtered with top 5% in this field

Create a Custom Filter

Learning Outcomes
- Filter records with multiple criteria
- Determine when to use AND and OR logical conditions

While AutoFilter lists can display records that are equal to certain amounts, you will often need more detailed filters. You can use more complex filters with the help of options in the Custom AutoFilter dialog box. For example, your criteria can contain comparison operators such as "greater than" or "less than" that let you display values above or below a certain amount. You can also use **logical conditions** like And and Or to narrow a search even further. You can have Excel display records that meet a criterion in a field *and* another criterion in that same field. This is often used to find records between two values. For example, by specifying an **And logical condition**, you can display records for customers with incomes between $40,000 *and* $70,000. You can also have Excel display records that meet either criterion in a field by specifying an Or condition. The **Or logical condition** is used to find records that satisfy either of two values. For example, in a table of book data you can use the Or condition to find records that contain either Beginning *or* Introduction in the title name. **CASE** *Kate wants to locate tours for customers who like active vacations. She also wants to find tours that depart between February 15, 2016, and April 15, 2016. She asks you to create custom filters to find the tours satisfying these criteria.*

STEPS

1. **Click the Tour list arrow, point to Text Filters, then click Contains**
   The Custom AutoFilter dialog box opens. You enter your criteria in the text boxes. The left text box on the first line currently displays "contains." You want to display tours that contain the word "sailing" in their names.
2. **Type sailing in the right text box on the first line**
   You want to see entries that contain either sailing or biking.
3. **Click the Or option button to select it, click the left text box list arrow on the second line, scroll to and select contains, then type biking in the right text box on the second line**
   Your completed Custom AutoFilter dialog box should match FIGURE H-4.
4. **Click OK**
   The dialog box closes, and only those records having "sailing" or "biking" in the Tour field appear in the worksheet. You want to find all tours that depart between February 15, 2016 and April 15, 2016.
5. **Click the Tour list arrow, click Clear Filter From "Tour", click the Depart Date list arrow, point to Date Filters, then click Custom Filter**
   The Custom AutoFilter dialog box opens. The word "equals" appears in the left text box on the first line. You want to find the departure dates that are between February 15, 2016 and April 15, 2016 (that is, after February 15 *and* before April 15).
6. **Click the left text box list arrow on the first line, click is after, then type 2/15/2016 in the right text box on the first line**
   The And condition is selected, which is correct.
7. **Click the left text box list arrow on the second line, select is before, type 4/15/2016 in the right text box on the second line, then click OK**
   The records displayed have departure dates between February 15, 2016, and April 15, 2016. Compare your records to those shown in FIGURE H-5.
8. **Click the Depart Date list arrow, click Clear Filter From "Depart Date", then add your name to the center section of the footer**
   You have cleared the filter, and all the tour records reappear.

QUICK TIP
When specifying criteria in the Custom Filter dialog box, you can use the (?) wildcard to represent any single character and the (*) wildcard to represent any series of characters.

FIGURE H-4: Custom AutoFilter dialog box

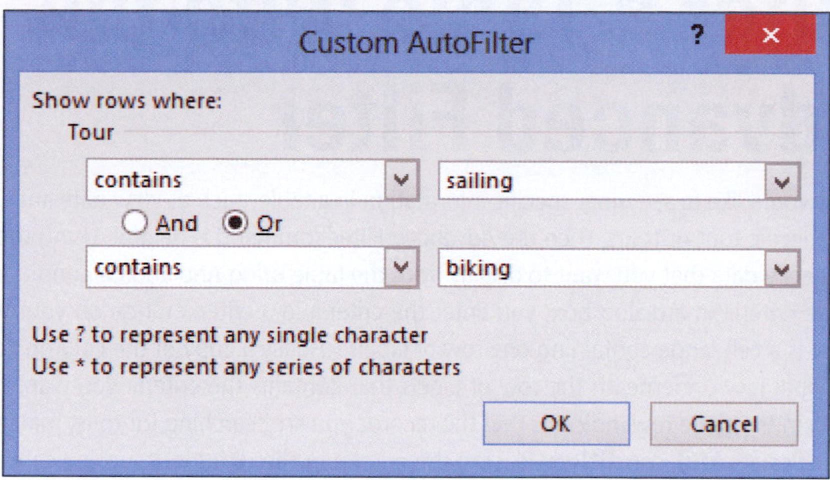

FIGURE H-5: Results of custom filter

	A	B	C	D	E	F	G	H
1	Tour	Depart Date	Number of Days	Seat Capacity	Seats Reserved	Price	Air Included	Insurance Included
6	Amazing Amazon	2/22/2016	14	43	39	$ 2,134	No	No
7	Hiking Patagonia	2/28/2016	7	20	15	$ 2,812	Yes	No
8	Pearls of the Orient	3/13/2016	14	45	15	$ 2,350	Yes	No
9	Silk Road Travels	3/19/2016	18	23	19	$ 2,110	Yes	Yes
10	Photographing France	3/20/2016	7	20	20	$ 1,755	Yes	Yes
11	Green Adventures in Ecuador	3/23/2016	18	25	22	$ 2,450	No	No
12	African National Parks	4/8/2016	30	12	10	$ 3,115	Yes	Yes
13	Experience Cambodia	4/11/2016	12	35	21	$ 2,441	Yes	No
65								

Departure dates are between 2/15 and 4/15

Using more than one rule when conditionally formatting data

You can apply conditional formatting to table cells in the same way that you can format a range of worksheet data. You can add multiple rules by clicking the HOME tab, clicking the Conditional Formatting button in the Styles group, then clicking New Rule for each additional rule that you want to apply. You can also add rules using the Conditional Formatting Rules Manager, which displays all of the rules for a data range. To use the Rules Manager, click the HOME tab, click the Conditional Formatting button in the Styles group, click Manage Rules, then click New Rule for each rule that you want to apply to the data range. After you have applied conditional formatting such as color fills, icon sets, or color scales to a numeric table range, you can use AutoFilter to sort or filter based on the colors or symbols.

Filter a Table with the Advanced Filter

Learning Outcomes
- Filter records using a criteria range and the And condition
- Filter records using a criteria range and the Or condition

If you would like to see more specific information in a table, such as view date and insurance information for a specific tour or tours, then the Advanced Filter command is helpful. Using the Advanced Filter, you can specify data that you want to display from the table using And and Or conditions. Rather than entering the criteria in a dialog box, you enter the criteria in a criteria range on your worksheet. A **criteria range** is a cell range containing one row of labels (usually a copy of the column labels) and at least one additional row underneath the row of labels that contains the criteria you want to match. Placing the criteria in the same row indicates that the records you are searching for must match both criteria; that is, it specifies an **And condition**. Placing the criteria in the different rows indicates that the records you are searching for must match only one of the criterion; that is, it specifies an **Or condition**. With the criteria range on the worksheet, you can easily see the criteria by which your table is sorted. You can also use the criteria range to create a macro using the Advanced Filter feature to automate the filtering process for data that you filter frequently. Another advantage of the Advanced Filter is that you can move filtered table data to a different area of the worksheet or to a new worksheet, as you will see in the next lesson. **CASE** *Kate wants to identify tours that depart after 6/1/2016 and that cost less than $2,000. She asks you to use the Advanced Filter to retrieve these records. You begin by defining the criteria range.*

STEPS

1. **Select table rows 1 through 6, click the Insert list arrow in the Cells group, click Insert Sheet Rows; click cell A1, type Criteria Range, then click the Enter button ✓ on the Formula bar**

   Six blank rows are added above the table. Excel does not require the label "Criteria Range", but it is useful to see the column labels as you organize the worksheet and use filters.

2. **Select the range A7:H7, click the Copy button in the Clipboard group, click cell A2, click the Paste button in the Clipboard group, then press [Esc]**

   Next, you want to insert criteria that will display records for only those tours that depart after June 1, 2016 and that cost under $2,000.

3. **Click cell B3, type >6/1/2016, click cell F3, type <2000, then click ✓**

   You have entered the criteria in the cells directly beneath the Criteria Range labels, as shown in FIGURE H-6.

4. **Click any cell in the table, click the DATA tab, then click the Advanced button in the Sort & Filter group**

   The Advanced Filter dialog box opens, with the table (list) range already entered. The default setting under Action is to filter the table in its current location ("in-place") rather than copy it to another location.

5. **Click the Criteria range text box, select the range A2:H3 in the worksheet, then click OK**

   You have specified the criteria range and used the filter. The filtered table contains eight records that match both criteria—the departure date is after 6/1/2016 and the price is less than $2,000, as shown in FIGURE H-7. You'll filter this table even further in the next lesson.

QUICK TIP
You can apply multiple criteria by using AutoFilter a second time on the results of the previously filtered data. Each additional filter builds on the results of the filtered data and filters the data further.

TROUBLE
If your filtered records don't match FIGURE H-7, make sure there are no spaces between the > symbol and the 6 in cell B3 and the < symbol and the 2 in cell F3.

FIGURE H-6: Criteria in the same row indicating an and condition

	A	B	C	D	E	F	G	H
1	Criteria Range							
2	Tour	Depart Date	Number of Days	Seat Capacity	Seats Reserved	Price	Air Included	Insurance Included
3		>6/1/2016				<2000		
4								
5								
6								
7	Tour	Depart Date	Number of Days	Seat Capacity	Seats Reserved	Price	Air Included	Insurance Included
8	Pacific Odyssey	1/12/2016	14	50	50	$ 2,255	Yes	No
9	Old Japan	1/13/2016	21	47	42	$ 1,984	Yes	No
10	Costa Rica	1/19/2016	10	31	28	$ 1,966	Yes	Yes

Filtered records will match these criteria

FIGURE H-7: Filtered table

	A	B	C	D	E	F	G	H
1	Criteria Range							
2	Tour	Depart Date	Number of Days	Seat Capacity	Seats Reserved	Price	Air Included	Insurance Included
3		>6/1/2016				<2000		
4								
5								
6								
7	Tour	Depart Date	Number of Days	Seat Capacity	Seats Reserved	Price	Air Included	Insurance Included
33	Exotic Morocco	6/12/2016	7	38	25	$ 1,900	Yes	No
34	Kayak Newfoundland	6/12/2016	7	20	15	$ 1,970	Yes	Yes
37	Wild River Escape	6/27/2016	10	21	21	$ 1,944	No	No
42	Kayak Newfoundland	7/12/2016	7	20	15	$ 1,970	Yes	Yes
44	Magnificent Montenegro	7/27/2016	10	48	0	$ 1,890	No	No
46	Kayak Newfoundland	8/12/2016	7	20	12	$ 1,970	Yes	Yes
49	Wild River Escape	8/27/2016	10	21	11	$ 1,944	No	No
61	Exotic Morocco	10/31/2016	7	38	15	$ 1,900	Yes	No
71								

Depart dates are after 6/1/2013

Prices are less than $2000

Using advanced conditional formatting options

You can emphasize top- or bottom-ranked values in a field using conditional formatting. To highlight the top or bottom values in a field, select the field data, click the Conditional Formatting button in the Styles group on the HOME tab, point to Top/Bottom Rules, select a Top or Bottom rule, if necessary enter the percentage or number of cells in the selected range that you want to format, select the format for the cells that meet the top or bottom criteria, then click OK. You can also format your worksheet or table data using icon sets and color scales based on the cell values. A **color scale** uses a set of two, three, or four fill colors to convey relative values. For example, red could fill cells to indicate they have higher values and green could signify lower values. To add a color scale, select a data range, click the HOME tab, click the Conditional Formatting button in the Styles group, then point to Color Scales. On the submenu, you can select preformatted color sets or click More Rules to create your own color sets. **Icon sets** let you visually communicate relative cell values by adding icons to cells based on the values they contain. An upward-pointing green arrow might represent the highest values, and downward-pointing red arrows could represent lower values. To add an icon set to a data range, select a data range, click the Conditional Formatting button in the Styles group, then point to Icon Sets. You can customize the values that are used as thresholds for color scales and icon sets by clicking the Conditional Formatting button in the Styles group, clicking Manage Rules, clicking the rule in the Conditional Formatting Rules Manager dialog box, then clicking Edit Rule.

Extract Table Data

Learning Outcomes
- Extract filtered records to another worksheet location
- Clear filtered records

Whenever you take the time to specify a complicated set of search criteria, it's a good idea to extract the matching records, rather than filtering it in place. When you **extract** data, you place a copy of a filtered table in a range that you specify in the Advanced Filter dialog box. This way, you won't accidentally clear the filter or lose track of the records you spent time compiling. To extract data, you use an Advanced Filter and enter the criteria beneath the copied field names, as you did in the previous lesson. You then specify the location where you want the extracted data to appear. **CASE** *Kate needs to filter the table one step further to reflect only the Wild River Escape or Kayak Newfoundland tours in the current filtered table. She asks you to complete this filter by specifying an Or condition, which you will do by entering two sets of criteria in two separate rows. You decide to save the filtered records by extracting them to a different location in the worksheet.*

STEPS

1. **In cell A3, enter Wild River Escape, then in cell A4, enter Kayak Newfoundland**
   The new sets of criteria need to appear in two separate rows, so you need to copy the previous filter criteria to the second row.
2. **Copy the criteria in B3:F3 to B4:F4**
   The criteria are shown in FIGURE H-8. When you use the Advanced Filter this time, you indicate that you want to copy the filtered table to a range beginning in cell A75, so that Kate can easily refer to the data, even if you use more filters later.
3. **If necessary, click the DATA tab, then click Advanced in the Sort & Filter group**
4. **Under Action, click the Copy to another location option button to select it, click the Copy to text box, then type A75**
   The last time you filtered the table, the criteria range included only rows 2 and 3, and now you have criteria in row 4.
5. **Edit the contents of the Criteria range text box to show the range $A$2:$H$4, click OK, then if necessary scroll down until row 75 is visible**
   The matching records appear in the range beginning in cell A75, as shown in FIGURE H-9. The original table, starting in cell A7, contains the records filtered in the previous lesson.
6. **Press [Ctrl][Home], then click the Clear button in the Sort & Filter group**
   The original table is displayed starting in cell A7, and the extracted table remains in A75:H80.
7. **Save the workbook**

QUICK TIP
Make sure the criteria range in the Advanced Filter dialog box includes the field names and the number of rows underneath the names that contain criteria. If you leave a blank row in the criteria range, Excel filters nothing and shows all records.

FIGURE H-8: Criteria in separate rows

	A	B	C	D	E	F	G
1	Criteria Range						
2	Tour	Depart Date	Number of Days	Seat Capacity	Seats Reserved	Price	Air Included
3	Wild River Escape	>6/1/2016				<2000	
4	Kayak Newfoundland	>6/1/2016				<2000	
5							

Criteria on two lines indicates an OR condition

FIGURE H-9: Extracted data records

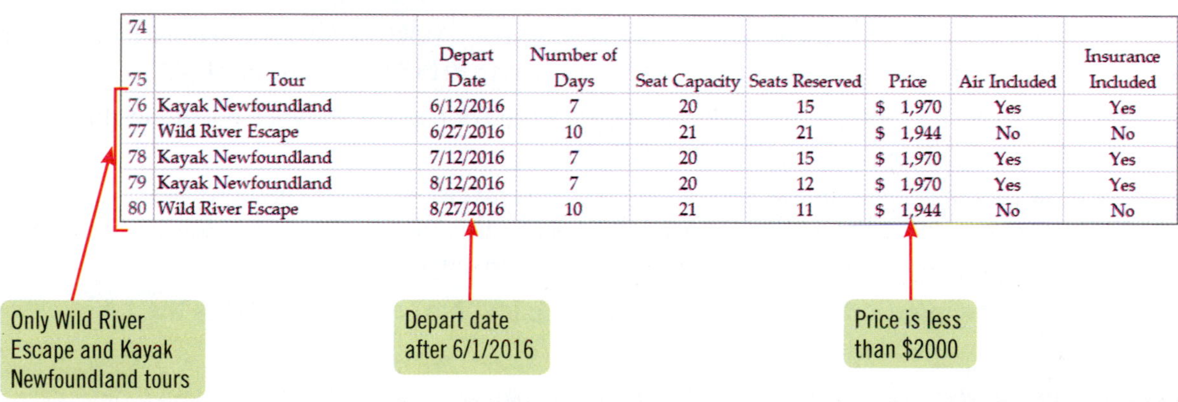

74								
75	Tour	Depart Date	Number of Days	Seat Capacity	Seats Reserved	Price	Air Included	Insurance Included
76	Kayak Newfoundland	6/12/2016	7	20	15	$ 1,970	Yes	Yes
77	Wild River Escape	6/27/2016	10	21	21	$ 1,944	No	No
78	Kayak Newfoundland	7/12/2016	7	20	15	$ 1,970	Yes	Yes
79	Kayak Newfoundland	8/12/2016	7	20	12	$ 1,970	Yes	Yes
80	Wild River Escape	8/27/2016	10	21	11	$ 1,944	No	No

Understanding the criteria range and the copy-to location

When you define the criteria range and the copy-to location in the Advanced Filter dialog box, Excel automatically creates the range names Criteria and Extract for these ranges in the worksheet. The Criteria range includes the field names and any criteria rows underneath them. The Extract range includes just the field names above the extracted table. You can select these ranges by clicking the Name box list arrow, then clicking the range name. If you click the Name Manager button in the Defined Names group on the FORMULAS tab, you will see these new names and the ranges associated with each one.

Excel 2013
UNIT H

Look Up Values in a Table

Learning Outcomes
- Use table references in a VLOOKUP formula
- Find table information using VLOOKUP

The Excel VLOOKUP function helps you locate specific values in a table. VLOOKUP searches vertically (V) down the far left column of a table, then reads across the row to find the value in the column you specify, much as you might look up a number in a name and address list: You locate a person's name, then read across the row to find the phone number you want. **CASE** *Kate wants to be able to find a tour destination by entering the tour code. You will use the VLOOKUP function to accomplish this task. You begin by viewing the table name so you can refer to it in a lookup function.*

STEPS

QUICK TIP
You can change table names to better represent their content so they are easier to use in formulas. Click the table in the list of names in the Name Manager text box, click Edit, type the new table name in the Name text box, then click OK.

1. **Click the Lookup sheet tab, click the FORMULAS tab in the Ribbon, then click the Name Manager button in the Defined Names group**

   The named ranges for the workbook appear in the Name Manager dialog box, as shown in FIGURE H-10. The Criteria and Extract ranges appear at the top of the range name list. At the bottom of the list is information about the three tables in the workbook. Table1 refers to the table on the Tours sheet, Table2 refers to the table on the Lookup sheet, and Table3 refers to the table on the Subtotals worksheet. The Excel structured reference feature automatically created these table names when the tables were created.

2. **Click Close**

   You want to find the tour represented by the code 830L. The VLOOKUP function lets you find the tour name for any trip code. You will enter a trip code in cell M1 and a VLOOKUP function in cell M2.

3. **Click cell M1, enter 830L, click cell M2, click the Lookup & Reference button in the Function Library group, then click VLOOKUP**

   The Function Arguments dialog box opens, with boxes for each of the VLOOKUP arguments. Because the value you want to find is in cell M1, M1 is the Lookup_value. The table you want to search is the table on the Lookup sheet, so its assigned name, Table2, is the Table_array.

QUICK TIP
If you want to find only the closest match for a value, enter TRUE in the Range_lookup text box. However, this can give misleading results if you are looking for an exact match. If you use FALSE and Excel can't find the value, you see an error message.

4. **With the insertion point in the Lookup_value text box, click cell M1, click the Table_array text box, then type Table2**

   The column containing the information that you want to find and display in cell M2 is the second column from the left in the table range, so the Col_index_num is 2. Because you want to find an exact match for the value in cell M1, the Range_lookup argument is FALSE.

5. **Click the Col_index_num text box, type 2, click the Range_lookup text box, then enter FALSE**

   Your completed Function Arguments dialog box should match FIGURE H-11.

6. **Click OK**

   Excel searches down the far-left column of the table until it finds a trip code that matches the one in cell M1. It then looks in column 2 of the table range and finds the tour for that record, Old Japan, and displays it in cell M2. You use this function to determine the tour for one other trip code.

7. **Click cell M1, type 325B, then click the Enter button ✓ on the formula bar**

   The VLOOKUP function returns the value of Biking In France in cell M2.

8. **Press [Ctrl][Home], then save the workbook**

Finding records using the DGET function

You can also use the DGET function to find a record in a table that matches specified criteria. For example, you could use the criteria of L1:L2 in the DGET function. When using DGET, you need to include [#All] after your table name in the formula to include the column labels that are used for the criteria range. Unlike VLOOKUP, you do not have the option of using a Range_Lookup value of TRUE to find an approximate match.

FIGURE H-10: Named ranges in the workbook

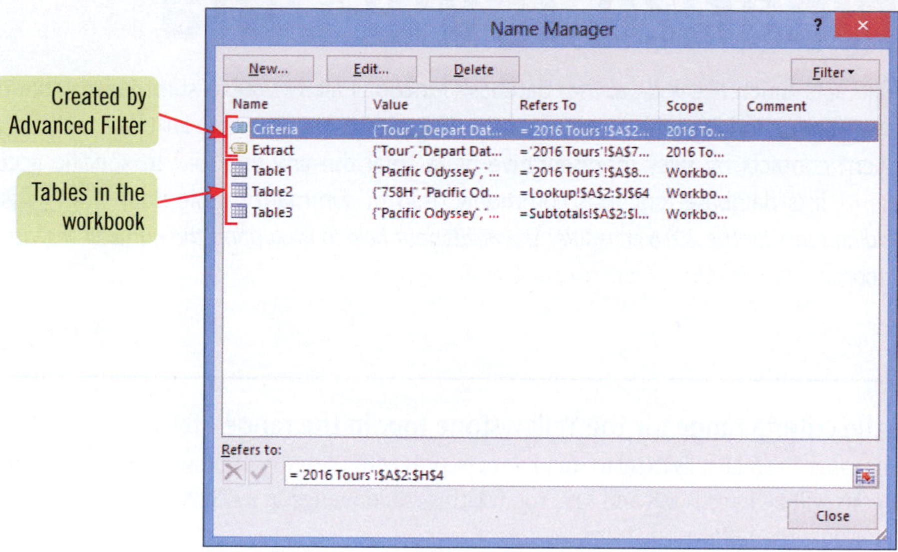

FIGURE H-11: Completed Function Arguments dialog box for VLOOKUP

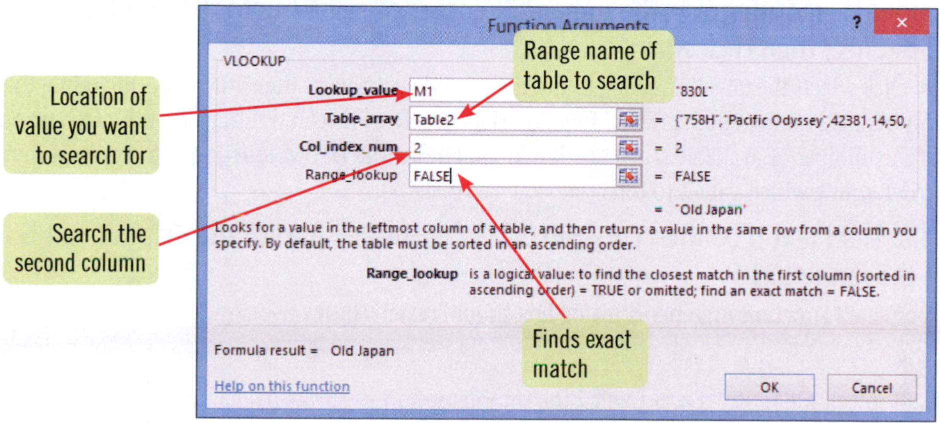

Using the HLOOKUP and MATCH functions

The VLOOKUP (Vertical Lookup) function is useful when your data is arranged vertically, in columns. When your data is arranged horizontally in rows, use the HLOOKUP (Horizontal Lookup) function. HLOOKUP searches horizontally across the upper row of a table until it finds the matching value, then looks down the number of rows you specify. The arguments for this function are identical to those for the VLOOKUP function, with one exception. Instead of a Col_index_number, HLOOKUP uses a Row_index_number, which indicates the location of the row you want to search. For example, if you want to search the fourth row from the top of the table range, the Row_index_number should be 4. You can use the MATCH function when you want the position of an item in a range. The MATCH function uses the syntax: MATCH (lookup_value,lookup_array,match_ type) where the lookup_value is the value you want to match in the lookup_array range. The match_type can be 0 for an exact match, 1 for matching the largest value that is less than or equal to lookup_value, or –1 for matching the smallest value that is greater than or equal to the lookup_value.

Summarize Table Data

Learning Outcomes
- Summarize table data using DSUM
- Summarize table data using DCOUNT or DCOUNTA

Because a table acts much like a database, database functions allow you to summarize table data in a variety of ways. When working with a sales activity table, for example, you can use Excel to count the number of client contacts by sales representative or to total the amount sold to specific accounts by month. **TABLE H-1** lists database functions commonly used to summarize table data. **CASE** *Kate is considering adding tours for the 2016 schedule. She needs your help in evaluating the number of seats available for scheduled tours.*

STEPS

1. **Review the criteria range for the Yellowstone tour in the range L5:L6**
   The criteria range in L5:L6 tells Excel to summarize records with the entry "Yellowstone" in the Tour column. The functions will be in cells M8 and M9. You use this criteria range in a DSUM function to sum the seats available for only the Yellowstone tours.

2. **Click cell M8, click the Insert Function button in the Function Library group, in the Search for a function text box type database, click Go, scroll to and click DSUM under Select a function, then click OK**
   The first argument of the DSUM function is the table, or database.

QUICK TIP
Because the DSUM formula uses the column headings to locate and sum the table data, the header row needs to be included in the database range.

3. **In the Function Arguments dialog box, with the insertion point in the Database text box, move the pointer over the upper-left corner of cell A1 until the pointer becomes ↘, click once, then click again**
   The first click selects the table's data range, and the second click selects the entire table, including the header row. The second argument of the DSUM function is the label for the column that you want to sum. You want to total the number of available seats. The last argument for the DSUM function is the criteria that will be used to determine which values to total.

QUICK TIP
You can move the Function Arguments dialog box if it overlaps a cell or range that you need to click. You can also click the Collapse Dialog Box button, select the cell or range, then click the Expand Dialog Box button to return to the Function Arguments dialog box.

4. **Click the Field text box, then click cell G1, Seats Available; click the Criteria text box and select the range L5:L6**
   Your completed Function Arguments dialog box should match **FIGURE H-12**.

5. **Click OK**
   The result in cell M8 is 129. Excel totaled the information in the Seats Available column for those records that meet the criterion of Tour equals Yellowstone. The DCOUNT and the DCOUNTA functions can help you determine the number of records meeting specified criteria in a database field. DCOUNTA counts the number of nonblank cells. You will use DCOUNTA to determine the number of tours scheduled.

6. **Click cell M9, click the Insert Function button on the formula bar, in the Search for a function text box type database, click Go, select DCOUNTA from the Select a function list, then click OK**

7. **With the insertion point in the Database text box, move the pointer over the upper-left corner of cell A1 until the pointer becomes ↘, click once, click again to include the header row, click the Field text box and click cell B1, click the Criteria text box and select the range L5:L6, then click OK**
   The result in cell M9 is 5, and it indicates that there are five Yellowstone tours scheduled for the year. You also want to display the number of seats available for the Old Japan tours.

8. **Click cell L6, type Old Japan, then click the Enter button on the formula bar**
   FIGURE H-13 shows that 67 seats are available in the four Old Japan tours, and there are four tours scheduled.

FIGURE H-12: Completed Function Arguments dialog box for DSUM

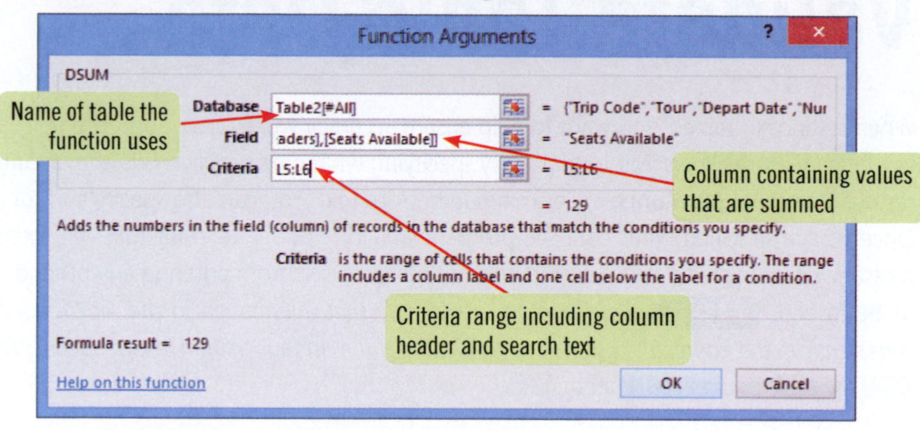

FIGURE H-13: Result generated by database functions

	G	H	I	J	K	L	M
1	Seats Available	Price	Air Included	Insurance Included		Trip Code	325B
2	0	$ 2,255	Yes	No		Tour	Biking in France
3	5	$ 1,984	Yes	No			
4	3	$ 1,966	Yes	Yes		Tour Information	
5	11	$ 1,850	Yes	Yes		Tour	
6	4	$ 2,134	No	No		Old Japan	
7	5	$ 2,812	Yes	No			
8	30	$ 2,350	Yes	No		Seats Available	67
9	4	$ 2,110	Yes	Yes		Number of tours scheduled	4
10	0	$ 1,755	Yes	Yes			
11	3	$ 2,450	No	No			

Information for Old Japan tours

TABLE H-1: Common database functions

function	result
DGET	Extracts a single record from a table that matches criteria you specify
DSUM	Totals numbers in a given table column that match criteria you specify
DAVERAGE	Averages numbers in a given table column that match criteria you specify
DCOUNT	Counts the cells that contain numbers in a given table column that match criteria you specify
DCOUNTA	Counts the cells that contain nonblank data in a given table column that match criteria you specify

Validate Table Data

Learning Outcomes
- Use data validation to restrict data entry to specified values
- Insert table data using data validation

When setting up tables, you want to help ensure accuracy when you or others enter data. The Excel data validation feature allows you to do this by specifying what data users can enter in a range of cells. You can restrict data to whole numbers, decimal numbers, or text. You can also specify a list of acceptable entries. Once you've specified what data the program should consider valid for that cell, Excel displays an error message when invalid data is entered and can prevent users from entering any other data that it considers to be invalid. **CASE** *Kate wants to make sure that information in the Air Included column is entered consistently in the future. She asks you to restrict the entries in that column to two options: Yes and No. First, you select the table column you want to restrict.*

STEPS

1. **Click the top edge of the Air Included column header**
   The column data is selected.
2. **Click the DATA tab, click the Data Validation button in the Data Tools group, click the Settings tab if necessary, click the Allow list arrow, then click List**
   Selecting the List option lets you type a list of specific options.

QUICK TIP
To specify a long list of valid entries, type the list in a column or row elsewhere in the worksheet, then type the list range in the Source text box.

3. **Click the Source text box, then type Yes, No**
   You have entered the list of acceptable entries, separated by commas, as shown in **FIGURE H-14**. You want the data entry person to be able to select a valid entry from a drop-down list.
4. **Click the In-cell dropdown check box to select it if necessary, then click OK**
   The dialog box closes, and you return to the worksheet.

TROUBLE
If you get an invalid data error, make sure that cell I1 is not included in the selection. If I1 is included, open the Data Validation dialog box, click Clear All, click OK, then begin with Step 1 again.

5. **Click the HOME tab, click any cell in the last table row, click the Insert list arrow in the Cells group, click Insert Table Row Below, click the last cell in the Air Included column, then click its list arrow to display the list of valid entries**
   The drop-down list is shown in **FIGURE H-15**. You could click an item in the list to have it entered in the cell, but you want to test the data restriction by entering an invalid entry.
6. **Click the list arrow to close the list, type Maybe, then press [Enter]**
   A warning dialog box appears and prevents you from entering the invalid data, as shown in **FIGURE H-16**.
7. **Click Cancel, click the list arrow, then click Yes**
   The cell accepts the valid entry. The data restriction ensures that records contain only one of the two correct entries in the Air Included column. The table is ready for future data entry.
8. **Delete the last table row, add your name to the center section of the footer, then save the workbook**

Restricting cell values and data length

In addition to providing an in-cell drop-down list for data entry, you can use data validation to restrict the values that are entered into cells. For example, if you want to restrict cells in a selected range to values less than a certain number, date, or time, click the DATA tab, click the Data Validation button in the Data Tools group, and on the Settings tab, click the Allow list arrow, select Whole number, Decimal, Date, or Time, click the Data list arrow, select less than, then in the bottom text box, enter the maximum value. You can also limit the length of data entered into cells by choosing Text length in the Allow list, clicking the Data list arrow and selecting less than, then entering the maximum length in the Maximum text box.

FIGURE H-14: Creating data restrictions

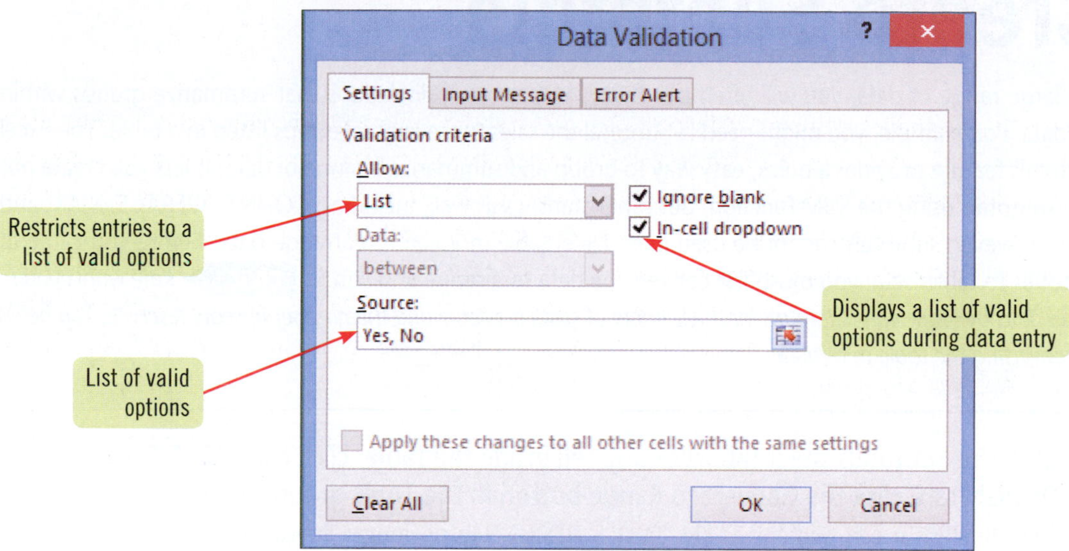

FIGURE H-15: Entering data in restricted cells

54	666B	Nepal Trekking	10/29/2016	14	18	8	10	$ 4,200	Yes	Yes
55	557N	Exotic Morocco	10/31/2016	7	38	15	23	$ 1,900	Yes	No
56	524Z	Experience Cambodia	10/31/2016	12	40	2	38	$ 2,908	Yes	No
57	509V	Treasures of Ethiopia	11/18/2016	10	41	12	29	$ 2,200	Yes	Yes
58	397S	Panama Adventure	12/18/2016	10	50	21	29	$ 2,204	Yes	Yes
59	621R	Panama Adventure	12/18/2016	10	50	21	29	$ 2,204	Yes	Yes
60	592D	Galapagos Adventure	12/20/2016	14	15	1	14	$ 2,100	Yes	Yes
61	793T	Galapagos Adventure	12/20/2016	14	15	1	14	$ 2,100	Yes	Yes
62	307R	Pacific Odyssey	12/21/2016	14	50	10	40	$ 2,105	Yes	No
63	927F	Yellowstone	12/30/2016	18	51	15	36	$ 2,922	Yes	Yes
64	448G	Old Japan	12/31/2016	21	47	4	43	$ 2,100	Yes	No
65							0			
66										

Dropdown list

Yes
No

FIGURE H-16: Invalid data warning

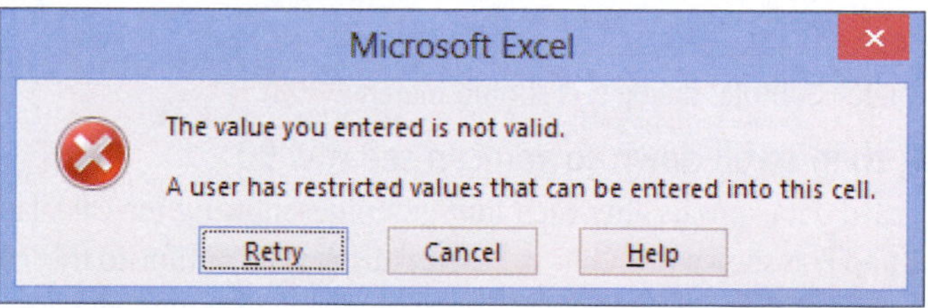

Adding input messages and error alerts

You can customize the way data validation works by using the two other tabs in the Data Validation dialog box: Input Message and Error Alert. The Input Message tab lets you set a message that appears when the user selects that cell. For example, the message might contain instructions about what type of data to enter. On the Input Message tab, enter a message title and message, then click OK. The Error Alert tab lets you set one of three alert levels if a user enters invalid data. The Information level displays your message with the information icon but allows the user to proceed with data entry. The Warning level displays your information with the warning icon and gives the user the option to proceed with data entry or not. The Stop level, which you used in this lesson, displays your message and only lets the user retry or cancel data entry for that cell.

Excel 2013
UNIT H

Create Subtotals

Learning Outcomes
- Summarize worksheet data using subtotals
- Use outline symbols
- Convert a table to a range

In a large range of data, you will often need ways to perform calculations that summarize groups within the data. For example, you might need to subtotal the sales for several sales reps listed in a table. The Excel Subtotals feature provides a quick, easy way to group and summarize a range of data. It lets you create not only subtotals using the SUM function, but other statistics as well, including COUNT, AVERAGE, MAX, and MIN. However, subtotals cannot be used in an Excel table, nor can it rearrange data. Before you can add subtotals to table data, you must first convert the data to a range and sort it. **CASE** *Kate wants you to group data by tours, with subtotals for the number of seats available and the number of seats reserved. You begin by converting the table to a range.*

STEPS

1. **Click the Subtotals sheet tab, click any cell inside the table, click the TABLE TOOLS DESIGN tab, click the Convert to Range button in the Tools group, then click Yes**
   The filter list arrows and the TABLE TOOLS DESIGN tab no longer appear. Before you can add the subtotals, you must first sort the data. You decide to sort it in ascending order, first by tour and then by departure date.
2. **Click the DATA tab, click the Sort button in the Sort & Filter group, in the Sort dialog box click the Sort by list arrow, click Tour, click the Add Level button, click the Then by list arrow, click Depart Date, verify that the order is Oldest to Newest, then click OK**
   You have sorted the range in ascending order, first by tour, then by departure date within each tour grouping.
3. **Click any cell in the data range if necessary, then click the Subtotal button in the Outline group**
   The Subtotal dialog box opens. Here you specify the items you want subtotaled, the function you want to apply to the values, and the fields you want to summarize.
4. **Click the At each change in list arrow, click Tour if necessary, click the Use function list arrow, click Sum; in the "Add subtotal to" list, click the Seats Reserved and Seats Available check boxes to select them, if necessary, then click the Insurance Included check box to deselect it**
5. **If necessary, click the Replace current subtotals and Summary below data check boxes to select them**
   Your completed Subtotal dialog box should match FIGURE H-17.
6. **Click OK, then scroll down so you can see row 90**
   The subtotaled data appears after each tour grouping, showing the calculated subtotals and grand total in columns E and F, as shown in FIGURE H-18. Excel displays an outline to the left of the worksheet, with outline buttons to control the level of detail that appears. The button number corresponds to the detail level that is displayed. You want to show the second level of detail, the subtotals and the grand total.
7. **Click the outline symbol 2**
   Only the subtotals and the grand total appear.
8. **Add your name to the center section of the footer, preview the worksheet, click the No Scaling list arrow, click Fit Sheet on One Page to scale the worksheet to print on one page, then save the workbook**
9. **Close the workbook, exit Excel, then submit the workbook to your instructor**

QUICK TIP
You can click the − button to hide or the + button to show a group of records in the subtotaled structure.

QUICK TIP
You can remove subtotals in a worksheet by clicking the Subtotal button and clicking Remove All. The subtotals no longer appear, and the Outline feature is turned off automatically.

FIGURE H-17: Completed Subtotal dialog box

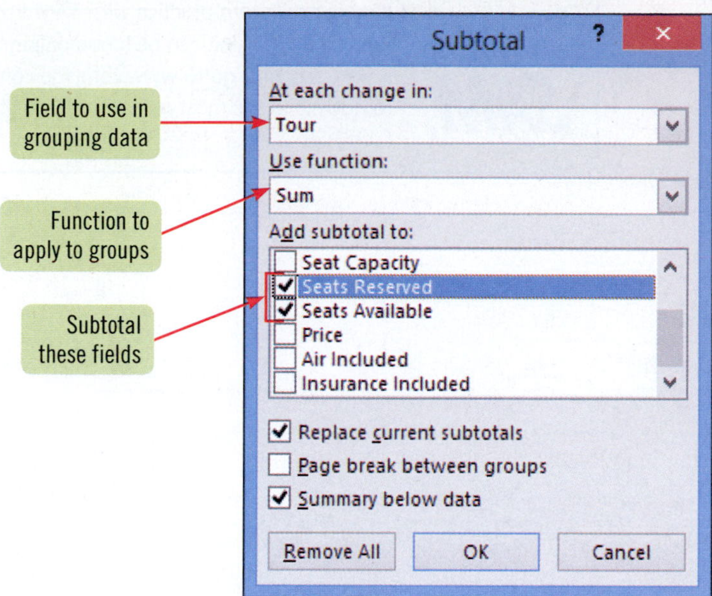

FIGURE H-18: Portion of subtotaled table

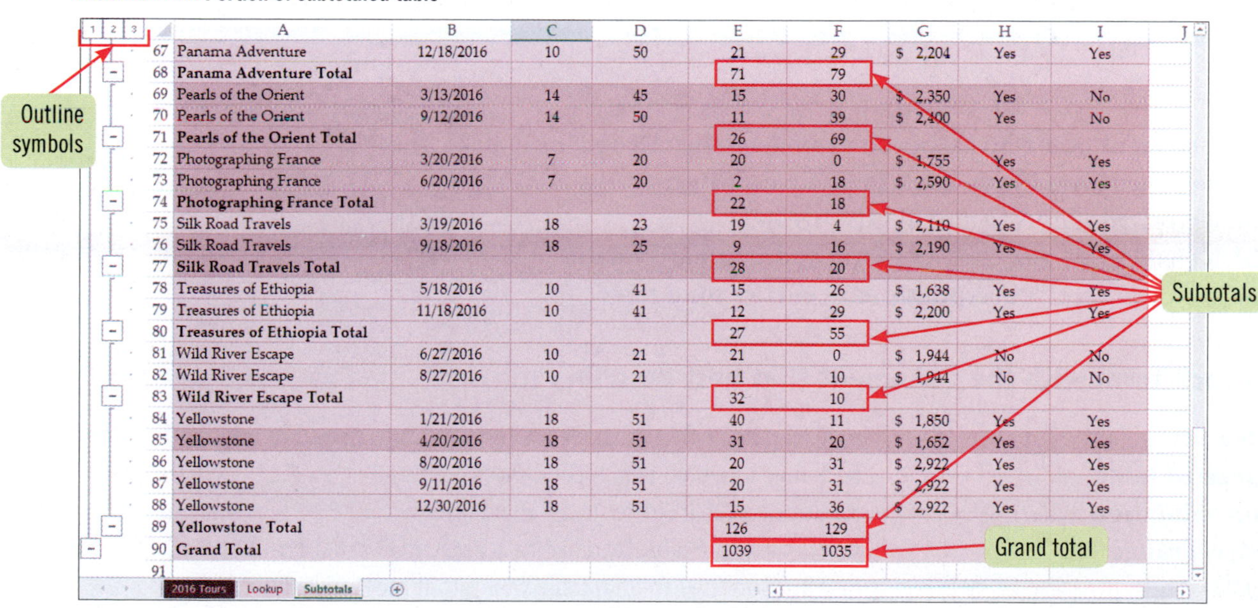

	A	B	C	D	E	F	G	H	I
67	Panama Adventure	12/18/2016	10	50	21	29	$ 2,204	Yes	Yes
68	**Panama Adventure Total**				71	79			
69	Pearls of the Orient	3/13/2016	14	45	15	30	$ 2,350	Yes	No
70	Pearls of the Orient	9/12/2016	14	50	11	39	$ 2,400	Yes	No
71	**Pearls of the Orient Total**				26	69			
72	Photographing France	3/20/2016	7	20	20	0	$ 1,755	Yes	Yes
73	Photographing France	6/20/2016	7	20	2	18	$ 2,590	Yes	Yes
74	**Photographing France Total**				22	18			
75	Silk Road Travels	3/19/2016	18	23	19	4	$ 2,110	Yes	Yes
76	Silk Road Travels	9/18/2016	18	25	9	16	$ 2,190	Yes	Yes
77	**Silk Road Travels Total**				28	20			
78	Treasures of Ethiopia	5/18/2016	10	41	15	26	$ 1,638	Yes	Yes
79	Treasures of Ethiopia	11/18/2016	10	41	12	29	$ 2,200	Yes	Yes
80	**Treasures of Ethiopia Total**				27	55			
81	Wild River Escape	6/27/2016	10	21	21	0	$ 1,944	No	No
82	Wild River Escape	8/27/2016	10	21	11	10	$ 1,944	No	No
83	**Wild River Escape Total**				32	10			
84	Yellowstone	1/21/2016	18	51	40	11	$ 1,850	Yes	Yes
85	Yellowstone	4/20/2016	18	51	31	20	$ 1,652	Yes	Yes
86	Yellowstone	8/20/2016	18	51	20	31	$ 2,922	Yes	Yes
87	Yellowstone	9/11/2016	18	51	20	31	$ 2,922	Yes	Yes
88	Yellowstone	12/30/2016	18	51	15	36	$ 2,922	Yes	Yes
89	**Yellowstone Total**				126	129			
90	**Grand Total**				1039	1035			
91									

Excel 2013

Practice

Put your skills into practice with **SAM Projects**! SAM Projects for this unit can be found online. If you have a SAM account, go to www.cengage.com/sam2013 to download the most recent Project Instruction and Start Files.

Concepts Review

FIGURE H-19

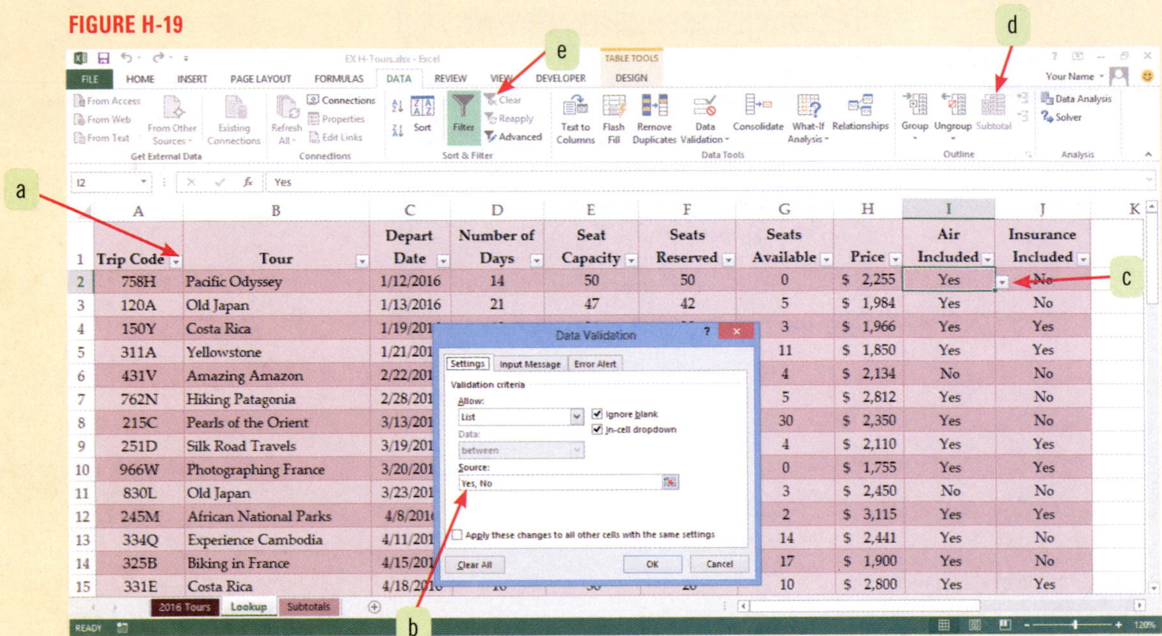

1. **Which element points to an in-cell drop-down list arrow?**
2. **Which element would you click to remove a filter?**
3. **Which element points to a field's list arrow?**
4. **Which element do you click to group and summarize data?**
5. **Where do you specify acceptable data entries for a table?**

Match each term with the statement that best describes it.

6. Table_array	**a.** Cell range when Advanced Filter results are copied to another location
7. Extracted table	**b.** Range in which search conditions are set
8. Data validation	**c.** Restricts table entries to specified options
9. Criteria range	**d.** Name of the table searched in a VLOOKUP function
10. DSUM	**e.** Function used to total table values that meet specified criteria

Select the best answer from the list of choices.

11. The ________ logical condition finds records matching both listed criteria.

a. True
b. Or
c. And
d. False

12. What does it mean when you select the Or option when creating a custom filter?

a. Both criteria must be true to find a match.
b. Neither criterion has to be 100% true.
c. Either criterion can be true to find a match.
d. A custom filter requires a criteria range.

13. What must a data range have before subtotals can be inserted?

a. Enough records to show multiple subtotals
b. Sorted data
c. Formatted cells
d. Grand totals

14. Which function finds the position of an item in a table?

a. VLOOKUP
b. MATCH
c. DGET
d. HLOOKUP

Skills Review

1. Filter a table.

a. Start Excel, open the file EX H-2.xlsx from the location where you store your Data Files, then save it as **EX H-Compensation**.

b. With the Compensation sheet active, filter the table to list only records for employees in the Boston branch.

c. Clear the filter, then add a filter that displays the records for employees in the Boston and Philadelphia branches.

d. Redisplay all employees, then use a filter to show the three employees with the highest annual salary.

e. Redisplay all the records.

2. Create a custom filter.

a. Create a custom filter showing employees hired before 1/1/2013 or after 12/31/2013.

b. Create a custom filter showing employees hired between 1/1/2013 and 12/31/2013.

c. Enter your name in the worksheet footer, then preview the filtered worksheet.

d. Redisplay all records.

e. Save the workbook.

3. Filter and extract a table with the Advanced Filter.

a. You want to retrieve a list of employees who were hired before 1/1/2014 and who have an annual salary of more than $75,000 a year. Define a criteria range by inserting six new rows above the table on the worksheet and copying the field names into the first row.

b. In cell D2, enter the criterion **<1/1/2014**, then in cell G2 enter **>75000**.

c. Click any cell in the table.

d. Open the Advanced Filter dialog box.

e. Indicate that you want to copy to another location, enter the criteria range **A1:J2**, verify that the List range is $A$7:$J$17, then indicate that you want to place the extracted list in the range starting at cell **A20**.

f. Confirm that the retrieved list meets the criteria as shown in FIGURE H-20.

g. Save the workbook, then preview the worksheet.

FIGURE H-20

	A	B	C	D	E	F	G	H	I	J
1	Employee Number	First Name	Last Name	Hire Date	Branch	Monthly Salary	Annual Salary	Annual Bonus	Benefits Dollars	Annual Compensation
2				<1/1/2014			>75000			
3										
4										
5										
6										
7	Employee Number	First Name	Last Name	Hire Date	Branch	Monthly Salary	Annual Salary	Annual Bonus	Benefits Dollars	Annual Compensation
8	1211	Mary	Lane	2/12/2013	New York	$ 4,650	$ 55,800	$ 1,370	$ 12,834	$ 70,004
9	4515	Leanne	Waters	4/1/2014	Boston	$ 5,970	$ 71,640	$ 5,725	$ 16,477	$ 93,842
10	4187	Debbie	Davie	5/6/2012	Philadelphia	$ 7,550	$ 90,600	$ 6,525	$ 20,838	$ 117,963
11	2599	Martha	Macky	12/10/2013	Boston	$ 8,450	$ 101,400	$ 7,550	$ 23,322	$ 132,272
12	2213	Jake	Green	2/15/2015	Boston	$ 2,950	$ 35,400	$ 680	$ 8,142	$ 44,222
13	6588	Paul	Early	3/25/2013	New York	$ 2,750	$ 33,000	$ 630	$ 7,590	$ 41,220
14	2120	Ellen	Meeb	6/23/2012	New York	$ 4,225	$ 50,700	$ 1,320	$ 11,661	$ 63,681
15	4450	Mark	Mollen	8/3/2015	Philadelphia	$ 6,750	$ 81,000	$ 5,900	$ 18,630	$ 105,530
16	9887	Hank	Randal	9/29/2014	Philadelphia	$ 8,500	$ 102,000	$ 7,650	$ 23,460	$ 133,110
17	3955	Jen	Richards	5/12/2013	Boston	$ 3,750	$ 45,000	$ 795	$ 10,350	$ 56,145
18										
19										
20	Employee Number	First Name	Last Name	Hire Date	Branch	Monthly Salary	Annual Salary	Annual Bonus	Benefits Dollars	Annual Compensation
21	4187	Debbie	Davie	5/6/2012	Philadelphia	$ 7,550	$ 90,600	$ 6,525	$ 20,838	$ 117,963
22	2599	Martha	Macky	12/10/2013	Boston	$ 8,450	$ 101,400	$ 7,550	$ 23,322	$ 132,272
23										

Skills Review (continued)

4. **Look up values in a table.**
   a. Click the Summary sheet tab. Use the Name Manager to view the table names in the workbook, then close the dialog box.
   b. You will use a lookup function to locate an employee's annual compensation; enter the Employee Number **2213** in cell A17.
   c. In cell B17, use the VLOOKUP function and enter **A17** as the Lookup_value, **Table2** as the Table_array, **10** as the Col_index_num, and **FALSE** as the Range_lookup; observe the compensation displayed for that employee number, then check it against the table to make sure it is correct.
   d. Replace the existing Employee Number in cell A17 with **4187**, and view the annual compensation for that employee.
   e. Format cell B17 with the Accounting format with the $ symbol and no decimal places.
   f. Save the workbook.
5. **Summarize table data.**
   a. You want to enter a database function to average the annual salaries by branch, using the New York branch as the initial criterion. In cell E17, use the DAVERAGE function, and click the upper-left corner of cell A1 twice to select the table and its header row as the Database, select cell G1 for the Field, and select the range D16:D17 for the Criteria. Verify that the average New York salary is 46500.
   b. Test the function further by entering the text **Philadelphia** in cell D17. When the criterion is entered, cell E17 should display 91200.
   c. Format cell E17 in Accounting format with the $ symbol and no decimal places.
   d. Save the workbook.
6. **Validate table data.**
   a. Select the data in column E of the table, and set a validation criterion specifying that you want to allow a list of valid options.
   b. Enter a list of valid options that restricts the entries to **New York**, **Boston**, and **Philadelphia**. Remember to use a comma between each item in the list.
   c. Indicate that you want the options to appear in an in-cell drop-down list, then close the dialog box.
   d. Add a row to the table. Go to cell E12, then select Boston in the drop-down list.
   e. Select the data in column F in the table, and indicate that you want to restrict the data entered to only whole numbers. In the Minimum text box, enter **1000**; in the Maximum text box, enter **10000**. Close the dialog box.
   f. Click cell F12, enter **15000**, then press [Enter]. You should get an error message.
   g. Click Cancel, then enter **7000**.
   h. Complete the new record by adding an Employee Number of **1119**, a First Name of **Cate**, a Last Name of **Smith**, a Hire Date of **2/1/2016**, and an Annual Bonus of **$5000**. Format the range F12:J12 as Accounting with no decimal places and using the $ symbol. Compare your screen to FIGURE H-21.
   i. Add your name to the center section of the footer, save the worksheet, then preview the worksheet.

FIGURE H-21

	A	B	C	D	E	F	G	H	I	J
1	Employee Number	First Name	Last Name	Hire Date	Branch	Monthly Salary	Annual Salary	Annual Bonus	Benefits Dollars	Annual Compensation
2	1211	Mary	Lane	2/12/2013	New York	$ 4,650	$ 55,800	$ 1,370	$ 12,834	$ 70,004
3	4515	Leanne	Waters	4/1/2014	Boston	$ 5,970	$ 71,640	$ 5,725	$ 16,477	$ 93,842
4	4187	Debbie	Davie	5/6/2012	Philadelphia	$ 7,550	$ 90,600	$ 6,525	$ 20,838	$ 117,963
5	2599	Martha	Macky	12/10/2013	Boston	$ 8,450	$101,400	$ 7,550	$ 23,322	$ 132,272
6	2213	Jake	Green	2/15/2015	Boston	$ 2,950	$ 35,400	$ 680	$ 8,142	$ 44,222
7	6588	Paul	Early	3/25/2013	New York	$ 2,750	$ 33,000	$ 630	$ 7,590	$ 41,220
8	2120	Ellen	Meeb	6/23/2012	New York	$ 4,225	$ 50,700	$ 1,320	$ 11,661	$ 63,681
9	4450	Mark	Mollen	8/3/2015	Philadelphia	$ 6,750	$ 81,000	$ 5,900	$ 18,630	$ 105,530
10	9887	Hank	Randal	9/29/2014	Philadelphia	$ 8,500	$102,000	$ 7,650	$ 23,460	$ 133,110
11	3955	Jen	Richards	5/12/2013	Boston	$ 3,750	$ 45,000	$ 795	$ 10,350	$ 56,145
12	1119	Cate	Smith	2/1/2016	Boston	$ 7,000	$ 84,000	$ 5,000	$ 19,320	$ 108,320
13										
14										
15										
16	Employee Number	Annual Compensation		Branch	Average Annual Salary					
17	4187	$ 117,963		Philadelphia	$ 91,200					
18										

Skills Review (continued)

7. **Create subtotals.**
   a. Click the Subtotals sheet tab.
   b. Use the Branch field list arrow to sort the table in ascending order by branch.
   c. Convert the table to a range.
   d. Group and create subtotals of the Annual Compensation data by branch, using the SUM function.
   e. Click the 2 outline button on the outline to display only the subtotals and the grand total. Compare your screen to FIGURE H-22.
   f. Enter your name in the worksheet footer, save the workbook, then preview the worksheet.
   g. Save the workbook, close the workbook, exit Excel, then submit your workbook to your instructor.

FIGURE H-22

	A	B	C	D	E	F	G	H	I	J
1	Employee Number	First Name	Last Name	Hire Date	Branch	Monthly Salary	Annual Salary	Annual Bonus	Benefits Dollars	Annual Compensation
6					Boston Total					$ 326,481
10					New York Total					$ 174,905
14					Philadelphia Total					$ 356,603
15					Grand Total					$ 857,989
16										

Independent Challenge 1

As the manager of Miami Dental, a dental supply company, you spend a lot of time managing your inventory. To help with this task, you have created an Excel table that you can extract information from using filters. You also need to add data validation and summary information to the table.

a. Start Excel, open the file EX H-3.xlsx from the location where you store your Data Files, then save it as **EX H-Dental**.
b. Using the table data on the Inventory sheet, create a filter to display information about only the product bond refill. Clear the filter.
c. Use a Custom Filter to generate a list of products with a quantity greater than 15. Clear the filter.
d. Copy the labels in cells A1:F1 into A16:F16. Type **Retention Pins** in cell A17, and type **Small** in cell C17. Use the Advanced Filter with a criteria range of A16:F17 to extract a table of small retention pins to the range of cells beginning in cell A20. Enter your name in the worksheet footer, save the workbook, then preview the worksheet.
e. On the Summary sheet tab, select the table data in column B. Open the Data Validation dialog box, then indicate you want to use a validation list with the acceptable entries of **Barnes**, **Blake**, **Lyon**, **Maxwell**. Make sure the In-cell dropdown check box is selected.
f. Test the data validation by trying to change a cell in column B of the table to **Lane**.
g. Using FIGURE H-23 as a guide, enter a function in cell E18 that calculates the total quantity of bond refill available in your inventory. Enter your name in the worksheet footer, preview the worksheet, then save the workbook.
h. On the Subtotals sheet, sort the table in ascending order by product. Convert the table to a range. Insert subtotals by product using the Sum function, then select Quantity in the "Add Subtotal to" box. Remove the check box for the Total field, if necessary. Use the appropriate button on the outline to display only the subtotals and grand total. Save the workbook, then preview the worksheet.
i. Submit the workbook to your instructor. Close the workbook, then exit Excel.

FIGURE H-23

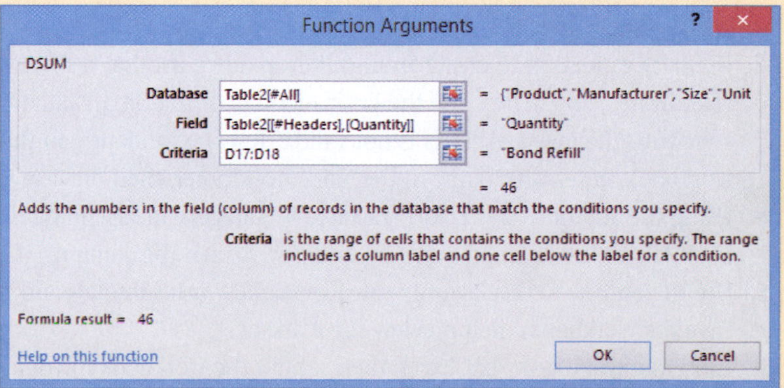

Excel 2013

Independent Challenge 2

As the senior accountant at Cambridge Electrical Supply you are adding new features to the company's accounts receivables workbook. The business supplies both residential and commercial electricians. You have put together an invoice table to track sales for the month of June. Now that you have this table, you would like to manipulate it in several ways. First, you want to filter the table to show only invoices over a certain amount with certain order dates. You also want to subtotal the total column by residential and commercial supplies. To prevent data entry errors you will restrict entries in the Order Date column. Finally, you would like to add database and lookup functions to your worksheet to efficiently retrieve data from the table.

a. Start Excel, open the file EX H-4.xlsx from the location where you store your Data Files, then save it as **EX H-Invoices**.

b. Use the Advanced Filter to show invoices with amounts more than $100.00 ordered before 6/15/2016, using cells A27:B28 to enter your criteria and extracting the results to cell A33. (*Hint*: You don't need to specify an entire row as the criteria range.) Enter your name in the worksheet footer.

c. Use the Data Validation dialog box to restrict entries to those with order dates between 6/1/2016 and 6/30/2016. Test the data restrictions by attempting to enter an invalid date in cell B25.

d. Enter **23698** in cell G28. Enter a VLOOKUP function in cell H28 to retrieve the total based on the invoice number entered in cell G28. Make sure you have an exact match with the invoice number. Format H28 using Accounting format with two decimal places. Test the function with the invoice number 23720.

e. Enter the date **6/1/2016** in cell J28. Use the database function, DCOUNT, in cell K28 to count the number of invoices for the date in cell J28. Save the workbook, then preview the worksheet.

f. On the Subtotals worksheet, sort the table in ascending order by Type, then convert the table to a range. Create subtotals showing the totals for commercial and residential invoices. Display only the subtotals for the commercial and residential accounts along with the grand total.

g. Save the workbook, preview the worksheet, close the workbook, then exit Excel. Submit the workbook to your instructor.

Independent Challenge 3

You are the manager of Nest, a paint and decorating store. You have created an Excel table that contains your order data, along with the amounts for each item ordered and the date the order was placed. You would like to manipulate this table to display product categories and ordered items meeting specific criteria. You would also like to add subtotals to the table and add database functions to total orders. Finally, you want to restrict entries in the Category column.

a. Start Excel, open the file EX H-5.xlsx from the location where you store your Data Files, then save it as **EX H-Nest**.

b. Create an advanced filter that extracts records with the following criteria to cell A42: orders greater than $1500 having dates either before 9/10/2016 or after 9/19/2016. (*Hint*: Recall that when you want records to meet one criterion or another, you need to place the criteria on separate lines.)

c. Use the DSUM function in cell H2 to let worksheet users find the total order amounts for the category entered in cell G2. Format the cell containing the total order using the Accounting format with the $ symbol and no decimals. Test the DSUM function using the Paint category name. (The sum for the Paint category should be $11,558.) Preview the worksheet.

d. Use data validation to create an in-cell drop-down list that restricts category entries to "Paint", "Wallpaper", "Hardware", and "Tile". Use the Error Alert tab of the Data Validation dialog box to set the alert level to the Warning style with the message "Data is not valid." Test the validation in the table with valid and invalid entries. Save the workbook, enter your name in the worksheet footer, then preview the worksheet.

e. Using the Subtotals sheet, sort the table by category in ascending order. Convert the table to a range, and add Subtotals to the order amounts by category. Widen the columns, if necessary.

f. Use the outline to display only category names with subtotals and the grand total.

g. Save the workbook, then preview the worksheet.

h. Close the workbook, exit Excel, then submit the workbook to your instructor.

Independent Challenge 4: Explore

You are an inventory manager at American Eyewear, an eyewear distributor. You track your inventory of eye products in an Excel worksheet. You would like to use conditional formatting in your worksheet to help track the products that need to be reordered as well as your inventory expenses. You would also like to prevent data entry errors using data validation. Finally, you would like to add an area to quickly lookup prices and quantities for customers.

a. Start Excel, open the file EX H-6.xlsx from the location where you store your Data Files, then save it as **EX H-Eyewear**.

b. Use conditional formatting to add icons to the quantity field using the following criteria: quantities greater than or equal to 300 are formatted with a green circle, quantities greater than or equal to 100 but less than 300 are formatted with a yellow circle, and quantities less than 100 are formatted with a red circle. If your icons are incorrect, select the data in the Quantity field, click the Conditional Formatting button in the Styles group of the HOME tab, click Manage Rules, click the Show formatting for list arrow, select Current Selection, then double click Icon Set and compare your formatting rule to FIGURE H-24. (*Hint*: You may need to click in the top Value text box for the correct value to display for the red circle.)

FIGURE H-24

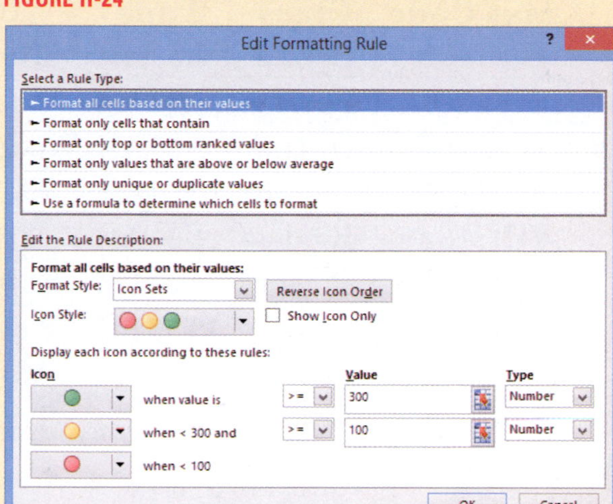

c. Conditionally format the Total data using Top/Bottom Rules to emphasize the cells containing the top 30 percent with red text.

d. Add another rule to format the bottom 20 percent in the Total column with purple text.

e. Restrict the Wholesale Price field entries to decimal values between 0 and 100. Add an input message of **Prices must be less than $100**. Add a Warning-level error message of **Please check price**. Test the validation entering a price of $105 in cell D3 and allow the new price to be entered.

f. Below the table, create a product lookup area with the following labels in adjacent cells: **Product Number**, **Wholesale Price**, **Quantity**.

g. Enter 1544 under the label Product Number in your products lookup area.

h. In the product lookup area, enter lookup functions to locate the wholesale price and quantity information for the product number that you entered in the previous step. Make sure you match the product number exactly. Format the wholesale price with the Accounting format with the $ symbol and two decimal places.

i. Enter your name in the center section of the worksheet header, save the workbook then preview the worksheet comparing it to FIGURE H-25.

j. Close the workbook, exit Excel, then submit the workbook to your instructor.

FIGURE H-25

Your Name

American Eyewear

Product Number	Category	Vendor	Wholesale Price	Quantity	Total
1122	Reading Glasses	Berkley	$105.00	125	$13,125.00
1132	Reading Glasses	Mallory	$10.66	68	$724.88
1184	Sports Eyewear	Bromen	$18.21	187	$3,405.27
1197	Sunglasses	Lincoln	$32.22	210	$6,766.20
1225	Frames	Berkley	$33.99	87	$2,957.13
1267	Frames	Mallory	$34.19	240	$8,205.60
1298	Sports Eyewear	Berkley	$21.97	375	$8,238.75
1345	Reading Glasses	Lincoln	$21.88	105	$2,297.40
1367	Safety Goggles	Lincoln	$17.18	168	$2,886.24
1398	Sports Eyewear	Bromen	$30.39	97	$2,947.83
1422	Sunglasses	Lincoln	$25.19	157	$3,954.83
1436	Cases	Mallory	$5.12	81	$414.72
1445	Sunglasses	Rand	$45.20	150	$6,780.00
1456	Custom	Berkley	$82.33	377	$31,038.41
1498	Safety Goggles	Rand	$19.22	51	$980.22
1521	Cases	Lincoln	$7.84	87	$682.08
1531	Lenses	Lincoln	$40.34	197	$7,946.98
1544	Reading Glasses	Bromen	$23.01	472	$10,860.72
1556	Frames	Bromen	$45.06	12	$540.72
1569	Sports Eyewear	Rand	$17.36	178	$3,090.08
1578	Sunglasses	Mallory	$63.22	35	$2,212.70
1622	Reading Glasses	Mallory	$25.33	874	$22,138.42
1634	Cases	Berkley	$18.47	501	$9,253.47
1657	Sunglasses	Bromen	$34.55	10	$345.50
1688	Safety Goggles	Rand	$18.66	73	$1,362.18
1723	Reading Glasses	Rand	$8.64	534	$4,613.76
1736	Sports Eyewear	Bromen	$25.66	15	$384.90
1798	Sports Eyewear	Mallory	$32.78	640	$20,979.20
1822	Cases	Mallory	$17.44	86	$1,499.84

Product Number	Wholesale Price	Quantity
1544	$ 23.01	472

Excel 2013

Visual Workshop

Open the file EX H-7.xlsx from the location where you save your Data Files, then save it as **EX H-Schedule**. Complete the worksheet as shown in FIGURE H-26. An in-cell drop-down list has been added to the data entered in the Room field. The range A18:G21 is extracted from the table using the criteria in cells A15:A16. Add your name to the worksheet footer, save the workbook, preview the worksheet, then submit the workbook to your instructor.

FIGURE H-26

	A	B	C	D	E	F	G
1	Spring 2016 Schedule of Yoga Classes						
2							
3	Class Code	Class	Time	Day	Room	Fee	Instructor
4	YOG100	Basics	7:30 AM	Monday	Mat Room	$15	Malloy
5	YOG101	Power	8:00 AM	Tuesday	Equipment Room	$20	Gregg
6	YOG102	Hatha	9:00 AM	Wednesday	Mat Room	$15	Malloy
7	YOG103	Kripalu	10:00 AM	Monday	Mat Room	$15	Brent
8	YOG104	Basics	11:00 AM	Friday	Mat Room	$15	Paulson
9	YOG105	Power	12:00 PM	Saturday	Equipment Room	$20	Dally
10	YOG106	Hatha	12:00 PM	Tuesday	Mat Room	$15	Rand
11	YOG107	Power	2:00 PM	Monday	Equipment Room	$20	Walton
12	YOG108	Basics	4:00 PM	Tuesday	Mat Room	15	Malloy
13					Please select Mat Room or Equipment Room		
14							
15	Class						
16	Basics						
17							
18	Class Code	Class	Time	Day	Room	Fee	Instructor
19	YOG100	Basics	7:30 AM	Monday	Mat Room	$15	Malloy
20	YOG104	Basics	11:00 AM	Friday	Mat Room	$15	Paulson
21	YOG108	Basics	4:00 PM	Tuesday	Mat Room	$15	Malloy
22							

Automating Worksheet Tasks

CASE Kate Morgan, the North America regional vice president of sales at Quest, wants you to automate a task in the sales workbooks by creating a macro for the sales division. Kate sees this as a timesaver for the sales group. The macro will automatically insert text that identifies the worksheet as a sales division document.

Unit Objectives

After completing this unit, you will be able to:

- Plan a macro
- Enable a macro
- Record a macro
- Run a macro
- Edit a macro
- Assign keyboard shortcuts to macros
- Use the Personal Macro Workbook
- Assign a macro to a button

Files You Will Need

EX I-1.xlsx
EX I-2.xlsm
EX I-3.xlsx

Plan a Macro

Learning Outcomes
- Plan a macro
- Determine the storage location for a macro

A **macro** is a named set of instructions you can create that performs tasks automatically, in an order you specify. You create macros to automate Excel tasks that you perform frequently. For example, you can create a macro to enter and format text or to save and print a worksheet. To create a macro, you record the series of actions using the macro recorder built into Excel, or you write the instructions in a special programming language. Because the sequence of actions in a macro is important, you need to plan the macro carefully before you record it. **CASE** *Kate wants you to create a macro for the sales division that inserts the text "Quest Sales" in the upper-left corner of any worksheet. You work with her to plan the macro.*

DETAILS

To plan a macro, use the following guidelines:

- **Assign the macro a descriptive name**
  The first character of a macro name must be a letter; the remaining characters can be letters, numbers, or underscores. Letters can be uppercase or lowercase. Spaces are not allowed in macro names; use underscores in place of spaces. Press [Shift][-] to enter an underscore character. Kate wants you to name the macro "DivStamp". See **TABLE I-1** for a list of macros that could be created to automate other tasks at Quest.
- **Write out the steps the macro will perform**
  This planning helps eliminate careless errors. Kate writes a description of the macro she wants, as shown in **FIGURE I-1**.
- **Decide how you will perform the actions you want to record**
  You can use the mouse, the keyboard, or a combination of the two. Kate wants you to use both the mouse and the keyboard.
- **Practice the steps you want Excel to record, and write them down**
  Kate has written down the sequence of actions she wants you to include in the macro.
- **Decide where to store the description of the macro and the macro itself**
  Macros can be stored in an active workbook, in a new workbook, or in the **Personal Macro Workbook**, a special workbook used only for macro storage. Kate asks you to store the macro in a new workbook.

FIGURE I-1: Handwritten description of planned macro

Macro to create stamp with the division name

Name: DivStamp

Description: Adds a stamp to the top left of the worksheet, identifying it as a Quest sales worksheet

Steps:
1. Position the cell pointer in cell A1.
2. Type Quest Sales, then click the Enter button.
3. Click the Format button, then click Cells.
4. Click the Font tab, under Font style, click Bold; under Underline, click Single; under Color, click Blue; then click OK.

TABLE I-1: Possible macros and their descriptive names

description of macro	descriptive name for macro
Enter a frequently used proper name, such as "Kate Morgan"	KateMorgan
Enter a frequently used company name, such as Quest	Company_Name
Print the active worksheet on a single page, in landscape orientation	FitToLand
Add a footer to a worksheet	FooterStamp
Add totals to a worksheet	AddTotals

Excel 2013
UNIT I

Enable a Macro

Learning Outcomes
- Create a macro-enabled workbook
- Enable macros by changing a workbook's security level

Because a macro may contain a **virus**—destructive software that can damage your computer files—the default security setting in Excel disables macros from running. Although a workbook containing a macro will open, if macros are disabled, they will not function. You can manually change the Excel security setting to allow macros to run if you know a macro came from a trusted source. When saving a workbook with a macro, you need to save it as a macro-enabled workbook with the extension .xlsm. **CASE** *Kate asks you to change the security level to enable all macros. You will change the security level back to the default setting after you create and run your macros.*

STEPS

QUICK TIP
If the DEVELOPER tab is displayed on your Ribbon, skip steps 2 and 3.

1. **Start Excel, open a blank workbook, click the Save button on the Quick Access toolbar, navigate to the location where you store your Data Files, in the Save As dialog box click the Save as type list arrow, click Excel Macro-Enabled Workbook (*.xlsm), in the File name text box type EX I-Macro Workbook, then click Save**

   The security settings that enable macros are available on the DEVELOPER tab. The DEVELOPER tab does not appear by default, but you can display it by customizing the Ribbon.

2. **Click the FILE tab, click Options, then click Customize Ribbon in the category list**

   The Customize the Ribbon options open in the Excel Options dialog box, as shown in FIGURE I-2.

3. **Click the Developer check box, if necessary, in the Main Tabs area on the right side of the screen to select it, then click OK**

   The DEVELOPER tab appears on the Ribbon. You are ready to change the security settings.

4. **Click the DEVELOPER tab, then click the Macro Security button in the Code group**

   The Trust Center dialog box opens.

5. **Click Macro Settings if necessary, click the Enable all macros (not recommended; potentially dangerous code can run) option button to select it as shown in FIGURE I-3, then click OK**

   The dialog box closes. Macros remain enabled until you disable them by deselecting the Enable all macros option. As you work with Excel, you should disable macros when you are not working with them.

FIGURE I-2: Excel Options dialog box

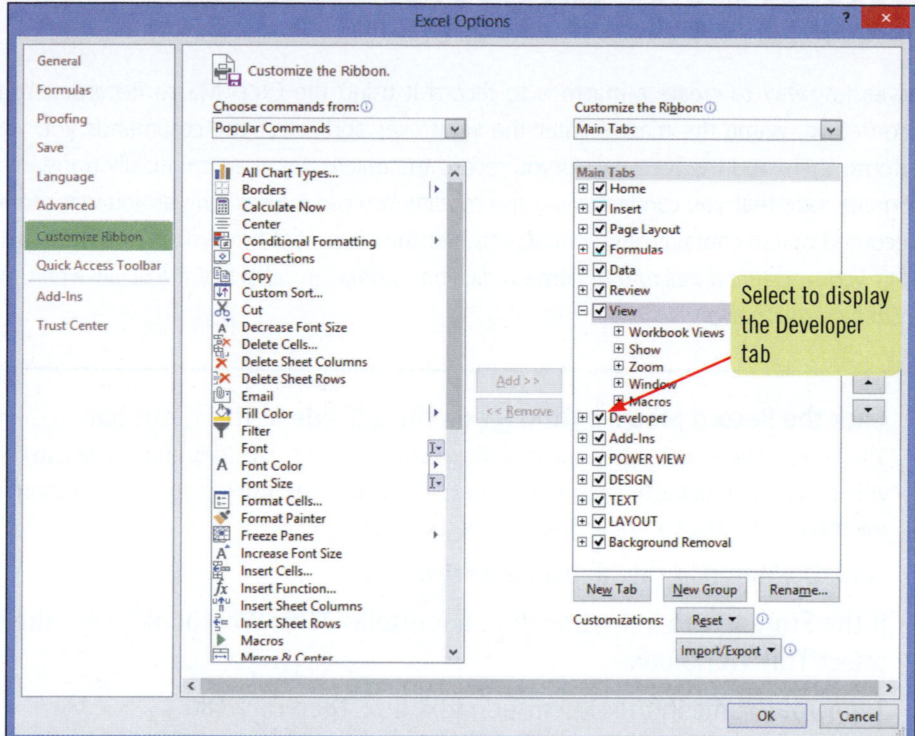

FIGURE I-3: Trust Center dialog box

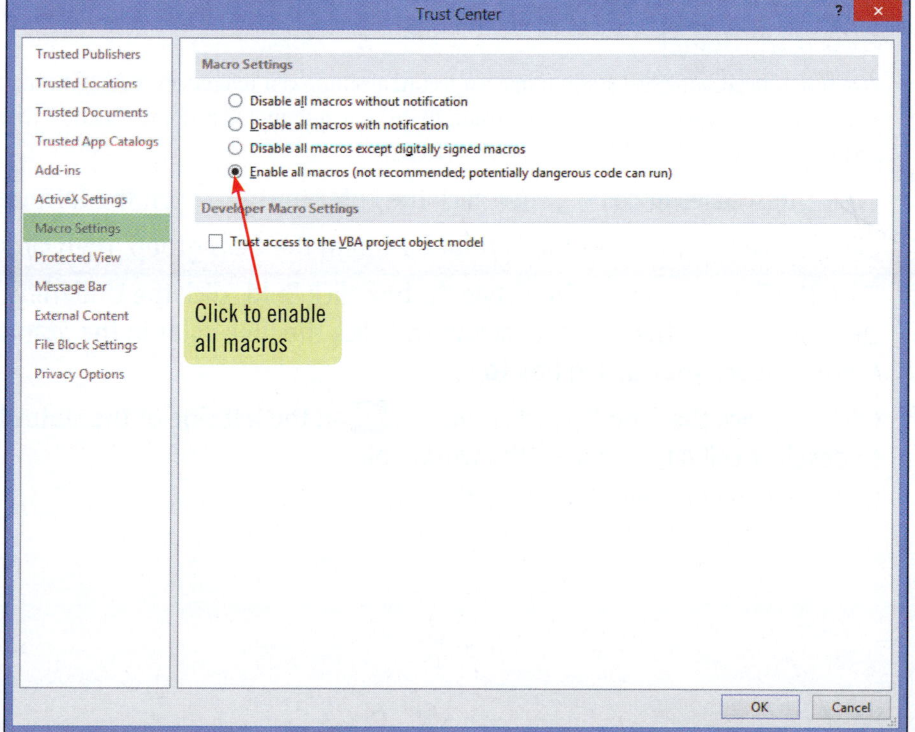

Disabling macros

To prevent viruses from running on your computer, you should disable all macros when you are not working with them. To disable macros, click the DEVELOPER tab, then click the Macro Security button in the Code group. Clicking any of the first three options disables macros. The first option disables all macros without notifying you. The second option notifies you when macros are disabled, and the third option allows only digitally signed macros to run.

Excel 2013

Record a Macro

Learning Outcomes
- Choose a macro storage location
- Create a macro by recording steps

The easiest way to create a macro is to record it using the Excel Macro Recorder. You turn the Macro Recorder on, name the macro, enter the keystrokes and select the commands you want the macro to perform, then stop the recorder. As you record the macro, Excel automatically translates each action into program code that you can later view and modify. You can take as long as you want to record the macro; a recorded macro contains only your actions, not the amount of time you took to record it. **CASE** *Kate wants you to create a macro that enters a division "stamp" in cell A1 of the active worksheet. You create this macro by recording your actions.*

STEPS

QUICK TIP
You can also click the Record Macro button in the Code group on the DEVELOPER tab, or the Macros button in the Macros group of the VIEW tab to record a new macro.

1. **Click the Record Macro button on the left side of the status bar**
   The Record Macro dialog box opens, as shown in FIGURE I-4. The default name Macro1 is selected. You can either assign this name or enter a new name. This dialog box also lets you assign a shortcut key for running the macro and assign a storage location for the macro.
2. **Type DivStamp in the Macro name text box**
3. **If the Store macro in list box does not display "This Workbook", click the list arrow and select This Workbook**
4. **Type your name in the Description text box, then click OK**
   The dialog box closes, and the Record Macro button on the status bar is replaced with a Stop Recording button. Take your time performing the steps below. Excel records every keystroke, menu selection, and mouse action that you make.
5. **Press [Ctrl][Home]**
   When you begin an Excel session, macros record absolute cell references. By beginning the recording with a command to move to cell A1, you ensure that the macro includes the instruction to select cell A1 as the first step, in cases where A1 is not already selected.
6. **Type Quest Sales in cell A1, then click the Enter button on the formula bar**
7. **Click the HOME tab, click the Format button in the Cells group, then click Format Cells**
8. **Click the Font tab, in the Font style list box click Bold, click the Underline list arrow and click Single, click the Color list arrow and click the Blue color in the Standard Colors row, then compare your dialog box to FIGURE I-5**
9. **Click OK, click the Stop Recording button on the left side of the status bar, click cell D1 to deselect cell A1, then save the workbook**
   FIGURE I-6 shows the result of recording the macro.

QUICK TIP
You can also click the Stop Recording button in the Code group on the DEVELOPER to stop recording a macro.

FIGURE I-4: Record Macro dialog box

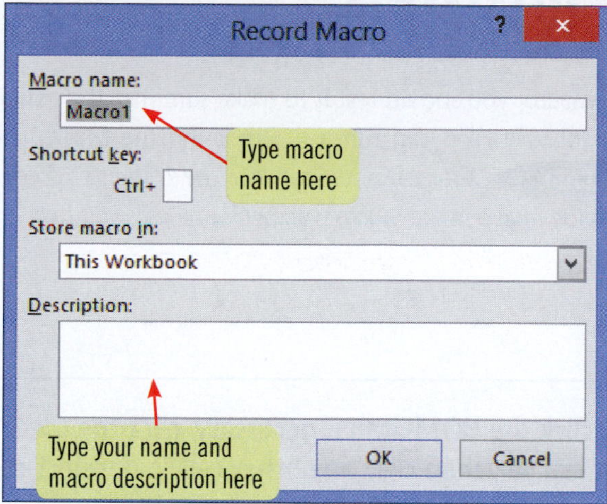

FIGURE I-5: Font tab of the Format Cells dialog box

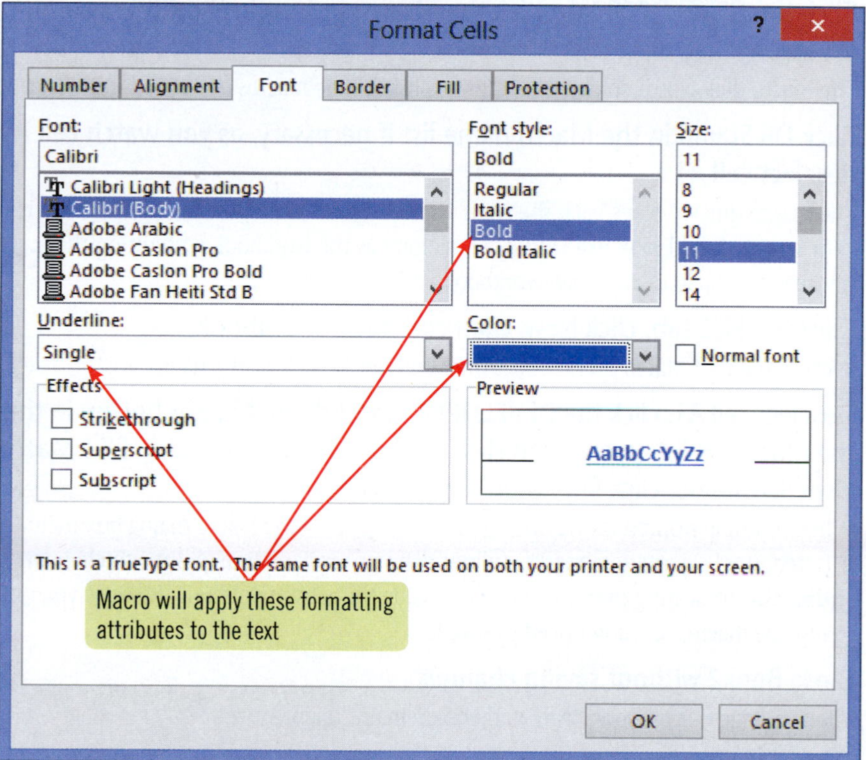

FIGURE I-6: Sales Division stamp

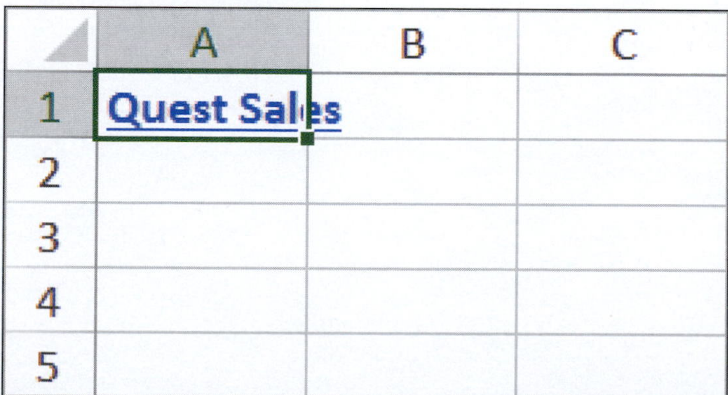

Excel 2013

Run a Macro

Learning Outcomes
- Display selected macros
- Run a macro using the Macro dialog box

Once you record a macro, you should test it to make sure that the actions it performs are correct. To test a macro, you **run** (play) it. You can run a macro using the Macros button in the Code group of the DEVELOPER tab. **CASE** *Kate asks you to clear the contents of cell A1, and then test the DivStamp macro. After you run the macro in the Macro workbook, she asks you to test the macro once more from a newly opened workbook.*

STEPS

1. **Click cell A1, click the HOME tab if necessary, click the Clear button in the Editing group, click Clear All, then click any other cell to deselect cell A1**
   When you delete only the contents of a cell, any formatting still remains in the cell. By using the Clear All option you can be sure that the cell is free of contents and formatting.
2. **Click the DEVELOPER tab, click the Macros button in the Code group, click the Macros in list arrow, then click This Workbook**
   The Macro dialog box, shown in FIGURE I-7, lists all the macros contained in the workbook.
3. **Click DivStamp in the Macro name list if necessary, as you watch cell A1 click Run, then deselect cell A1**
   The macro quickly plays back the steps you recorded in the previous lesson. When the macro is finished, your screen should look like FIGURE I-8. As long as the workbook containing the macro remains open, you can run the macro in any open workbook.
4. **Click the FILE tab, click New, then click Blank workbook**
   Because the EX I-Macro Workbook.xlsm is still open, you can use its macros.
5. **Deselect cell A1, click the DEVELOPER tab, click the Macros button in the Code group, click the Macros in list arrow, then click All Open Workbooks, click 'EX I-Macro Workbook.xlsm'!DivStamp, click Run, then deselect cell A1**
   When multiple workbooks are open, the macro name in the Macro dialog box includes the workbook name between single quotation marks, followed by an exclamation point which is an **external reference indicator**, indicating that the macro is outside the active workbook. Because you only used this workbook to test the macro, you don't need to save it.
6. **Close Book2 without saving changes**
   The EX I-Macro Workbook.xlsm workbook remains open.

QUICK TIP
To create a custom button on the Quick Access toolbar that will run a macro, right-click the Ribbon, click Customize Quick Access Toolbar, click the Choose commands from list arrow, select Macros, select the macro to assign to a custom button in the macro list on the left, click Add to move the macro to the list of buttons on the Quick Access Toolbar, then click OK.

FIGURE I-7: Macro dialog box

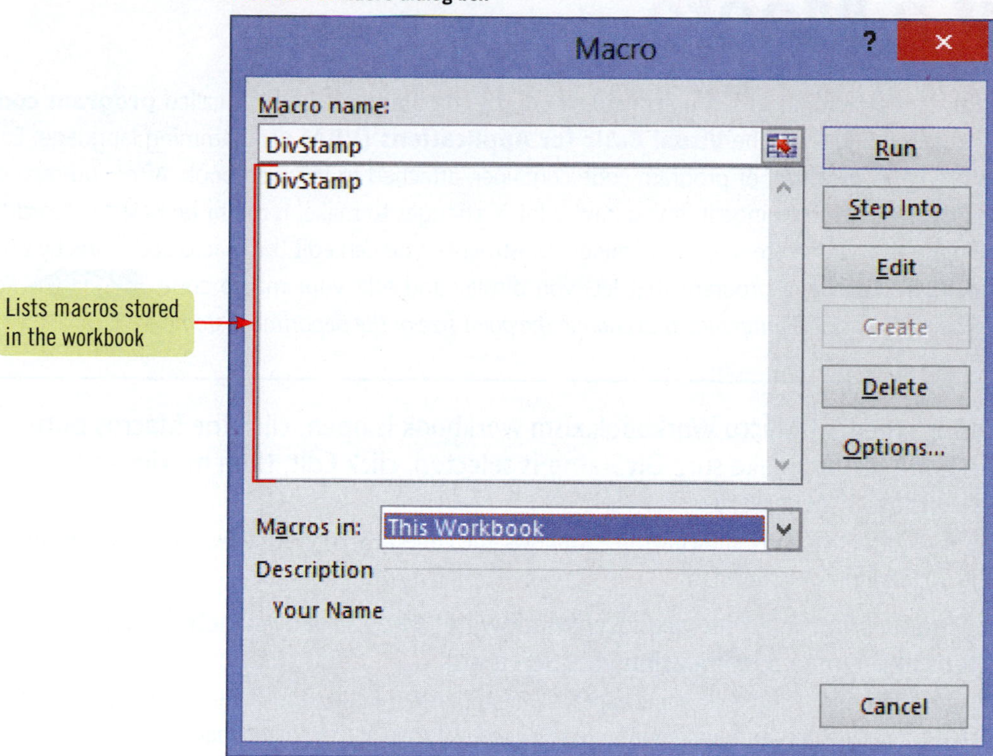

FIGURE I-8: Result of running DivStamp macro

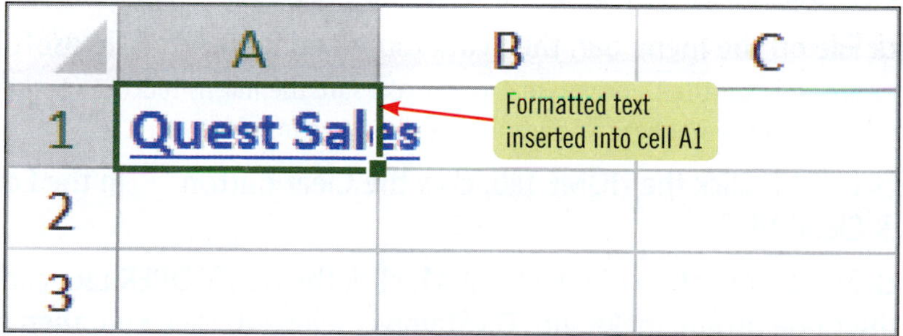

Running a macro automatically

You can create a macro that automatically performs certain tasks when the workbook in which it is saved is opened. This is useful for actions you want to do every time you open a workbook. For example, you may import data from an external data source into the workbook or format the worksheet data in a certain way. To create a macro that will automatically run when the workbook is opened, you need to name the macro Auto_Open and save it in that workbook.

Excel 2013
UNIT I

Edit a Macro

Learning Outcomes
- Edit a macro using VBA
- Add comments to Visual Basic Code

When you use the Macro Recorder to create a macro, the program instructions, called **program code**, are recorded automatically in the **Visual Basic for Applications (VBA)** programming language. Each macro is stored as a **module**, or program code container, attached to the workbook. After you record a macro, you might need to change it. If you have a lot of changes to make, it might be best to record the macro again. But if you need to make only minor adjustments, you can edit the macro code directly using the **Visual Basic Editor**, a program that lets you display and edit your macro code. **CASE** *Kate wants you to modify the DivStamp macro to change the point size of the department stamp to 12.*

STEPS

1. **Make sure the EX I-Macro Workbook.xlsm workbook is open, click the Macros button in the Code group, make sure DivStamp is selected, click Edit, then maximize the Code window, if necessary**
   The Visual Basic Editor starts, showing three windows: the Project Explorer window, the Properties window, and the Code window, as shown in FIGURE I-9.
2. **Click Module 1 in the Project Explorer window if it's not already selected, then examine the steps in the macro, comparing your screen to FIGURE I-9**
   The name of the macro and your name appear at the top of the Code window. Below this area, Excel has translated your keystrokes and commands into macro code. When you open and make selections in a dialog box during macro recording, Excel automatically stores all the dialog box settings in the macro code. For example, the line .FontStyle = "Bold" was generated when you clicked Bold in the Format Cells dialog box. You also see lines of code that you didn't generate directly while recording the DivStamp macro, for example, .Name = "Calibri".
3. **In the line .Size = 11, double-click 11 to select it, then type 12**
   Because Module1 is attached to the workbook and not stored as a separate file, any changes to the module are saved automatically when you save the workbook.
4. **Review the code in the Code window**
5. **Click File on the menu bar, then click Close and Return to Microsoft Excel**
   You want to rerun the DivStamp macro to make sure the macro reflects the change you made using the Visual Basic Editor. You begin by clearing the division name from cell A1.
6. **Click cell A1, click the HOME tab, click the Clear button in the Editing group, then click Clear All**
7. **Click any other cell to deselect cell A1, click the DEVELOPER tab, click the Macros button in the Code group, make sure DivStamp is selected, click Run, then deselect cell A1**
   The department stamp is now in 12-point type, as shown in FIGURE I-10.
8. **Save the workbook**

TROUBLE
If the Properties window does not appear in the lower-left portion of your screen, click the Properties Window button on the Visual Basic Standard toolbar, then resize it as shown in the figure if necessary.

QUICK TIP
You can return to Excel without closing the module by clicking the View Microsoft Excel button on the Visual Basic Editor toolbar.

QUICK TIP
Another way to start the Visual Basic Editor is to click the DEVELOPER tab, then click the Visual Basic button in the Code group.

FIGURE I-9: Visual Basic Editor showing Module1

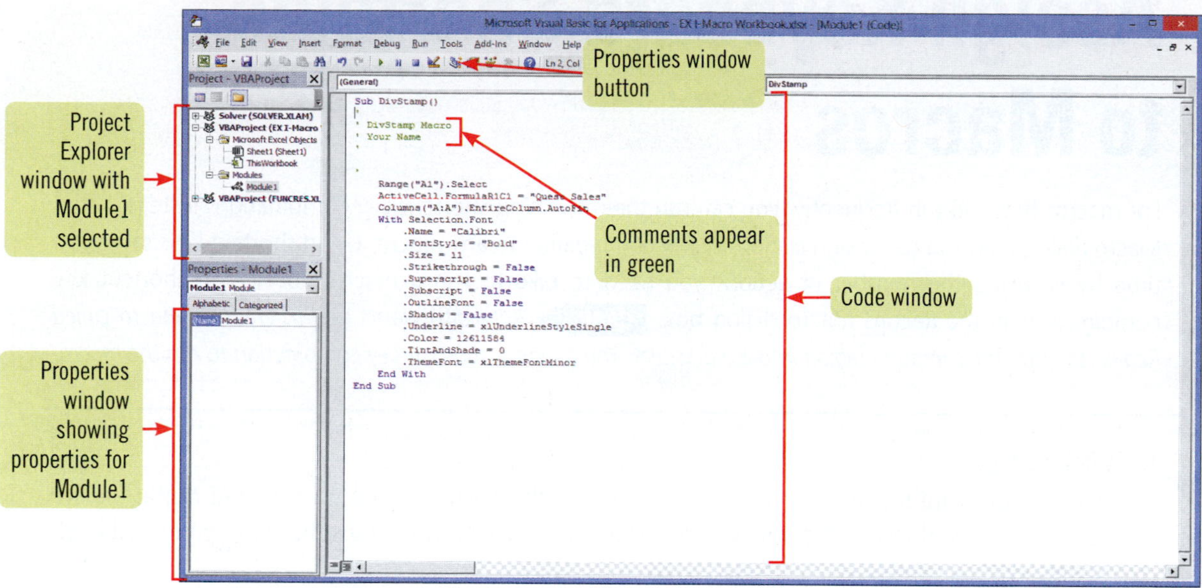

FIGURE I-10: Result of running edited DivStamp macro

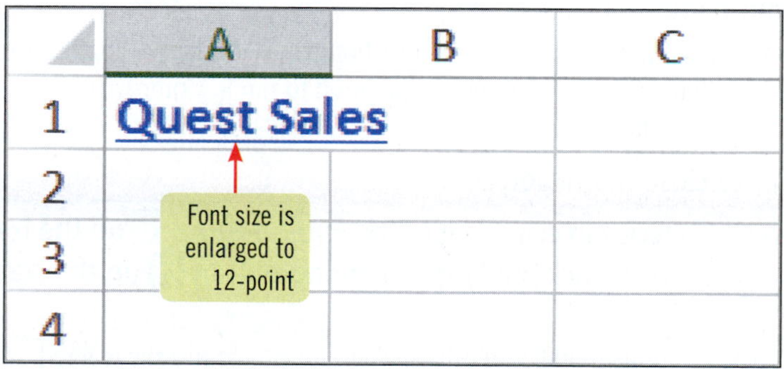

Adding comments to Visual Basic code

With practice, you will be able to interpret the lines of macro code. Others who use your macro, however, might want to review the code to, for example, learn the function of a particular line. You can explain the code by adding comments to the macro. **Comments** are explanatory text added to the lines of code. When you enter a comment, you must type an apostrophe (') before the comment text. Otherwise, the program tries to interpret it as a command. On the screen, comments appear in green after you press [Enter], as shown in **FIGURE I-9**. You can also insert blank lines as comments in the macro code to make the code more readable. To do this, type an apostrophe, then press [Enter].

Learning Outcomes
- Run a macro using shortcut key combinations

Assign Keyboard Shortcuts to Macros

For macros that you run frequently, you can run them by using shortcut key combinations instead of the Macro dialog box. You can assign a shortcut key combination to any macro. Using shortcut keys saves you time by reducing the number of actions you need to take to run a macro. You assign shortcut key combinations in the Record Macro dialog box. **CASE** *Kate also wants you to create a macro called Region to enter the company region into a worksheet. You assign a shortcut key combination to run the macro.*

STEPS

1. **Click cell B2**

   You want to record the macro in cell B2, but you want the macro to enter the region of North America anywhere in a worksheet. Therefore, you do not begin the macro with an instruction to position the cell pointer, as you did in the DivStamp macro.

2. **Click the Record Macro button on the status bar**

   The Record Macro dialog box opens. Notice the option Shortcut key: Ctrl+ followed by a blank box. You can type a letter (A–Z) in the Shortcut key text box to assign the key combination of [Ctrl] plus that letter to run the macro. Because some common Excel shortcuts use the [Ctrl][*letter*] combination, such as [Ctrl][C] for Copy, you decide to use the key combination [Ctrl][Shift] plus a letter to avoid overriding any of these shortcut key combinations.

QUICK TIP
Be careful when choosing letters for a keyboard shortcut. The letters entered in the shortcut key text box are case sensitive.

3. **With the default macro name selected, type Region in the Macro name text box, click the Shortcut key text box, press and hold [Shift], type C, then in the Description box type your name**

   You have assigned the shortcut key combination [Ctrl][Shift][C] to the Region macro. After you create the macro, you will use this shortcut key combination to run it. Compare your screen with **FIGURE I-11**. You are ready to record the Region macro.

4. **Click OK to close the dialog box**

5. **Type North America in cell B2, click the Enter button on the formula bar, press [Ctrl][I] to italicize the text, click the Stop Recording button on the status bar, then deselect cell B2**

   North America appears in italics in cell B2. You are ready to run the macro in cell A5 using the shortcut key combination.

6. **Click cell A5, press and hold [Ctrl][Shift], type C, then deselect the cell**

   The region appears in cell A5, as shown in **FIGURE I-12**. The macro played back in the selected cell (A5) instead of the cell where it was recorded (B2) because you did not begin recording the macro by clicking cell B2.

FIGURE I-11: Record Macro dialog box with shortcut key assigned

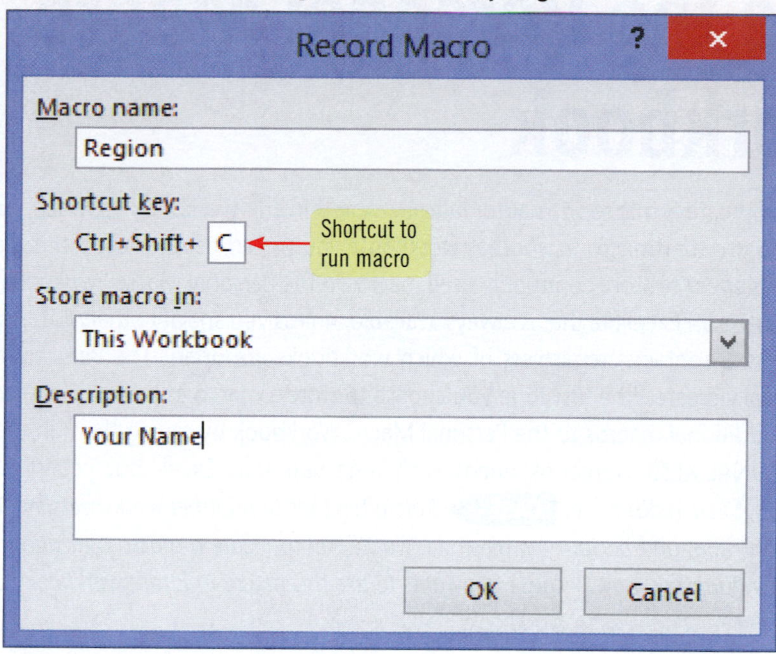

FIGURE I-12: Result of running the Region macro

	A	B	C	D	E	F	G
1	Quest Sales						
2		*North America* ← Result of recording macro in cell B2					
3							
4							
5	*North America* ← Result of running macro in cell A5						
6							
7							

Using relative referencing when creating a macro

By default, Excel records absolute cell references in macros. You can record a macro's actions based on the relative position of the active cell by clicking the Use Relative References button in the Code group prior to recording the action. For example, when you create a macro using the default setting of absolute referencing, bolding the range A1:D1 will always bold that range when the macro is run. However, if you click the Use Relative References button when recording the macro before bolding the range, then running the macro will not necessarily result in bolding the range A1:D1. The range that will be bolded will depend on the location of the active cell when the macro is run. If the active cell is A4, then the range A4:D4 will be bolded. Selecting the Use Relative References button highlights the button name, indicating it is active, as shown in FIGURE I-13. The button remains active until you click it again to deselect it. This is called a toggle, meaning that it acts like an off/on switch: it retains the relative reference setting until you click it again to turn it off or you exit Excel.

FIGURE I-13: Use Relative References button selected

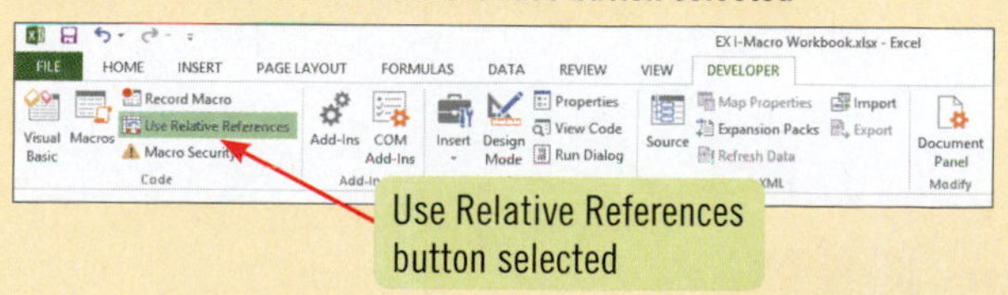

Excel 2013

Use the Personal Macro Workbook

Learning Outcomes
- Determine when when to use the Personal Macro Workbook
- Save a macro in the Personal Macro Workbook

When you create a macro, it is automatically stored in the workbook in which you created it. But if you wanted to use that macro in another workbook, you would have to copy the macro to that workbook. Instead, it's easier to store commonly used macros in the Personal Macro Workbook. The **Personal Macro Workbook** is an Excel file that is always available, unless you specify otherwise, and gives you access to all the macros it contains, regardless of which workbooks are open. The Personal Macro Workbook file is automatically created the first time you choose to store a macro in it, and is named PERSONAL.XLSB. You can add additional macros to the Personal Macro Workbook by saving them in the workbook. By default, the PERSONAL.XLSB workbook opens each time you start Excel, but you don't see it because Excel designates it as a hidden file. **CASE** *Kate often likes to print her worksheets in landscape orientation with 1" left, right, top, and bottom margins. She wants you to create a macro that automatically formats a worksheet for printing this way. Because she wants to use this macro in future workbooks, she asks you to store the macro in the Personal Macro Workbook.*

STEPS

1. **Click the Record Macro button on the status bar**
   The Record Macro dialog box opens.
2. **Type FormatPrint in the Macro name text box, click the Shortcut key text box, press and hold [Shift], type F, then click the Store macro in list arrow**
   You have named the macro FormatPrint and assigned it the shortcut combination [Ctrl][Shift][F]. The "This Workbook" storage option is selected by default, indicating that Excel automatically stores macros in the active workbook, as shown in FIGURE I-14. You can also choose to store the macro in a new workbook or in the Personal Macro Workbook.
3. **Click Personal Macro Workbook, in the Description text box enter your name, then click OK**
   The recorder is on, and you are ready to record the macro keystrokes.
4. **Click the PAGE LAYOUT tab, click the Orientation button in the Page Setup group, click Landscape, click the Margins button in the Page Setup group, click Custom Margins, then enter 1 in the Top, Left, Bottom, and Right text boxes**
   Compare your margin settings to FIGURE I-15.
5. **Click OK, then click the Stop Recording button on the status bar**
   You want to test the macro.
6. **Add a new worksheet, in cell A1 type Macro Test, press [Enter], press and hold [Ctrl][Shift], then type F**
   The FormatPrint macro plays back the sequence of commands.
7. **Preview Sheet2 and verify in the Settings that the orientation is landscape and the Last Custom Margins are 1" on the left, right, top, and bottom**
8. **Click the Back button then save the workbook**

TROUBLE
If a dialog box appears saying that a macro is already assigned to this shortcut combination, choose another letter for a keyboard shortcut. If a dialog box appears with the message that a macro named FormatPrint already exists, click Yes to replace it.

TROUBLE
You may have to wait a few moments for the macro to finish. If you are using a different letter for the shortcut key combination, type that letter instead of the letter F.

FIGURE I-14: Record Macro dialog box showing macro storage options

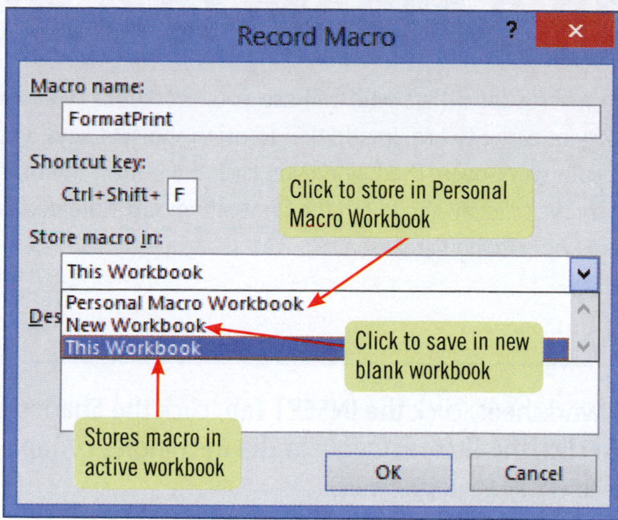

FIGURE I-15: Margin settings for the FormatPrint macro

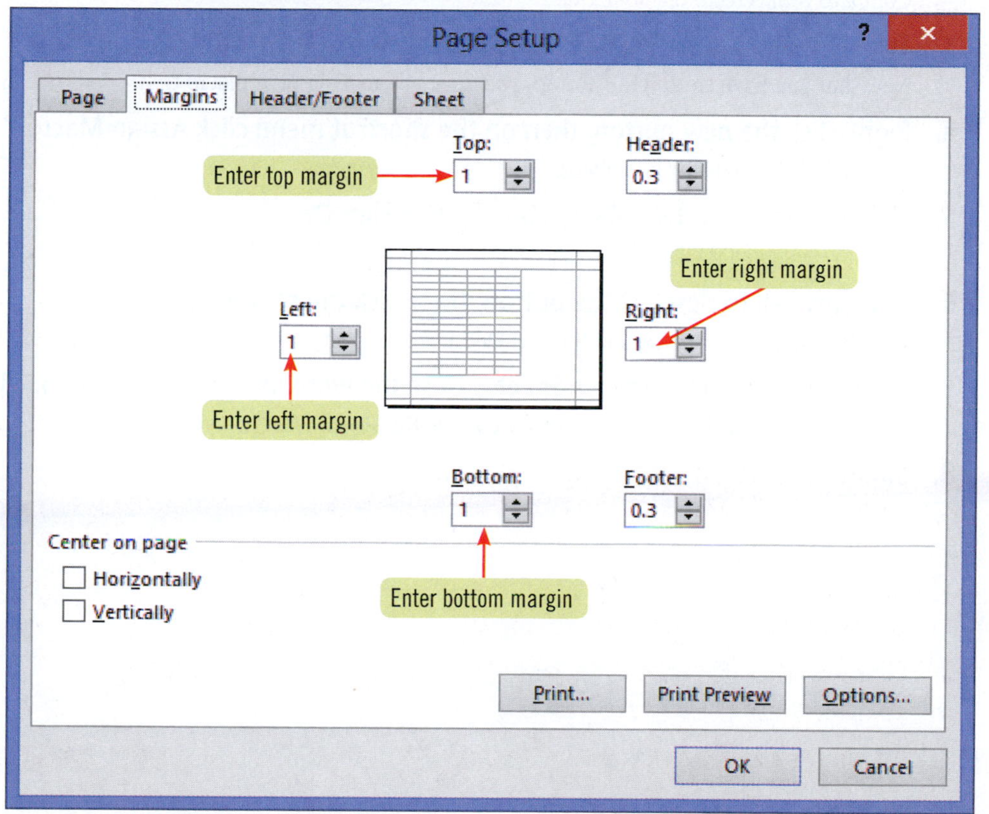

Working with the Personal Macro Workbook

Once you use the Personal Macro Workbook, it opens automatically each time you start Excel so you can add macros to it. By default, the Personal Macro Workbook is hidden in Excel as a precautionary measure so you don't accidentally delete anything from it. If you need to delete a macro from the Personal Macro Workbook, click the VIEW tab, click Unhide in the Window group, click PERSONAL.XLSB, then click OK. To hide the Personal Macro Workbook, make it the active workbook, click the VIEW tab, then click Hide in the Window group. If you should see a message that Excel is unable to record to your Personal Macro Workbook, check to make sure it is enabled: Click the FILE tab, click Options, click Add-ins, click the Manage list arrow, click Disabled Items, then click Go. If your Personal Macro Workbook is listed in the Disabled items dialog box, click its name, then click Enable.

Assign a Macro to a Button

Learning Outcomes
- Create a button shape in a worksheet
- Assign a macro to a button

When you create macros for others who will use your workbook, you might want to make the macros more visible so they're easier to use. In addition to using shortcut keys, you can run a macro by assigning it to a button on your worksheet. Then when you click the button the macro will run. **CASE** *To make it easier for people in the sales division to run the DivStamp macro, Kate asks you to assign it to a button on the workbook. You begin by creating the button.*

STEPS

1. **Add a new worksheet, click the INSERT tab, click the Shapes button in the Illustrations group, then click the first rectangle in the Rectangles group**
   The mouse pointer changes to a + symbol.
2. **Click at the top-left corner of cell A8, and drag the pointer to the lower-right corner of cell B9**
   Compare your screen to FIGURE I-16.
3. **Type Division Macro to label the button**
   Now that you have created the button, you are ready to assign the macro to it.
4. **Right-click the new button, then on the shortcut menu click Assign Macro**
   The Assign Macro dialog box opens.
5. **Click DivStamp under "Macro name", then click OK**
   You have assigned the DivStamp macro to the button.
6. **Click any cell to deselect the button, then click the button**
   The DivStamp macro plays, and the text Quest Sales appears in cell A1, as shown in FIGURE I-17.
7. **Save the workbook, preview Sheet3, close the workbook, then exit Excel, clicking Don't Save when asked to save changes to the Personal Macro Workbook**
8. **Submit the workbook to your instructor**

QUICK TIP

To format a macro button using 3-D effects, clip art, photographs, fills, and shadows, right-click it, select Format Shape from the shortcut menu, then select features such as Fill, Line Color, Line Style, Shadow, Reflection, Glow and Soft Edges, 3-D Format, 3-D Rotation, Picture Color, and Text Box in the Format Shape pane.

FIGURE I-16: Button shape

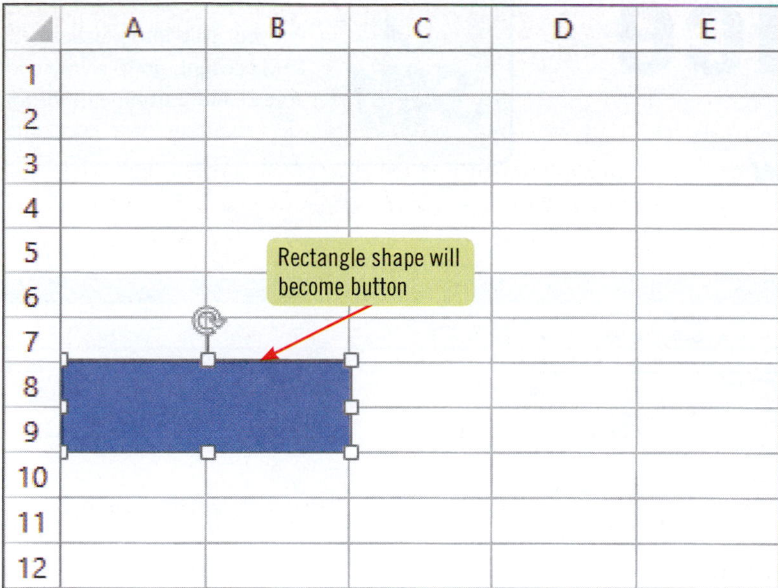

FIGURE I-17: Sheet3 with the Sales Division text

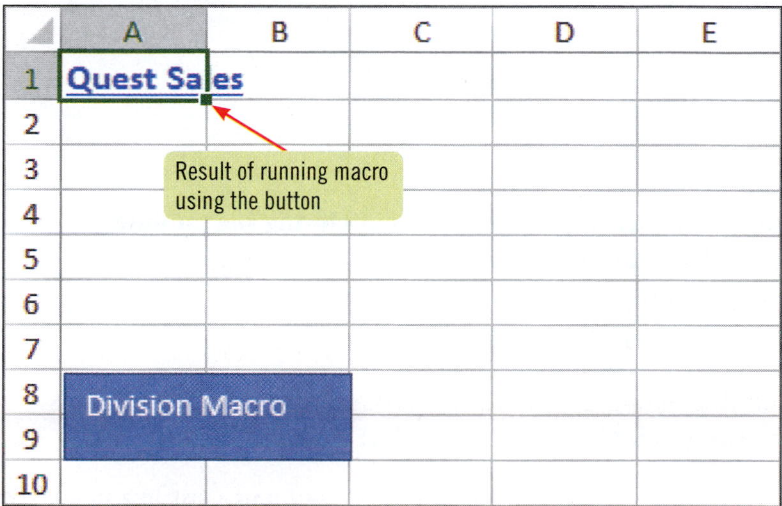

Creating and formatting a form control

You can add an object called a **form control** to an Excel worksheet to make it easier for users to enter or select data. Click the DEVELOPER tab on the Ribbon, click the Insert button in the Controls group, click the desired control in the Form Controls area of the Insert gallery, then draw the shape on the worksheet. After adding a control to a worksheet, you need to link it to a cell or cells in the worksheet. To do this, right-click it, select Format Control, then click the Control tab. For example, if you add a list box form control, the input range is the location of the list box selections and the cell link is the cell with the numeric value for the current position of the list control. To edit the form control's positioning properties (such as moving, sizing, and printing) right-click the form control, select Format Control and click the Properties tab. See **FIGURE I-18**.

FIGURE I-18: Properties tab of the Format Control dialog box

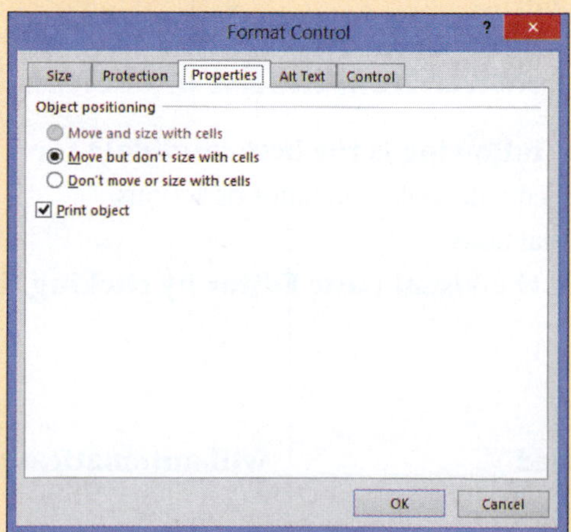

Excel 2013

Practice

Put your skills into practice with SAM! If you have a SAM account, go to www.cengage.com/sam2013 to access SAM assignments for this unit.

Concepts Review

FIGURE I-19

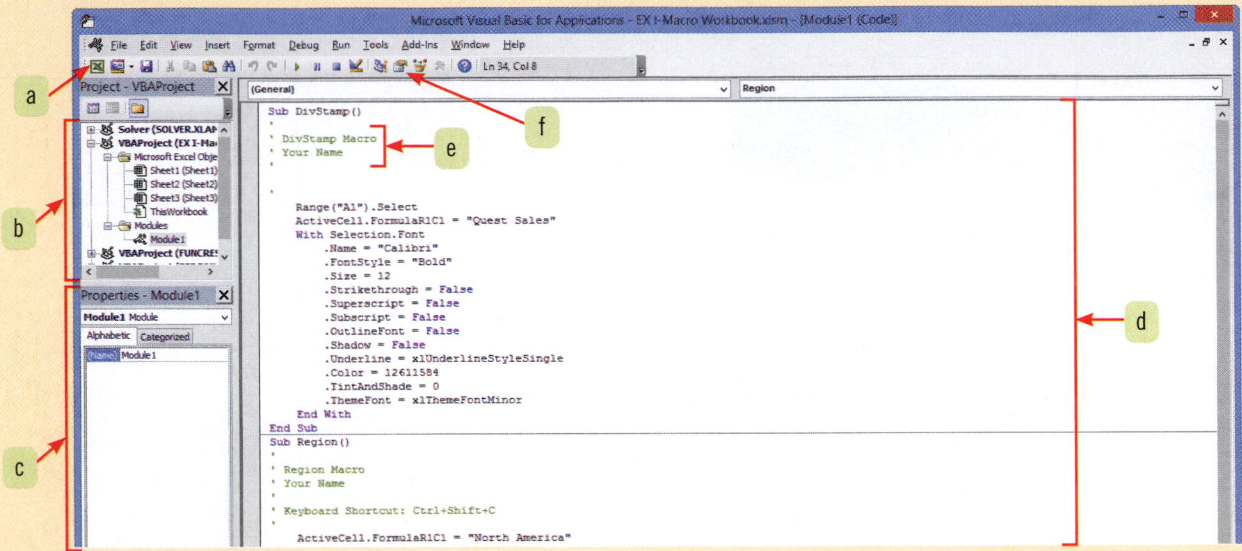

1. **Which element points to comments?**
2. **Which element do you click to return to Excel without closing the module?**
3. **Which element points to the Code window?**
4. **Which element points to the Properties Window button?**
5. **Which element points to the Project Explorer window?**
6. **Which element points to the Properties window?**

Match each term or button with the statement that best describes it.

7. **Macro**
8. **Virus**
9. **Comments**
10. **Personal Macro Workbook**
11. **Visual Basic Editor**

- **a.** Set of instructions that performs a task in a specified order
- **b.** Statements that appear in green explaining the macro
- **c.** Destructive software that can damage computer files
- **d.** Used to make changes to macro code
- **e.** Used to store frequently used macros

Select the best answer from the list of choices.

12. **Which of the following is the best candidate for a macro?**
    - **a.** Often-used sequences of commands or actions
    - **b.** Nonsequential tasks
    - **c.** Seldom-used commands or tasks
    - **d.** One-button or one-keystroke commands
13. **You can open the Visual Basic Editor by clicking the ______________ button in the Macro dialog box.**
    - **a.** Edit
    - **b.** Programs
    - **c.** Modules
    - **d.** Visual Basic Editor
14. **A Macro named ______________ will automatically run when the workbook it is saved in opens.**
    - **a.** Default
    - **b.** Auto_Open
    - **c.** Macro1
    - **d.** Open_Macro

15. Which of the following is *not* true about editing a macro?

- **a.** You edit macros using the Visual Basic Editor.
- **b.** A macro cannot be edited and must be recorded again.
- **c.** You can type changes directly in the existing program code.
- **d.** You can make more than one editing change in a macro.

16. Why is it important to plan a macro?

- **a.** Macros can't be deleted.
- **b.** Planning helps prevent careless errors from being introduced into the macro.
- **c.** It is impossible to edit a macro.
- **d.** Macros won't be stored if they contain errors.

17. Macros are recorded with relative references:

- **a.** Only if the Use Relative References button is selected.
- **b.** In all cases.
- **c.** By default.
- **d.** Only if the Use Absolute References button is not selected.

18. You can run macros:

- **a.** From the Macro dialog box.
- **b.** From shortcut key combinations.
- **c.** From a button on the worksheet.
- **d.** Using all of the above.

19. Macro security settings can be changed using the ______________ tab.

- **a.** Home
- **b.** Developer
- **c.** Security
- **d.** Review

Skills Review

1. Plan and enable a macro.

- **a.** You need to plan a macro that enters and formats your name and e-mail address in a worksheet.
- **b.** Write out the steps the macro will perform.
- **c.** Write out how the macro could be used in a workbook.
- **d.** Start Excel, open a new workbook, then save it as a Macro-Enabled workbook named **EX I-Macros** in the location where you store your Data Files. (*Hint*: The file will have the file extension .xlsm.)
- **e.** Use the Excel Options feature to display the DEVELOPER tab if it is not showing in the Ribbon.
- **f.** Using the Trust Center dialog box, enable all macros.

2. Record a macro.

- **a.** You want to record a macro that enters and formats your name and e-mail address in the range A1:A2 in a worksheet using the steps below.
- **b.** Name the macro **MyEmail**, store it in the current workbook, and make sure your name appears in the Description text box as the person who recorded the macro.
- **c.** Record the macro, entering your name in cell A1 and your e-mail address in cell A2. (*Hint*: You need to press [Ctrl][Home] first to ensure cell A1 will be selected when the macro runs.)
- **d.** Resize column A to fit the information entirely in that column.
- **e.** Add an outside border around the range A1:A2 and format the font using Green from the Standard Colors.
- **f.** Add bold formatting to the text in the range A1:A2.
- **g.** Stop the recorder and save the workbook.

3. Run a macro.

- **a.** Clear cell entries and formats in the range affected by the macro, resize the width of column A to 8.43, then select cell B3.
- **b.** Run the MyEmail macro to place your name and e-mail information in the range A1:A2.
- **c.** On the worksheet, clear all the cell entries and formats generated by running the MyEmail macro. Resize the width of column A to 8.43.
- **d.** Save the workbook.

Skills Review (continued)

4. Edit a macro.

- **a.** Open the MyEmail macro in the Visual Basic Editor.
- **b.** Change the line of code above the last line from Selection.Font.Bold = True to Selection.Font.Bold = False.
- **c.** Use the Close and Return to Microsoft Excel command on the File menu to return to Excel.
- **d.** Test the macro on Sheet1, and compare your worksheet to FIGURE I-20 verifying that the text is not bold.
- **e.** Save the workbook.

FIGURE I-20

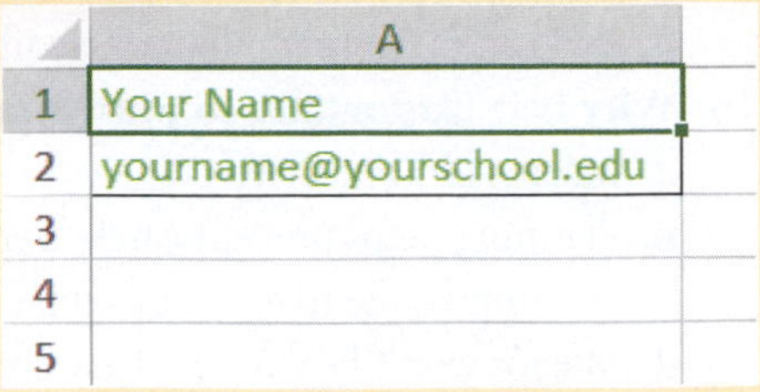

	A
1	Your Name
2	yourname@yourschool.edu
3	
4	
5	

5. Assign keyboard shortcuts to macros.

- **a.** Create a macro named **EmailStamp** in the current workbook, assign your macro the shortcut key combination [Ctrl][Shift][Q], enter your name in the description. (*Hint*: If you get an error when trying to use [Ctrl][Shift][Q], select another key combination.)
- **b.** Begin recording, enter your e-mail address, format it in italics with a font color of red, without underlining, in the selected cell of the current worksheet. Stop recording.
- **c.** After you record the macro, clear the contents and formats from the cell containing your e-mail address that you used to record the macro.
- **d.** Use the shortcut key combination to run the EmailStamp macro in a cell other than the one in which it was recorded. Compare your macro result to FIGURE I-21. Your e-mail address may appear in a different cell.
- **e.** Save the workbook.

FIGURE I-21

C	D	E
yourname@yourschool.edu		

6. Use the Personal Macro Workbook.

- **a.** Using Sheet1, record a new macro called **FitToLand** and store it in the Personal Macro Workbook with your name in the Description text box. If you already have a macro named FitToLand replace that macro. The macro should set the print orientation to landscape.
- **b.** After you record the macro, Add a new worksheet, and enter **Test data for FitToLand macro** in cell A1.
- **c.** Preview Sheet2 to verify that the orientation is set to portrait.
- **d.** Run the FitToLand macro. (You may have to wait a few moments.)
- **e.** Add your name to the Sheet2 footer, then preview Sheet2 and verify that it is now in Landscape orientation.
- **f.** Save the workbook.

7. Assign a macro to a button.

- **a.** Add a new worksheet and enter **Button Test** in cell A1.
- **b.** Using the rectangle shape, draw a rectangle in the range A7:B8.
- **c.** Label the button with the text **Landscape**. Compare your worksheet to FIGURE I-22.
- **d.** Assign the macro PERSONAL.XLSB!FitToLand to the button.
- **e.** Verify that the orientation of Sheet3 is set to portrait.
- **f.** Run the FitToLand macro using the button.
- **g.** Preview the worksheet, and verify that it is in landscape view.
- **h.** Add your name to the Sheet3 footer, then save the workbook.
- **i.** Close the workbook, exit Excel without saving the FitToLand macro in the Personal Macro Workbook, then submit your workbook to your instructor.

FIGURE I-22

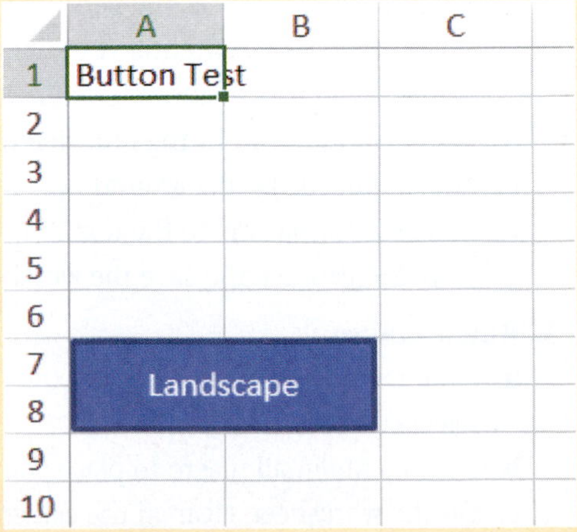

	A	B	C
1	Button Test		
2			
3			
4			
5			
6			
7	Landscape		
8			
9			
10			

Independent Challenge 1

As the office manager of Ocean Point Consulting Group, you need to develop ways to help your fellow employees work more efficiently. Employees have asked for Excel macros that can do the following:

- Adjust the column widths to display all column data in a worksheet.
- Place the company name of Ocean Point Consulting Group in the header of a worksheet.

a. Plan and write the steps necessary for each macro.

b. Start Excel, open the Data File EX I-1.xlsx from the location where you store your Data Files, then save it as a macro-enabled workbook called **EX I-Consulting**.

c. Check your macro security on the DEVELOPER tab to be sure that macros are enabled.

d. Create a macro named **ColumnFit**, save it in the EX I-Consulting.xlsm workbook, assign the ColumnFit macro a shortcut key combination of [Ctrl][Shift][X], and add your name in the description area for the macro. Record the macro using the following instructions:

- Record the ColumnFit macro to adjust a worksheet's column widths to display all data. (*Hint*: Select the entire sheet, click the HOME tab, click the Format button in the Cells group, select AutoFit Column Width, then click cell A1 to deselect the worksheet.)
- End the macro recording.

e. Format the widths of columns A through G to 8.43, then test the ColumnFit macro with the shortcut key combination [Ctrl][Shift][X].

f. Create a macro named **CompanyName**, and save it in the EX I-Consulting.xlsm workbook. Assign the macro a shortcut key combination of [Ctrl][Shift][Y], and add your name in the description area for the macro.

g. Record the CompanyName macro. The macro should place the company name of Ocean Point Consulting Group in the center section of the worksheet header.

h. Enter **CompanyName test data** in cell A1 of Sheet2, and test the CompanyName macro using the shortcut key combination [Ctrl][Shift][Y]. Preview Sheet2 to view the header.

i. Edit the CompanyName macro in the Visual Basic Editor to change the company name from Ocean Point Consulting Group to **Shore Consulting Group**. Close the Visual Basic Editor and return to Excel.

j. Add a rectangle button to Sheet3 in the range A6:B7. Label the button with the text **Company Name**.

k. Assign the CompanyName macro to the button.

l. Enter **New CompanyName Test** in cell A1. Compare your screen to FIGURE I-23. Use the button to run the CompanyName macro. Preview the worksheet, checking the header to be sure it is displaying the new company name.

m. Enter your name in the footers of all three worksheets. Save the workbook, close the workbook, then submit the workbook to your instructor and exit Excel.

FIGURE I-23

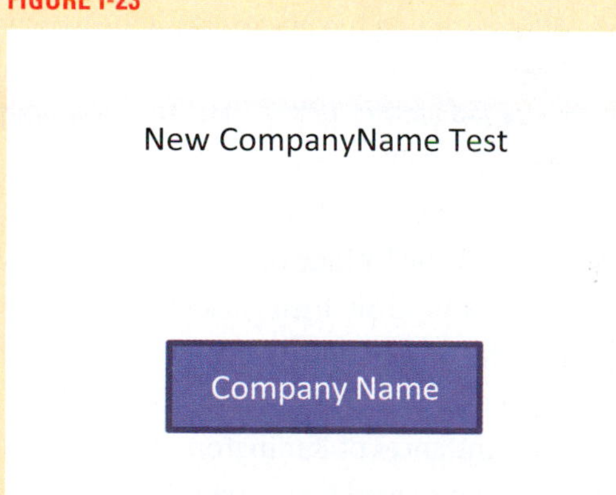

Excel 2013

Independent Challenge 2

You are an assistant to the VP of Sales at Twin Cities Beverage Company, a distributor of juices, water, and soda to 'supermarkets. As part of your work, you create spreadsheets with sales projections for different regions of the company. You frequently have to change the print settings so that workbooks print in landscape orientation with custom margins of 1" on the top and bottom. You also add a header with the company name on every worksheet. You have decided that it's time to create a macro to streamline this process.

a. Plan and write the steps necessary to create the macro.

b. Check your macro security settings to confirm that macros are enabled.

Independent Challenge 2 (continued)

c. Start Excel, create a new workbook, then save it as a macro-enabled file named **EX I-Sales Macro** in the location where you store your Data Files.

d. Create a macro that changes the page orientation to landscape, adds custom margins of 1" on the top and bottom of the page, adds a header of **Twin Cities Beverage Company** in the center section formatted as Bold with a font size of 14 points. Name the macro **Format**, add your name in the description, assign it the shortcut key combination [Ctrl][Shift][W], and store it in the current workbook.

e. Add a new worksheet and enter the text **Format Test** in cell A1. Test the macro using the shortcut key combination of [Ctrl][Shift][W]. Preview Sheet2 to check the page orientation, margins, and the header.

f. Add a new worksheet, enter the text **Format Test** in cell A1 add a rectangular button with the text **Format Worksheet** to run the Format macro, then test the macro using the button.

g. Preview the Visual Basic code for the macro.

h. Save the workbook, close the workbook, exit Excel, then submit the workbook to your instructor.

Independent Challenge 3

You are the Northeast regional sales manager of New England Technology, a technology consulting firm. You manage the New England operations and frequently create workbooks with data from the office locations. It's tedious to change the tab names and colors every time you open a new workbook, so you decide to create a macro that will add the office locations and colors to the three office location worksheet tabs, as shown in FIGURE I-24.

FIGURE I-24

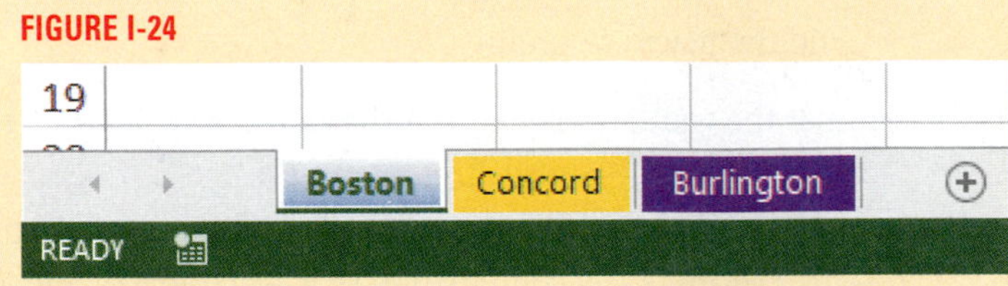

a. Plan and write the steps to create the macro described above.

b. Start Excel and open a new workbook.

c. Create the macro using the plan you created in Step a, name it **SheetFormat**, assign it the shortcut key combination [Ctrl][Shift][Q], store it in the Personal Macro Workbook, and add your name in the description area.

d. After recording the macro, close the workbook without saving it. Save the changes to the Personal Macro workbook.

e. Open a new workbook, then save it as a macro-enabled workbook named **EX I-Office Test** in the location where you store your Data Files. Use the shortcut key combination of [Ctrl][Shift][Q] to test the macro in the new workbook.

f. Unhide the PERSONAL.XLSB workbook. (*Hint*: Click the VIEW tab, click the Unhide button in the Window group, click PERSONAL.XLSB, then click OK.)

g. Edit the SheetFormat macro using FIGURE I-25 as a guide, changing the Burlington sheet name to Portland. (*Hint*: There are three instances of Burlington that need to be changed.)

h. Open a new workbook, then save it as a macro-enabled workbook named **EX I-Office Test New** in the location where you store your Data Files. Test the edited macro using the shortcut key combination of [Ctrl][Shift][Q].

i. Add a new sheet in the workbook, and name it **Code**. Copy the SheetFormat macro code from the Personal Macro Workbook, and paste it in the Code sheet beginning in cell A1. Save the workbook, close the workbook, then submit the EX I-Office Test New workbook to your instructor.

FIGURE I-25

```
Sub SheetFormat()
'
' SheetFormat Macro
' Your Name
'
' Keyboard Shortcut: Ctrl+Shift+Q
'
    Sheets("Sheet1").Select
    Sheets("Sheet1").Name = "Boston"
    Sheets("Boston").Select
    With ActiveWorkbook.Sheets("Boston").Tab
        .Color = 12611584
        .TintAndShade = 0
    End With
    Sheets("Sheet2").Select
    Sheets("Sheet2").Name = "Concord"
    Sheets("Concord").Select
    With ActiveWorkbook.Sheets("Concord").Tab
        .Color = 65535
        .TintAndShade = 0
    End With
    Sheets("Sheet3").Select
    Sheets("Sheet3").Name = "Portland"
    Sheets("Portland").Select
    With ActiveWorkbook.Sheets("Portland").Tab
        .Color = 10498160
        .TintAndShade = 0
    End With
End Sub
```

Independent Challenge 3 (continued)

j. Hide the PERSONAL.XLSB workbook. (*Hint*: With the PERSONAL.XLSB workbook active, click the VIEW tab, then click the Hide button in the Window group.)

k. Close the workbook without saving changes to the PERSONAL.XLSB workbook, then exit Excel.

Independent Challenge 4: Explore

As the owner of a yoga studio you manage your courses using an Excel workbook. You have created a macro that will display available classes when a type of class is entered. You have been manually entering the class name and then running the macro. You have hired an assistant and would like to simplify the process of displaying class information by adding a form control to help select the data in the worksheet and then run the macro. Specifically, you will ask your assistant to use a list box which will return a numeric value for the current position of the control. That numeric value can be used with an Index function to insert the selected data in the necessary location for the macro which will use it as criteria to filter your data to return the requested course information.

a. Start Excel, open the Data File EX I-2.xlsm from the location where you store your Data Files, then save it as **EX I-Classes**.

b. Test the macro FindClass by entering **Power** in cell A20 and running the macro. Scroll down to cell A23 to see the results.

c. Insert a button form control in cells B19:C20 and assign the FindClass macro to the form control button. Label the button with the text **Find Classes**.

d. Enter **Basics** in cell A20 and test the button.

e. On the Controls sheet create a list for a List Box form control by entering **Basics** in cell A1, **Power** in cell A2, **Hatha** in cell A3, and **Kripalu** in cell A4.

f. On the Yoga Classes sheet enter **Select Class** in cell A1. Insert a list box form control in cells B1:B4. Format the control to set the Input range to A1:A4 of the Controls sheet and the Cell link to cell B1 in the Controls sheet. Compare your controls to FIGURE I-26.

g. Test the list box by clicking different classes and viewing the position in the list displayed in cell B1 of the Controls sheet, the cell link used in the previous step.

h. Replace the class in cell A20 with the index formula **=INDEX(Controls!A1:A4,Controls!B1,0)**. This will use the list position displayed in cell B1 of the Controls sheet to find the class in the range A1:A4 of the Controls sheet and display the class name in cell A20. Test the index formula by selecting different classes in the list box and verifying cell A20 matches the selection.

i. Delete the form control button in cells B19:C20.

j. Assign the FindClass macro to the list box form control.

k. Select a class from the list box and verify the macro is working properly.

l. Enter your name in the footers of both worksheets. Save the workbook, close the workbook, then submit the workbook to your instructor and exit Excel.

FIGURE I-26

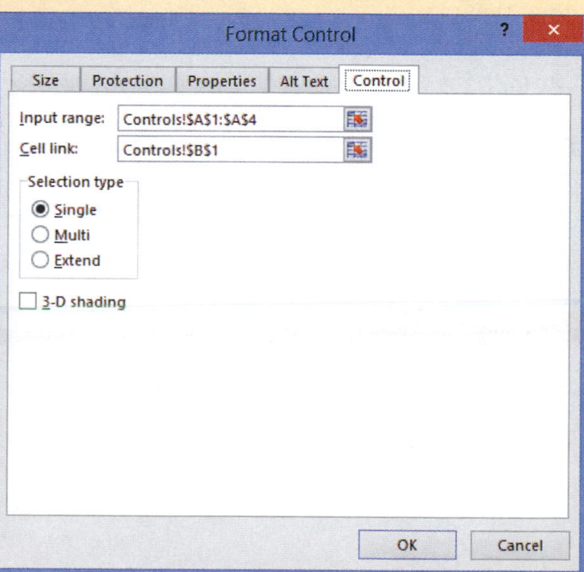

Excel 2013

Visual Workshop

Start Excel, open the Data File EX I-3.xlsx from the location where you store your Data Files, then save it as a macro-enabled workbook called **EX I-Payroll**. Create a macro with the name **TotalHours**, save the macro in the EX I-Payroll workbook that does the following:

- Totals the weekly hours for each employee by totaling the hours for the first employee and copying that formula for the other employees
- Adds a row at the top of the worksheet and inserts a label of **Hours** in a font size of 14 point, centered across all columns
- Adds your name in the worksheet footer

Test the TotalHours macro by opening the Data File EX I-3.xlsx from the location where you store your Data Files and running the macro. Compare your macro results to **FIGURE I-27**. Close the Data File EX I-3 without saving it, then save the EX I-Payroll workbook. Submit the EX I-Payroll workbook to your instructor.

FIGURE I-27

	A	B	C	D	E	F	G	H	I
1	Hours								
2		Monday	Tuesday	Wednesday	Thursday	Friday	Saturday	Sunday	Total
3	Mary Jacobs	7	8	6	8	5	0	1	35
4	John Malone	5	7	8	7	7	6	2	42
5	Ken Duffy	6	5	7	6	3	5	0	32
6	Sally Landry	8	7	6	5	5	1	0	32
7	Kathy Bane	8	7	5	8	7	7	0	42
8	Jacki Rand	8	7	5	5	7	8	0	40
9	Cindy Healy	7	5	2	6	8	5	3	36
10	Randy Thomas	2	7	8	6	7	2	0	32
11	Ken Yang	0	4	4	4	4	4	1	21
12	Linda Regan	7	8	2	8	8	1	0	34
13									

Enhancing Charts

CASE Quest's vice president of sales, Kate Morgan, has requested charts comparing sales and trends in the Quest regions over the first two quarters. You will produce these charts and enhance them to improve their appearance, clarify the display, and make the worksheet data more accessible.

Unit Objectives

After completing this unit, you will be able to:

- Customize a data series
- Change a data source and add a chart style
- Add chart elements
- Format chart axes
- Create a combination chart
- Enhance a chart
- Summarize data with sparklines
- Identify data trends

Files You Will Need

EX J-1.xlsx
EX J-2.xlsx
EX J-3.xlsx
EX J-4.xlsx
EX J-5.xlsx
EX J-6.xlsx
EX J-7.xlsx

Excel 2013
UNIT J

Customize a Data Series

Learning Outcomes

- Switch row and column data
- Format a data series

A **data series** is the sequence of values that Excel uses to **plot**, or create, a chart. As with other Excel elements, you can change the data series presentation to get another view of your data. For example, you can reverse the data charted on the x and y axes. You can also format a chart's data series to make the chart more attractive and easier to read. **CASE** *Kate wants you to create a chart showing the sales for each region in January and February. You begin by creating a column chart, which you will customize to make it easier to compare the sales for each region.*

STEPS

1. **Start Excel, open the file EX J-1.xlsx from the location where you store your Data Files, then save it as EX J-Region Sales**

   To begin, Kate wants to see how each region performed over January and February. The first step is to select the data you want to appear in the chart.

2. **Select the range A2:C6**

3. **Click the Quick Analysis tool at the lower right corner of the selected range, click the CHARTS tab at the top of the Quick Analysis gallery, move the mouse pointer over the recommended charts to view your data in different visual presentations, then point to the Clustered Column option**

   A clustered column chart preview comparing the January and February sales for each branch appears, as shown in FIGURE J-1. You decide to use this option to compare the monthly sales for each branch.

> **QUICK TIP**
> You can also click the INSERT tab and click the Recommended Charts button in the Charts group on the Ribbon to explore the available charts.

4. **Click Clustered Column, then on the CHART TOOLS DESIGN tab in the Ribbon, click the Switch Row/Column button in the Data group**

   The legend now contains the region data, and the horizontal axis groups the bars by month. Kate can now easily compare the branch sales for each month. You want to see how the graph looks with the U.S. data series plotted in a green color.

5. **Double-click the Jan U.S. data series bar (the far-left bar on the graph), click the Fill & Line button in the Format Data Series pane, click Fill, click the Solid fill option button, click the Fill Color list arrow, select Dark Green, Accent 5 in the Theme Colors group, then close the Format Data Series pane**

6. **Point to the edge of the chart, then drag the chart to place its upper-left corner in cell A8**

7. **Drag the chart's lower-right sizing handle to fit the chart in the range A8:H20, then compare your chart to FIGURE J-2**

   You can resize a chart by dragging its corner sizing handles.

8. **Save the workbook**

Adding width and depth to data series

You can change the gap depth and the gap width in column charts by double-clicking one of the chart's data series and dragging the Gap Width or depth sliders in the Format Data Series pane. Increasing the gap width adds space between each set of data on the chart by decreasing the width of the chart's data series. If you are working with 3-D charts, you will have the option to increase the gap depth to add depth to all categories of data.

FIGURE J-1: Clustered column chart comparing January and February sales for each region

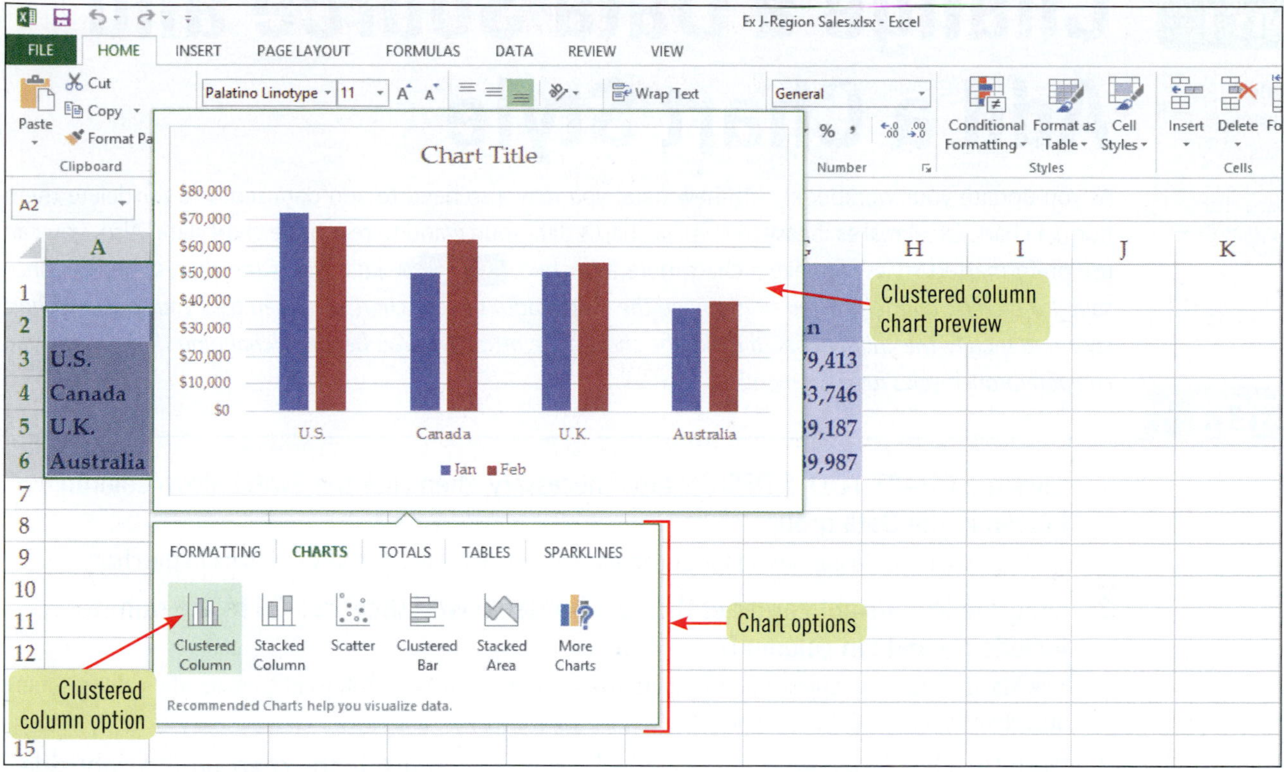

FIGURE J-2: Chart comparing region sales in January and February

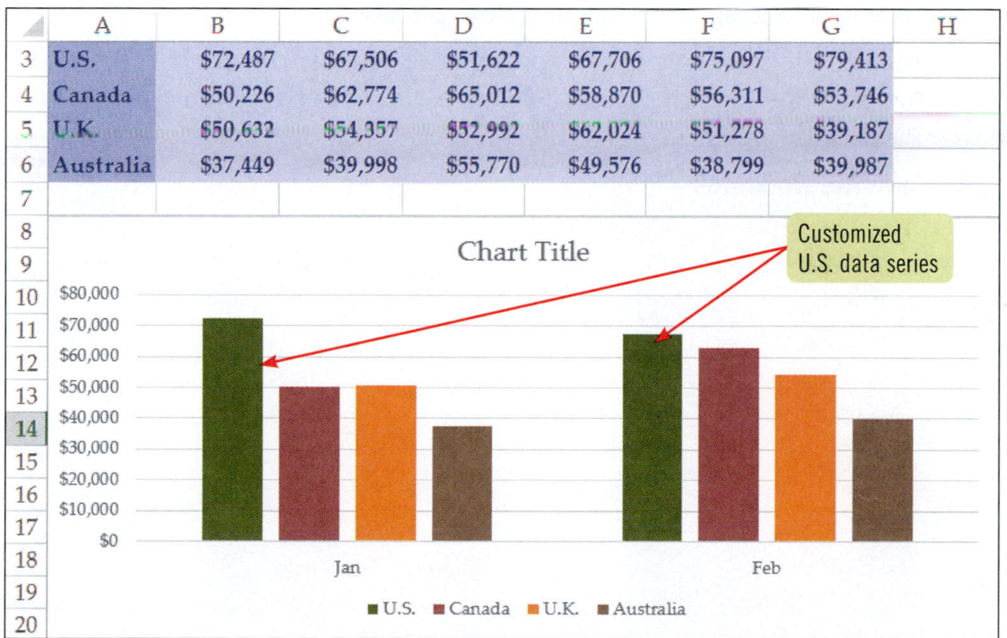

	A	B	C	D	E	F	G
3	U.S.	$72,487	$67,506	$51,622	$67,706	$75,097	$79,413
4	Canada	$50,226	$62,774	$65,012	$58,870	$56,311	$53,746
5	U.K.	$50,632	$54,357	$52,992	$62,024	$51,278	$39,187
6	Australia	$37,449	$39,998	$55,770	$49,576	$38,799	$39,987

Excel 2013

Excel 2013
UNIT J

Learning Outcomes
- Add data to a chart
- Format a chart with a chart style

Change a Data Source and Add a Chart Style

As you update your workbooks with new data, you may also need to add data series to (or delete them from) a chart. Excel makes it easy to revise a chart's data source and to rearrange chart data. Also, you can use preformatted styles to make a chart more attractive. **CASE** *Kate wants the chart to show branch sales for the first quarter, so you need to add the March data to your chart. She then asks you to add a chart style and modify the chart colors to make the chart more attractive. You begin by changing the data view to compare branch sales for each month.*

STEPS

1. **Click the CHART TOOLS DESIGN tab if necessary, then click the Switch Row/Column button in the Data group**

   The region data again appears on the horizontal axis. You want to add the March data to the chart.

2. **Drag the lower-right corner of the data border in worksheet cell C6 to the right to include the data in column D**

   The March data series appears on the chart, as shown in FIGURE J-3. You want to make the columns more attractive using one of the chart styles.

3. **With the chart selected, click Chart Styles button outside the chart on the right side, then scroll down to and click Style 14 (the last style)**

   The data bars have an appearance of depth and the January data bars are now a blue color again. The menu remains open. You want to change the colors of the data bars.

4. **Click COLOR at the top of the Chart Styles gallery**

   There are colorful and monochromatic galleries available.

5. **Point to the color galleries and preview the data bar colors, click Color 2 (the second row from the top), then click the Chart Styles button again to close the gallery**

   The data bars appear in the new color scheme. Compare your chart to FIGURE J-4.

6. **Save the workbook**

FIGURE J-3: Chart with March data series added

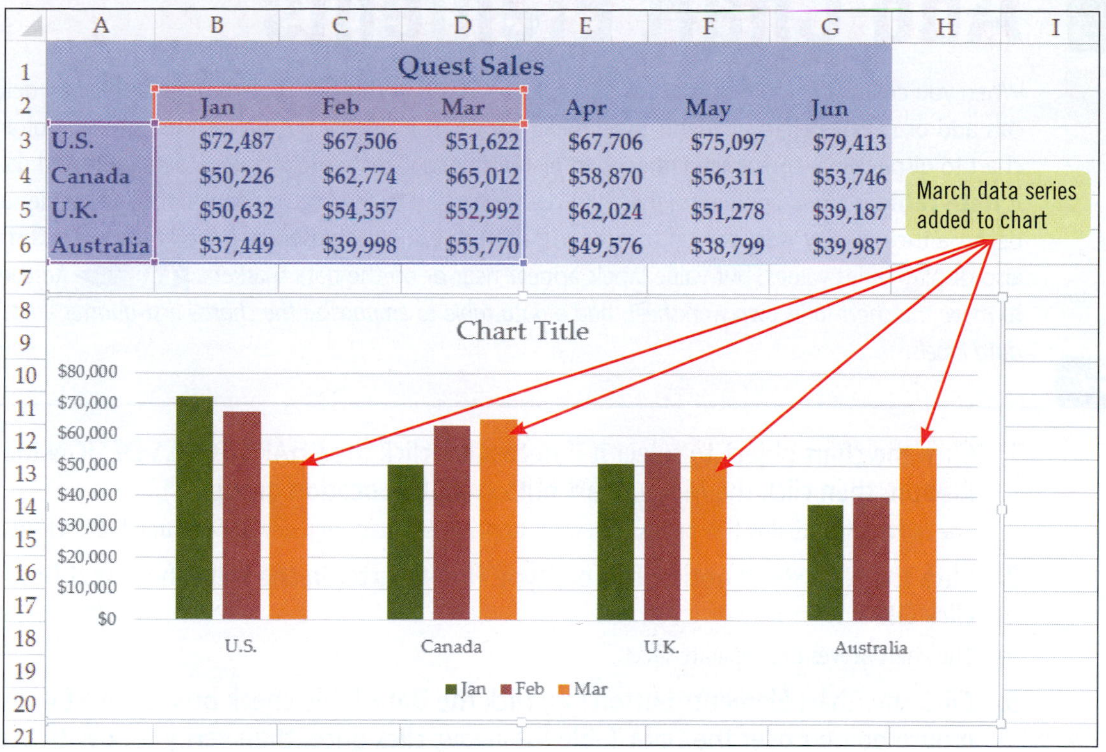

FIGURE J-4: Chart with new color scheme

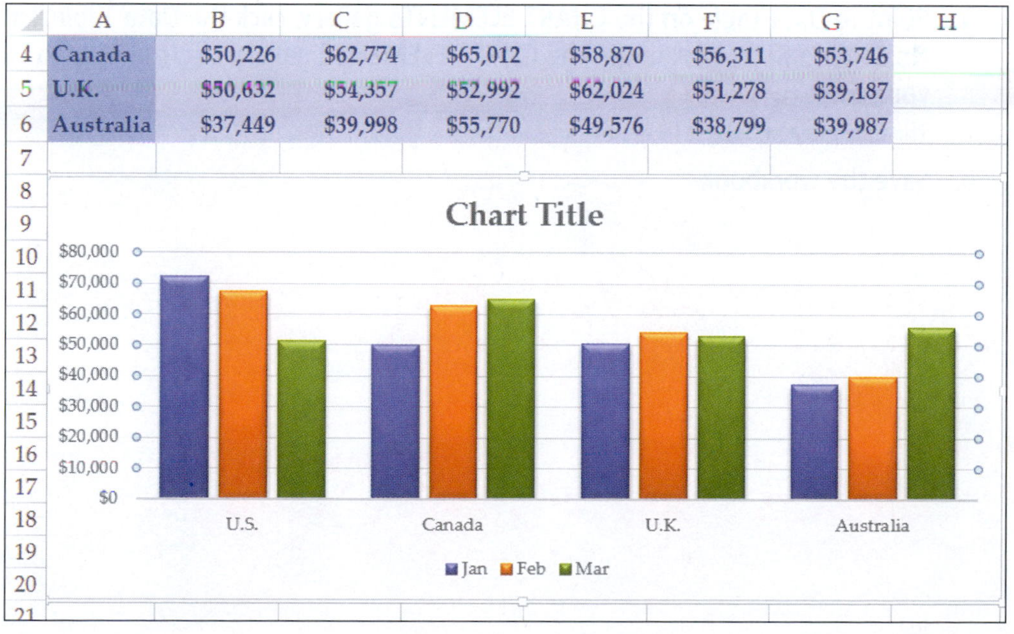

Excel 2013

Add Chart Elements

Learning Outcomes

- Move a chart to a different worksheet
- Add a data table to a chart
- Add data labels to a chart

When you create a chart, **chart elements** such as the chart title and legend often appear by default. You can add or remove chart elements by clicking the Chart Elements button on the right side of a selected chart to display an element list. Other chart elements you can choose include a data table and data labels. A **data table** is a grid containing the chart data, attached to the bottom of a chart. Data tables are useful because they display—directly on the chart itself—the values you used to generate a chart. **Data labels** also display series values, but value labels appear near or on the data markers. CASE *Kate wants you to move the chart to its own worksheet, add a data table to emphasize the chart's first-quarter data, and add data labels.*

STEPS

1. **Click the chart object to select it if necessary, click the CHART TOOLS DESIGN tab on the Ribbon, then click the Move Chart button in the Location group**

   The Move Chart dialog box opens. You want to place the chart on a new sheet named First Quarter.

2. **Click the New sheet option button, type First Quarter in the New sheet text box, then click OK**

   The chart moves to a separate sheet.

3. **Click the Chart Elements button [+], click the Data Table check box to select it, move the mouse pointer over the Data Table list arrow, click once, then verify that With Legend Keys is selected**

   A data table with the first-quarter data and a key to the legend appears at the bottom of the chart, as shown in FIGURE J-5. You will add data labels to clarify the exact amount of sales represented by each data bar.

4. **Click the Data Labels check box in the CHART ELEMENTS gallery**

   Data labels appear above the data bars. You don't need the legend keys in the data table so you decide to remove them.

5. **Point to Data Table on the CHART ELEMENTS gallery, click the Data Table list arrow, click No Legend Keys, click under the CHART ELEMENTS gallery to close it, then compare your chart to FIGURE J-6**

   The data table no longer shows the legend keys.

6. **Save the workbook**

FIGURE J-5: Chart with data table

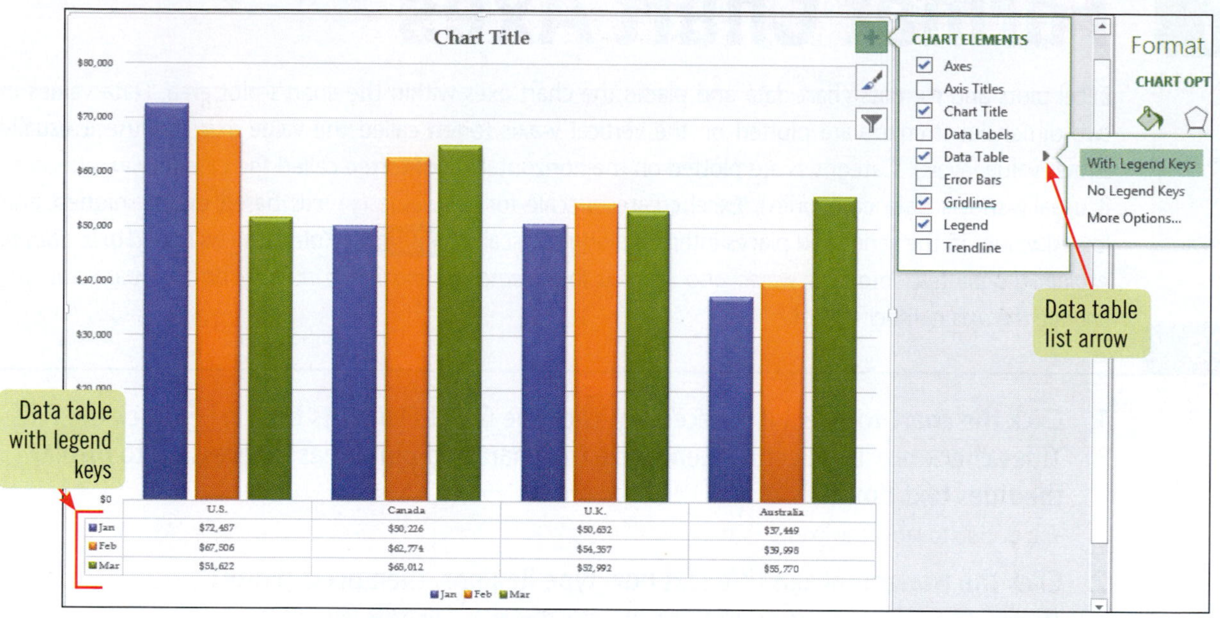

FIGURE J-6: Chart with data table legend keys removed

Formatting legends

To format a legend's fill, border, color, or shadows, click the Chart Elements button point to Legend, click the Legend list arrow, then click More Options. Using the options in the Format Legend pane, you can use the LEGEND OPTIONS tab and TEXT OPTIONS tab to customize the legend. For example, you can add a picture to the legend by clicking the Fill & Line button, clicking the Picture or texture fill option button, clicking the File button under Insert picture from, then browsing to your image. The legend in **FIGURE J-7** has a textured fill background. You can also drag a legend to any location. To change a legend's font size, color, or style right-click the legend text, click Font on the shortcut menu, then adjust the settings in the Font dialog box.

FIGURE J-7: Formatted legend

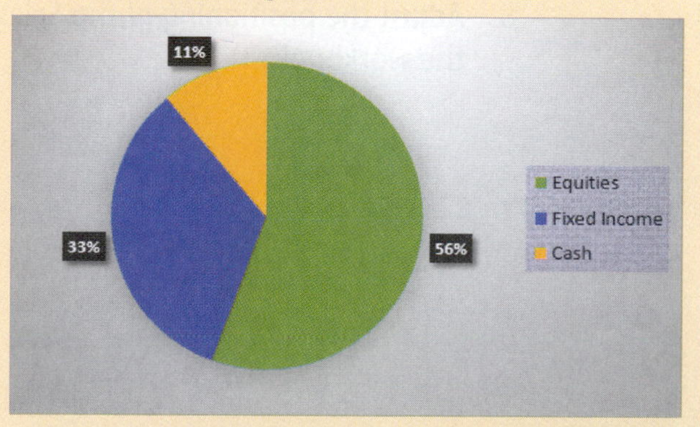

Excel 2013

Excel 2013
UNIT J

Format Chart Axes

Learning Outcomes
- Add axis titles
- Change the vertical axis maximum value

Excel plots and formats chart data and places the chart axes within the chart's plot area. Data values in two-dimensional charts are plotted on the vertical y-axis (often called the value axis because it usually shows value levels). Categories are plotted on the horizontal x-axis (often called the category axis because it usually shows data categories). Excel creates a scale for the value (y) axis based on the highest and lowest values in the series and places intervals along the scale. **CASE** *Kate asks you to add axes titles to explain the plotted data. She would also like you to increase the maximum number on the value axis and change the axis number format.*

STEPS

1. **Click the chart to select it if necessary, click the Chart Elements button [+], click the Axis Titles check box to select it, then resize the chart and plot areas if necessary to display the titles text boxes**
   You decide to label the axes.
2. **Click the Horizontal axis title text box, type Regions, then press [Enter]**
   The word "Regions" appears as the Horizontal axis title after you press [Enter].
3. **Click the Vertical axis title text box, type Sales, then press [Enter]**
   The word "Sales" appears in the Vertical axis title as shown in FIGURE J-8. You decide to change the maximum number on the value axis. The maximum number on the value axis is currently $80,000.
4. **Click [+], point to Axes, click the Axes list arrow, then click More Options**
   The Format Axis pane opens.
5. **Click the AXIS OPTIONS list arrow near the top of the pane, click the Vertical (Value) Axis, in the Maximum text box type 90000, then press [Enter]**
   Now 90000.0 appears as the maximum value on the value axis, and the chart bar heights adjust to reflect the new value. Next, you want the vertical axis values to appear without additional zeroes to make the chart data easier to read.
6. **Click the Display units list arrow, click Thousands, then make sure the Show display units label on chart check box is selected**
   The values are reduced to two digits and the word "Thousands" appears in a text box to the left of the values. You will increase the font size of the axes titles and unit label to make them easier to see.
7. **Right-click the Sales title, in the shortcut menu click Font, enter 16 in the Size text box in the Font dialog box, click OK, right-click the Regions title, in the shortcut menu click Font, enter 16 in the Size text box in the Font dialog box, click OK, right-click the Thousands title, in the shortcut menu click Font, enter 12 in the Size text box in the Font dialog box, then click OK**
8. **Adjust the positioning of the Sales and Thousands titles to match FIGURE J-9, then save the workbook**

FIGURE J-8: Chart with axes titles

	U.S.	Canada	U.K.	Australia
Jan	$72,487	$50,226	$50,632	$37,449
Feb	$67,506	$62,774	$54,357	$39,998
Mar	$51,622	$65,012	$52,992	$55,770

FIGURE J-9: Chart with formatted axes

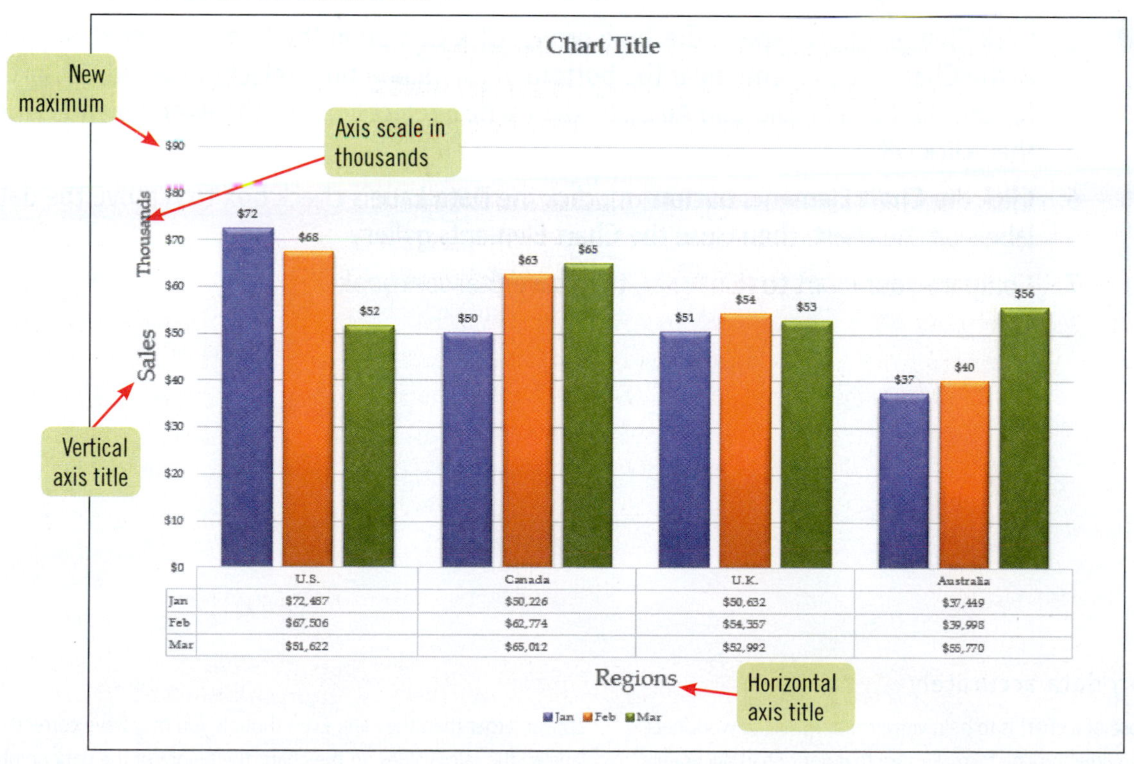

	U.S.	Canada	U.K.	Australia
Jan	$72,487	$50,226	$50,632	$37,449
Feb	$67,506	$62,774	$54,357	$39,998
Mar	$51,622	$65,012	$52,992	$55,770

Create a Combination Chart

Learning Outcomes
- Add chart data
- Create a chart with two types of graphs

A combination chart is a chart that combines two or more chart types in a single chart. This is helpful if you have different types of data in a chart and you want to emphasize the different data types. An example of a combination chart is a line and bar combination chart showing profits and sales. **CASE** *Kate wants you to create a combination chart by adding a line chart showing the averages of sales for the first quarter months.*

STEPS

1. **Click the Sales sheet tab to select it, select the range A2:D6, click the Quick Analysis tool, click the TOTALS tab, then click the Average button**
   Averages for the months appear in row 7.
2. **Click the First Quarter sheet tab, click the chart if necessary to select it, click the CHART TOOLS DESIGN tab, click the Select Data button in the Data group, edit the Chart data range to =Sales!$A$2:$D$7, then click OK**
   The average data bars are included in the chart as shown in FIGURE J-10. To create more room on the chart you will move the legend into the data table.
3. **Click the Chart Elements button [+], click the Data Table list arrow, click With Legend Keys, click the Legend check box to remove the legend, then click the Chart Elements button to close the gallery**
   You want to switch the axes data to show average amounts for each month.
4. **Click the Switch Row/Column button in the Data group**
   The average amounts for each month will be easier to distinguish if they are on a different type of graph.
5. **Click Change Chart Type in the Type group, click Combo in the Change Type dialog box, in the Chart Type column near the bottom of the dialog box, select Clustered Column for the US, Canada, UK, and Australia data series, select Line for the Average data series, then click OK**
6. **Click the Chart Elements button [+], click the Data Labels check box to remove the data labels on the chart, then close the Chart Elements gallery**
7. **Compare your chart to FIGURE J-11, then save the workbook**

QUICK TIP
You can plot two data sets on different axes by creating a combination chart, selecting the Secondary Axis checkbox next to one of the data series, then clicking OK.

Charting data accurately

The purpose of a chart is to help viewers interpret the worksheet data. When creating charts, make sure that your chart accurately portrays your data. Charts can sometimes misrepresent data and thus mislead people. For example, it is possible to change the y-axis units or its starting value to make charted sales values appear larger than they are. Even though you may have correctly labeled the sales values on the chart, the height of the data points will lead people viewing the chart to think the sales are higher than the labeled values. So use caution when you modify charts to make sure you accurately represent your data.

FIGURE J-10: Chart with average data series

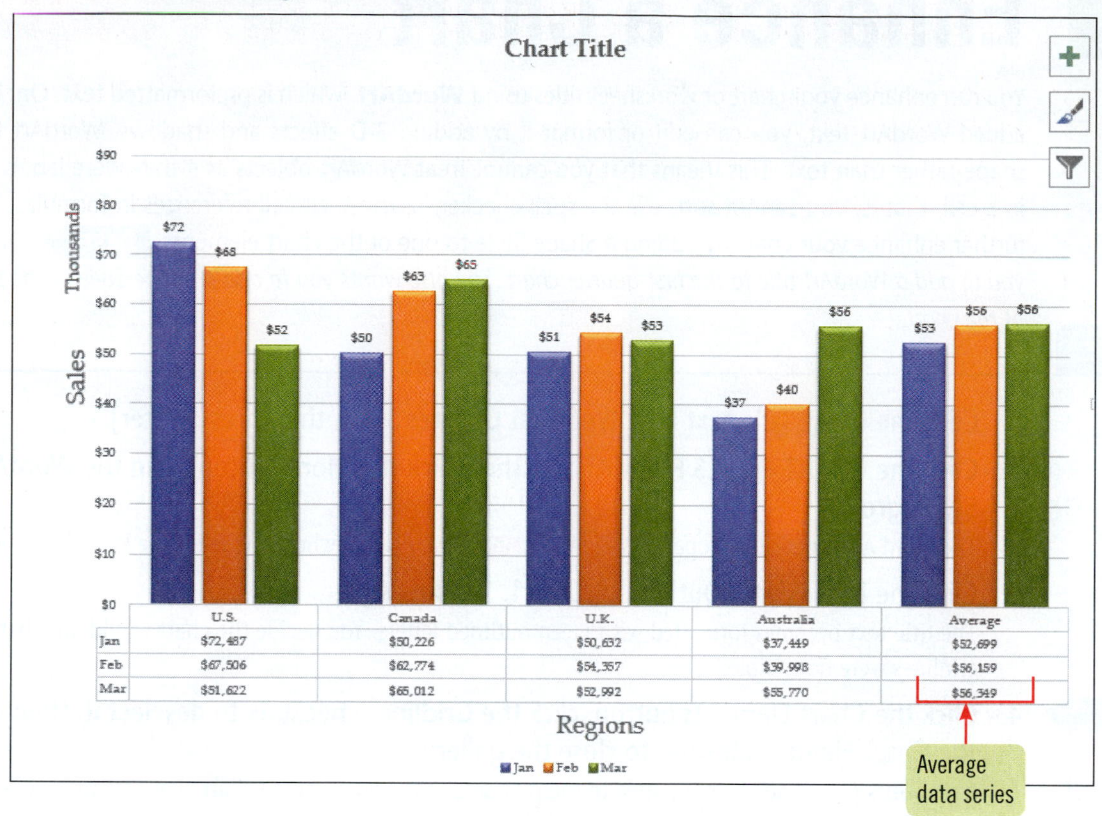

	U.S.	Canada	U.K.	Australia	Average
Jan	$72,487	$50,226	$50,632	$37,449	$52,699
Feb	$67,506	$62,774	$54,357	$39,998	$56,159
Mar	$51,622	$65,012	$52,992	$55,770	$56,349

FIGURE J-11: Combination chart with two types of graphs

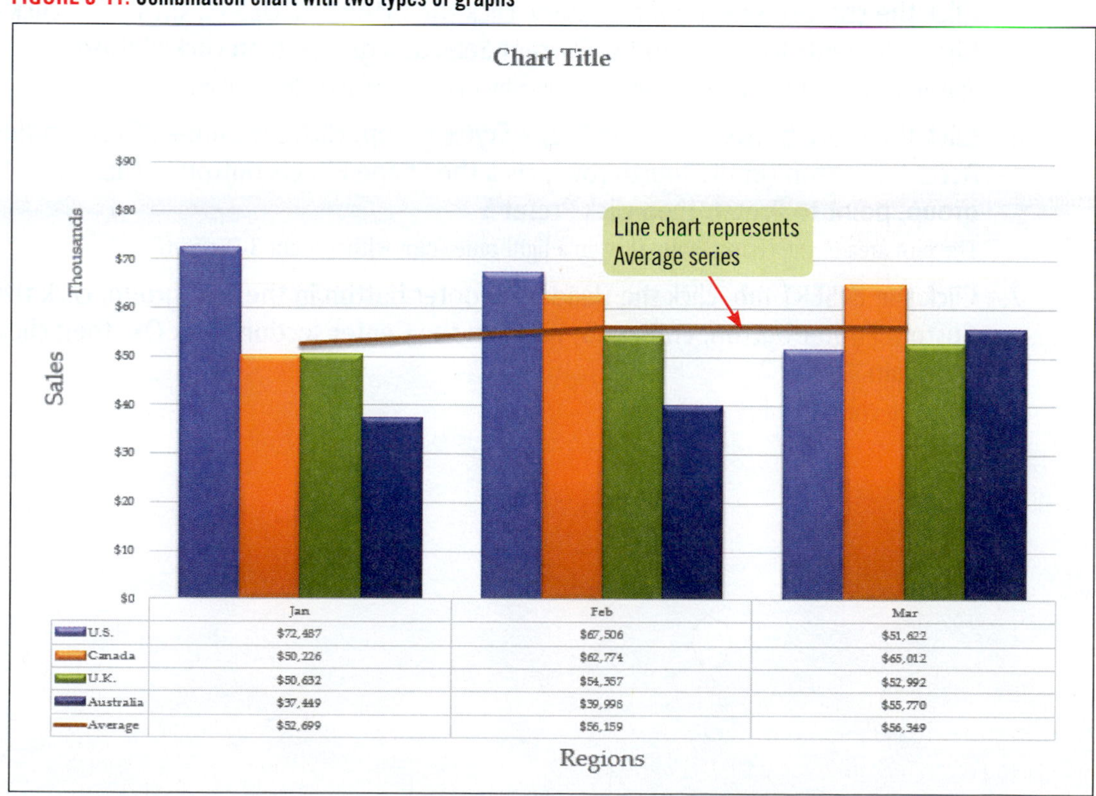

	Jan	Feb	Mar
U.S.	$72,487	$67,506	$51,622
Canada	$50,226	$62,774	$65,012
U.K.	$50,632	$54,357	$52,992
Australia	$37,449	$39,998	$55,770
Average	$52,699	$56,159	$56,349

Excel 2013

Excel 2013
UNIT J

Enhance a Chart

Learning Outcomes
- Add a WordArt title to a chart
- Add a shape style to the plot area

You can enhance your chart or worksheet titles using **WordArt**, which is preformatted text. Once you've added WordArt text, you can edit or format it by adding 3-D effects and shadows. WordArt text is a shape rather than text. This means that you cannot treat WordArt objects as if they were labels entered in a cell; that is, you cannot sort, use the spell checker, or use their cell references in formulas. You can further enhance your chart by adding a Shape Style to one of the chart elements. **CASE** *Kate wants you to add a WordArt title to the first-quarter chart. She also wants you to add a Shape Style to the plot area of the chart.*

STEPS

1. **Click the Chart Title text box, type First Quarter Sales, then press [Enter]**
2. **Click the CHART TOOLS FORMAT tab, then click the More button in the WordArt Styles group**

   The Word Art styles gallery opens, as shown in FIGURE J-12. This is where you select the WordArt for your text.
3. **Click the Fill - White, Outline - Accent 1, Shadow style**

   The title text becomes formatted with green outlined letters. You decide the chart would look better if the gridlines were not visible.

QUICK TIP
You can also enhance a chart by adding a picture to one of the chart elements.

4. **Click the Chart Elements button, click the Gridlines checkbox to deselect it, then click the Chart Elements button to close the gallery**

   Kate wants you to add a shape style to the plot area of the chart. Some chart elements cannot be selected using the CHART ELEMENTS gallery on the chart; instead you need to use the Chart Elements list arrow on the Ribbon.
5. **Click the chart to select it if necessary, click the CHART TOOLS FORMAT tab, click the Chart Elements list arrow in the Current Selection group, then click Plot Area**

   The plot area of the chart is selected, as shown by the four small circles on its corners.
6. **Click the More button in the Shape Styles group, click the Subtle Effect - Indigo, Accent 1 button (in the fourth row), click the Shape Effects button in the Shape Styles group, point to Preset, then click Preset 5**

   The plot area of the chart is formatted in a light blue color with a slight 3-D effect.
7. **Click the INSERT tab, click the Header & Footer button in the Text group, click the Custom Footer button, enter your name in the Center section, click OK, then click OK again**

   Compare your chart to FIGURE J-13.

FIGURE J-12: WordArt Styles gallery

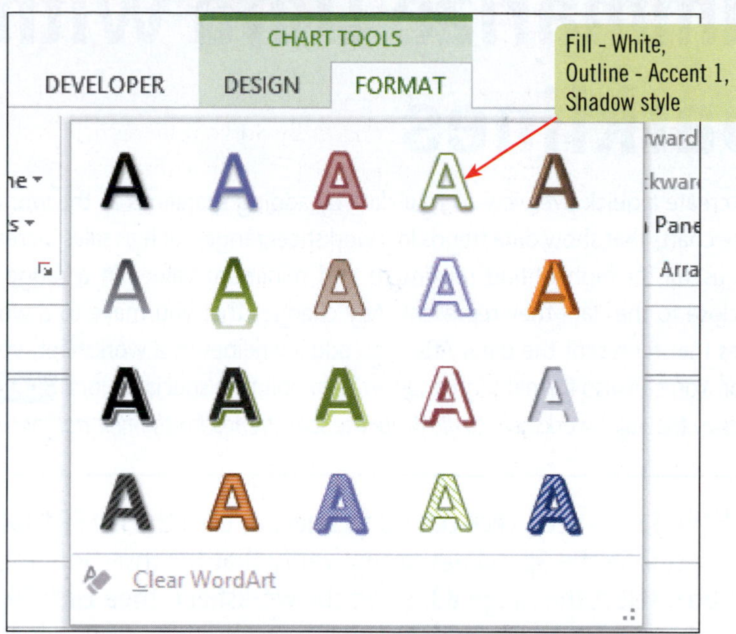

FIGURE J-13: Chart with formatted title and plot area

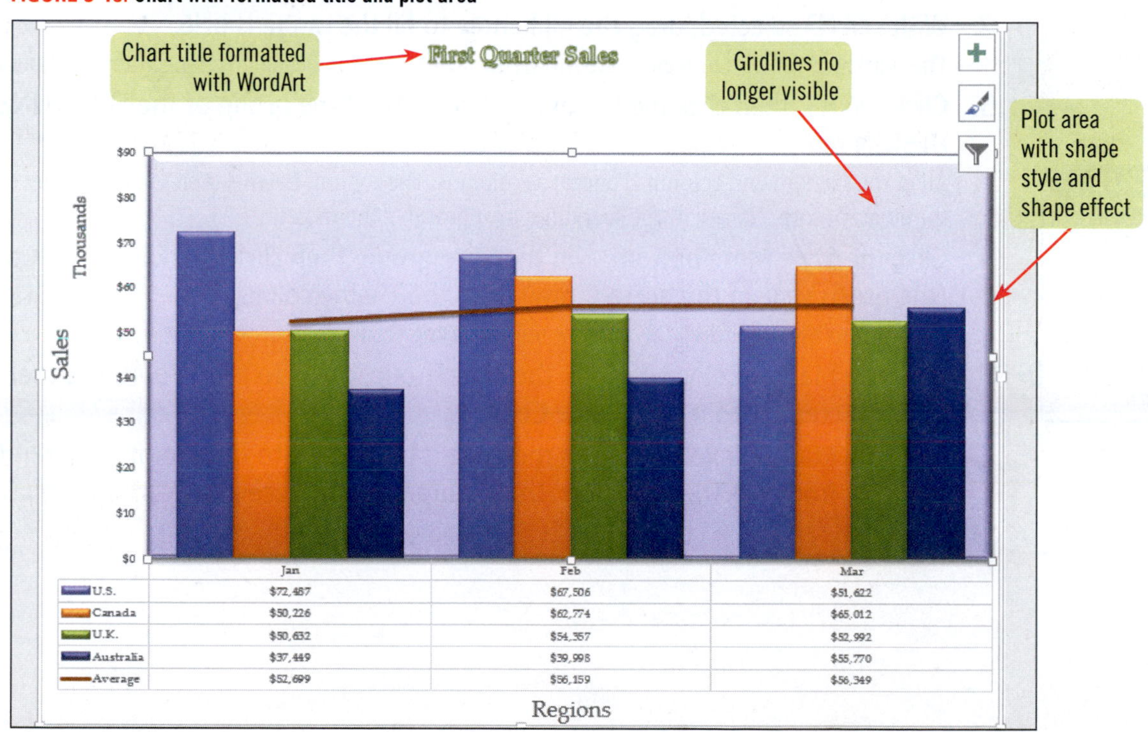

	Jan	Feb	Mar
U.S.	$72,487	$67,506	$51,622
Canada	$50,226	$62,774	$65,012
U.K.	$50,632	$54,357	$52,992
Australia	$37,449	$39,998	$55,770
Average	$52,699	$56,159	$56,349

Working with Shapes

Shapes are wonderful additions to any worksheet, and can make your data more visually interesting. To create a shape, click the INSERT tab, click the Shapes button in the Illustrations group, click any shape, then drag across the worksheet to create a shape object. Once you create a shape, you can rotate it by selecting the shape if necessary, clicking the Rotate button in the Arrange group on the DRAWING TOOLS FORMAT tab, then clicking one of the rotation options. You can change a shape type by selecting it, clicking the Edit Shape button in the Insert Shapes group on the Drawing Tools Format tab, pointing to Change Shape, then clicking the new shape. To modify the shape of the existing shape, click the Edit Shape button in the Insert Shapes group, click Edit Points, then drag any of the existing points that appear as small black squares on the shape's perimeter to a new location. You can also add a new point by clicking the perimeter, then dragging the new point to a new location.

Excel 2013
UNIT J

Learning Outcomes
- Add sparklines to a worksheet
- Format sparklines
- Add markers to sparklines

Summarize Data with Sparklines

You can create a quick overview of your data by adding sparklines to the worksheet cells. **Sparklines** are miniature charts that show data trends in a worksheet range, such as sales increases or decreases. Sparklines are also useful for highlighting maximum and minimum values in a range of data. Sparklines usually appear close to the data they represent. Any changes that you make to a worksheet are reflected in the sparklines that represent the data. After you add sparklines to a worksheet, you can change the sparkline and color. You can also format high and low data points in special colors. **CASE** *Kate wants you to add sparklines to the Sales worksheet to illustrate the sales trends for the first half of the year.*

STEPS

1. **Click the Sales sheet, click cell H3 to select it, click the INSERT tab if necessary, click the Line button in the Sparklines group, verify that the insertion point is in the Data Range text box, select the range B3:G3 on the worksheet, then click OK**
   A sparkline showing the sales trend for the U.S. appears in cell H3. You can copy the sparkline to cells representing other regions.
2. **With cell H3 selected, drag the fill handle to fill the range H4:H6**
   The sparklines for all four regions are shown in FIGURE J-14. You decide to change the sparklines to columns.
3. **Click cell H3, then click the Column button in the Type group of the SPARKLINE TOOLS DESIGN tab**
   All of the sparklines in column H appear as columns. The column heights represent the values of the data in the adjacent rows. You want the sparklines to appear in a theme color.
4. **Click the Style More button in the Style group, then click Sparkline Style Colorful #4 (the green style in the bottom row) from the Theme colors**
   You want to highlight the high and low months using theme colors.
5. **Click the Marker Color button in the Style group, point to High Point, then select Dark Green, Accent 5 from the Theme Colors**
6. **Click the Marker Color button in the Style group, point to Low Point, select Indigo Accent 1 from the Theme Colors, then compare your screen to FIGURE J-15**

QUICK TIP
To display or hide data markers on a Sparkline, select or deselect the Markers check box in the Show group on the SPARKLINE TOOLS DESIGN tab.

FIGURE J-14: Sales trend sparklines

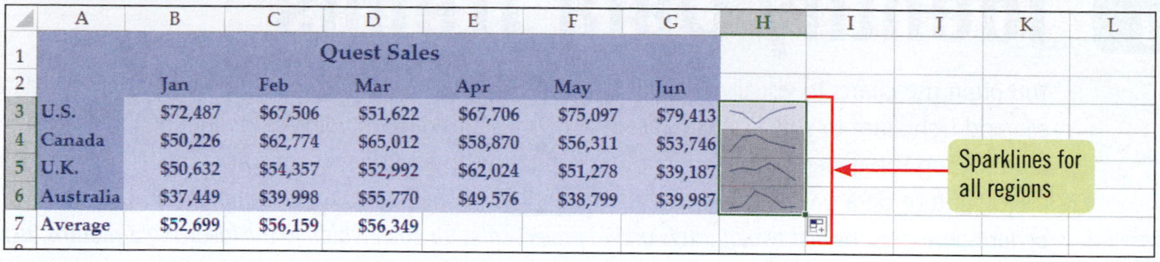

	A	B	C	D	E	F	G	H	I	J	K	L
1	Quest Sales											
2		Jan	Feb	Mar	Apr	May	Jun					
3	U.S.	$72,487	$67,506	$51,622	$67,706	$75,097	$79,413					
4	Canada	$50,226	$62,774	$65,012	$58,870	$56,311	$53,746					
5	U.K.	$50,632	$54,357	$52,992	$62,024	$51,278	$39,187					
6	Australia	$37,449	$39,998	$55,770	$49,576	$38,799	$39,987					
7	Average	$52,699	$56,159	$56,349								

Sparklines for all regions

FIGURE J-15: Formatted sparklines

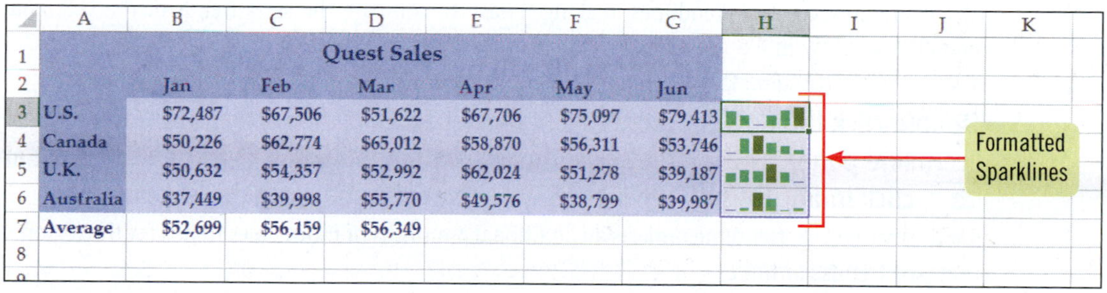

	A	B	C	D	E	F	G	H	I	J	K
1	Quest Sales										
2		Jan	Feb	Mar	Apr	May	Jun				
3	U.S.	$72,487	$67,506	$51,622	$67,706	$75,097	$79,413				
4	Canada	$50,226	$62,774	$65,012	$58,870	$56,311	$53,746				
5	U.K.	$50,632	$54,357	$52,992	$62,024	$51,278	$39,187				
6	Australia	$37,449	$39,998	$55,770	$49,576	$38,799	$39,987				
7	Average	$52,699	$56,159	$56,349							
8											

Formatted Sparklines

Identify Data Trends

Learning Outcomes
- Compare chart data using trendlines
- Format a trendline
- Forecast future trends using trendlines

You often use charts to visually represent data over a period of time. To emphasize patterns in data, you can add trendlines to your charts. A **trendline** is a series of data points on a line that shows data values representing the general direction in a data series. In some business situations, you can use trendlines to project future data based on past trends. **CASE** *Kate wants you to compare the U.S. and U.K. sales performance over the first two quarters and to project sales for each region in the following 3 months, assuming past trends. You begin by charting the 6-months sales data in a 2-D Column chart.*

STEPS

1. **On the Sales sheet, select the range A2:G6, click the Quick Analysis tool, click the CHARTS tab, then click the Clustered Column button**

2. **Drag the chart left until its upper-left corner is at the upper-left corner of cell A8, then drag the middle-right sizing handle right to the border between column G and column H**

   You are ready to add a trendline for the U.S. data series.

3. **Click the Chart Elements button click Trendline, verify that U.S. is selected in the Add Trendline dialog box, then click OK**

   A linear trendline identifying U.S. sales trends in the first 6 months is added to the chart, along with an entry in the legend identifying the line. You need to compare the U.S. sales trend with the U.K. sales trend.

4. **Make sure the U.S. trendline is not selected, click the Chart Elements button if necessary, point to Trendline, click the Trendline list arrow, click Linear, click U.K. in the Add Trendline dialog box, then click OK**

   The chart now has two trendlines, making it easy to compare the sales trends of the U.S. and the U.K. branches as show in FIGURE J-16. Now you want to project the next 3-months sales for the U.S. and U.K. sales branches based on the past 6-month trends.

5. **Double-click the U.S. data series trendline, enter 3 in the Forward textbox in the Format Trendline pane, press [Enter], click the Fill & Line button, click the Color list arrow, click Indigo Accent 1, Darker 50%, then close the Format Trendline pane**

   The formatted U.S. trendline projects an additional 3 months of future sales trends for the region, assuming that past trends continue.

6. **Double-click the U.K. data series trendline, enter 3 in the Forward textbox in the Format Trendline pane, press [Enter], click , click the Color list arrow, click Orange, Accent 3, Darker 25%, then click Chart Title in the CHART ELEMENTS gallery to deselect it**

   The formatted U.K. trendline also projects an additional 3 months of future sales trends for the region, assuming that past trends continue, and the chart title is removed. You will change the UK June data. When chart data is changed you will view the **chart animation** showing the resulting changes to the chart.

7. **Type 80,000 in cell G5, view the chart as you press [Enter], enter your name in the center section of the Sales sheet footer, save the workbook, preview the Sales sheet, close the workbook, submit the workbook to your instructor, then exit Excel**

   The completed worksheet is shown in FIGURE J-17.

FIGURE J-16: Chart with two trendlines

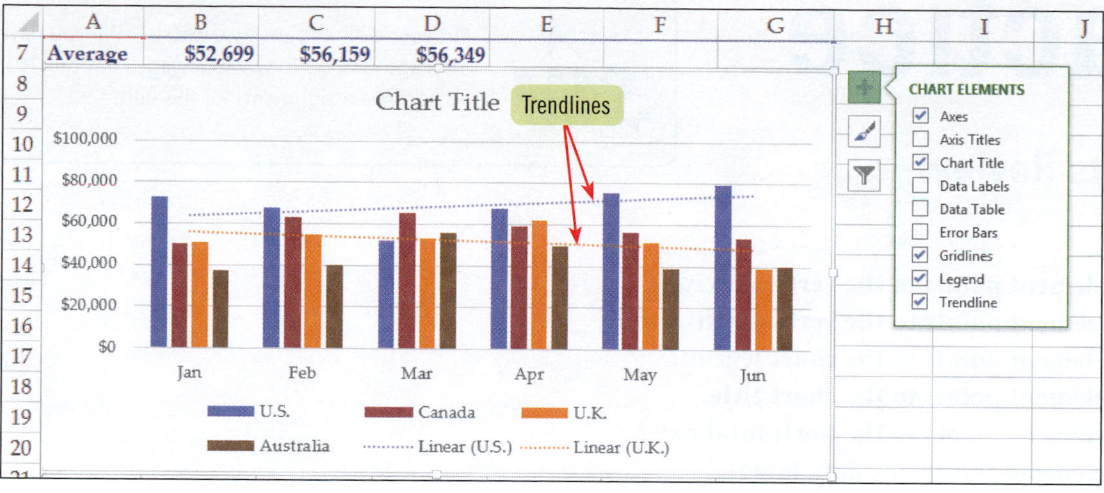

FIGURE J-17: Sales chart with trendlines for U.S. and U.K. data

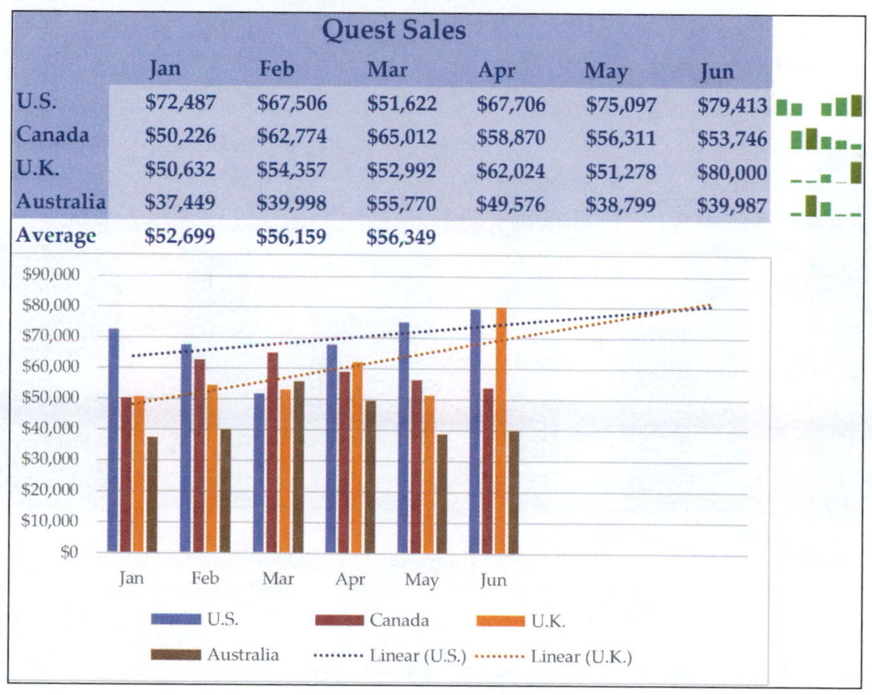

Quest Sales	Jan	Feb	Mar	Apr	May	Jun
U.S.	$72,487	$67,506	$51,622	$67,706	$75,097	$79,413
Canada	$50,226	$62,774	$65,012	$58,870	$56,311	$53,746
U.K.	$50,632	$54,357	$52,992	$62,024	$51,278	$80,000
Australia	$37,449	$39,998	$55,770	$49,576	$38,799	$39,987
Average	$52,699	$56,159	$56,349			

Choosing the right trendline for your chart

Trendlines can help you forecast where your data is headed and understand its past values. You can choose from six types of trendlines: Linear, Exponential, logarithmic, power, polynomial, and Two-Period Moving Average. A linear trendline is used for data series with data points that have the pattern of a line. An exponential or power trendline is a curved line that is used when data values increase or decrease in an arc shape. A polynomial trendline is also curved but changes direction more than one time. A two-period moving average smooths out fluctuations in data by averaging the data points. Logarithmic trendlines are useful for data that increases or decreases before leveling out.

Practice

Put your skills into practice with SAM! If you have a SAM account, go to www.cengage.com/sam2013 to access SAM assignments for this unit.

Concepts Review

1. **Which element points to the vertical axis?**
2. **Which element points to the vertical axis title?**
3. **Which element points to the chart legend?**
4. **Which element points to the chart title?**
5. **Which element points to the horizontal axis?**
6. **Which element points to a data label?**

FIGURE J-18

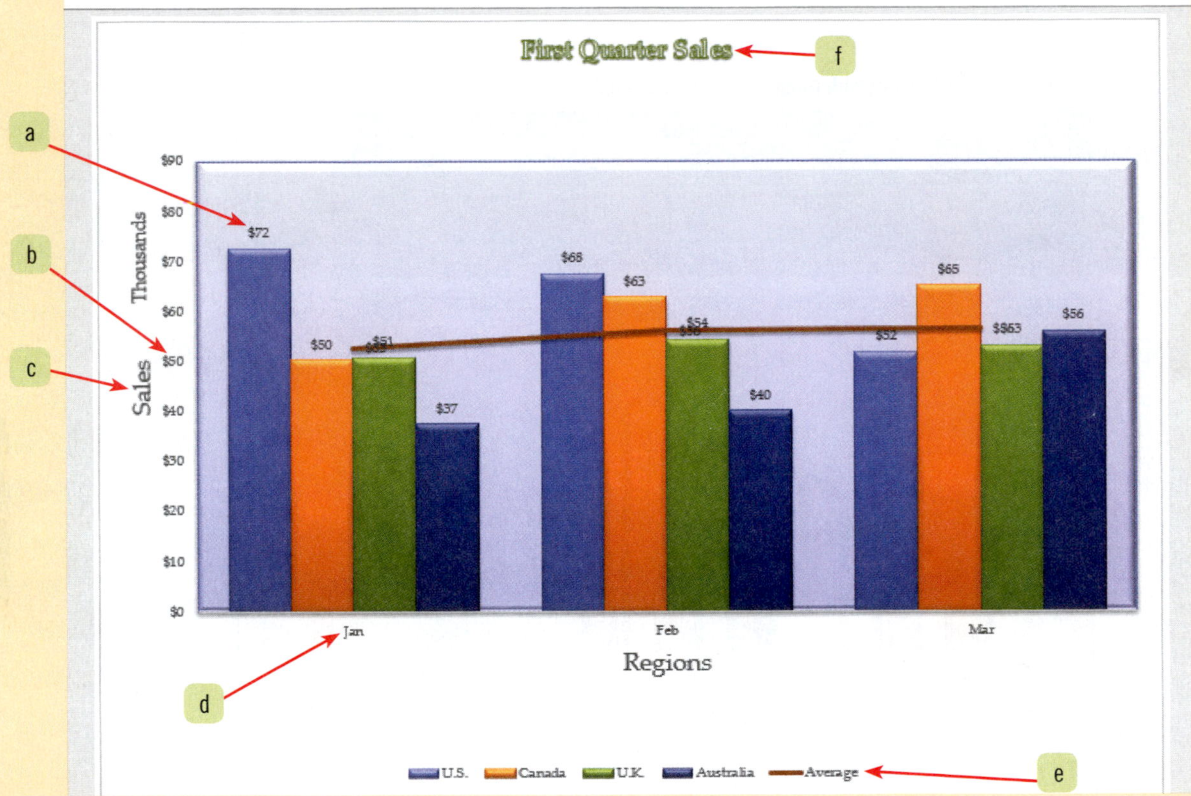

Match each term with the statement that best describes it.

7. Data series	**a.** Category axis
8. Plot area	**b.** Miniature charts that show data trends
9. Sparklines	**c.** Line charts that can be used to project future data
10. X-axis	**d.** Sequence of values plotted on a chart
11. Trendlines	**e.** Location holding data charted on the axes

Select the best answer from the list of choices.

12. Which of the following is true regarding WordArt?
- **a.** Cell references to WordArt can be used in formulas.
- **b.** WordArt is a shape.
- **c.** Spelling errors in WordArt can be detected by the spell checker.
- **d.** Cells containing WordArt can be sorted.

13. Descriptive text that appears above a data marker is called a:
- **a.** Data series.
- **b.** Data label.
- **c.** High point.
- **d.** Period.

14. A chart's scale:
- **a.** Can be adjusted.
- **b.** Always has a maximum of 80000.
- **c.** Always has a minimum of 0.
- **d.** Always appears in units of 10.

15. Which Chart feature shows how a change in data values affects a chart?
- **a.** Visualization
- **b.** Animation
- **c.** Update
- **d.** Format

16. What is a data table?
- **a.** A customized data series
- **b.** The data used to create a chart, displayed in a grid
- **c.** A grid with chart data displayed above a chart
- **d.** A three-dimensional arrangement of data on the y-axis

17. A chart that combines two or more chart types is a:
- **a.** Combination chart
- **b.** Grouped chart
- **c.** Clustered chart
- **d.** Complex chart

18. Which of the following is false regarding trendlines?
- **a.** Trendlines visually represent patterns in past data.
- **b.** Trendlines are used to project future data.
- **c.** Six types of trendlines can be added to a chart.
- **d.** Trendlines can be formatted to stand out on a chart.

Skills Review

1. Customize a data series.
- **a.** Start Excel, open the file EX J-2.xlsx from the location where you save your Data Files, then save it as **EX J-Pastry Sales**.
- **b.** On the Sales sheet select the range A2:D6.
- **c.** Create a clustered column chart using the selected data.
- **d.** Move and resize the chart to fit in the range A8:G20.
- **e.** Change the color of the January data series to Tan, Accent 1, Darker 50% in the Theme Colors.
- **f.** Change the chart view by exchanging the row and column data.
- **g.** Save the workbook.

2. Change a data source and add a chart style.
- **a.** Add the April, May, and June data to the chart.
- **b.** Resize the chart to fill the range A8:J20 to display the new data.
- **c.** Change the chart view back to show the months in the legend by exchanging the row and column data.
- **d.** Apply Chart Style 14.
- **e.** Save the workbook.

3. Add chart elements.
- **a.** Move the chart to its own sheet named **Sales Chart**.
- **b.** Add a data table with legend keys.
- **c.** Add data labels to your chart.

Skills Review (continued)

d. Remove the data table legend keys.

e. Save the workbook, then compare your screen to FIGURE J-19.

4. Format chart axes.

a. Remove the data table.

b. Set the value axis maximum to 5000.

c. Add a horizontal axis title and label it **Products**.

d. Add a vertical axis title and label it **Sales**.

e. Format both axes titles in 12-point bold.

f. Save the workbook.

5. Create a combination chart.

a. On the Sales sheet enter **Average** in cell A7.

b. Select the range B3:G6 and use the Quick Analysis tool to place averages in row 7.

c. On the Sales chart, change the chart data to **A2:G7** on the Sales sheet.

d. Switch the row and column chart view.

e. Create a combination chart with the muffins, cookies, brownies, and biscotti data as clustered column charts and the average data as a line chart.

f. Remove the data labels.

g. Save the workbook.

FIGURE J-19

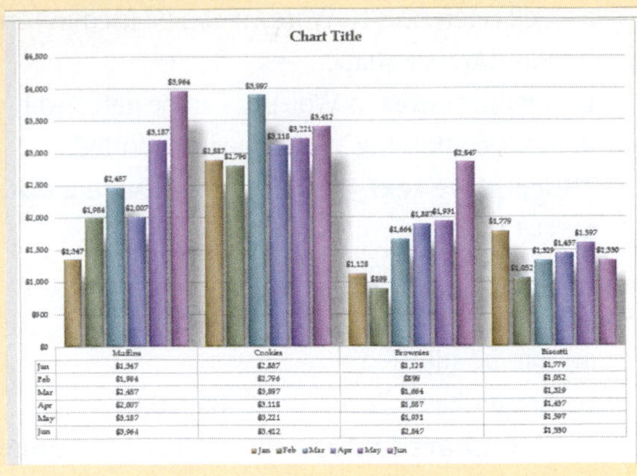

6. Enhance a chart.

a. Add a chart title of **Pastry Sales** to the top of the chart.

b. Format the chart title with the WordArt style Fill – Tan, Accent 1, Shadow.

c. Add a shape style of Subtle Effect - Lavender, Accent 6 to the plot area.

d. Remove the gridlines.

e. Compare your chart to FIGURE J-20.

f. Add your name to the chart footer, then save the workbook.

FIGURE J-20

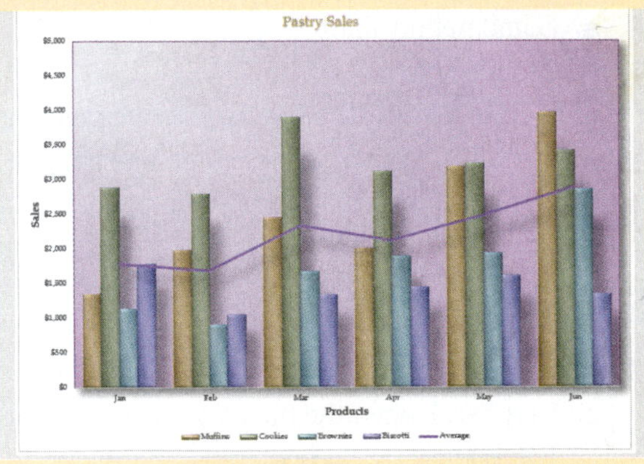

7. Summarize data with Sparklines.

a. On the Sales worksheet, add a Line sparkline to cell H3 that represents the data in the range B3:G3.

b. Copy the sparkline in cell H3 into the range H4:H6.

c. Change the sparklines to columns.

d. Apply the sparkline style Colorful #4.

e. Add high point markers with the color of Lavender, Accent 6 from the theme colors.

f. Save the workbook.

8. Identify data trends.

a. Create a line chart using the data in the range A2:G6, then move and resize the chart to fit in the range A8:G20.

b. Add linear trendlines to the Muffins and Cookies data series.

c. Change the Cookies trendline color to red and the Muffins trendline color to purple.

d. Set the forward option to six periods for both trendlines to view the future trend, increase the width of the chart to the border between columns J and K, remove the chart title, then compare your screen to FIGURE J-21.

FIGURE J-21

	A	B	C	D	E	F	G	H	I	J
1	Main Street Pastry									
2		Jan	Feb	Mar	Apr	May	Jun			
3	Muffins	$1,347	$1,984	$2,457	$2,007	$3,187	$3,964			
4	Cookies	$2,887	$2,796	$3,897	$3,118	$3,221	$3,412			
5	Brownies	$1,128	$899	$1,664	$1,887	$1,931	$2,847			
6	Biscotti	$1,779	$1,052	$1,329	$1,437	$1,597	$1,330			
7	Average	$1,785	$1,683	$2,337	$2,112	$2,484	$2,888			

Skills Review (continued)

e. Add your name to the center footer section, save the workbook, preview the worksheet, close the workbook, then submit the workbook to your instructor.

f. Exit Excel.

Independent Challenge 1

You are the assistant to the vice president of marketing at a local radio station. The vice president has asked you to chart some information from a recent survey of the station's customers. Your administrative assistant has entered the survey data in an Excel worksheet, which you will use to create two charts.

a. Start Excel, open the file titled EX J-3.xlsx from the location where you store your Data Files, then save it as **EX J-Customer Demographics**.

b. Using the data in A2:B7 of the Education Data worksheet, create a pie chart on the worksheet.

c. Move the chart to a separate sheet named **Education Chart**. Format the chart using chart Style 9.

d. Add a title of **Education Data** above the chart. Format the title using WordArt Fill – White, Outline - Accent 1, Glow - Accent 1. Change the chart title font to a size of 28. (*Hint*: Right click the title and select Font from the shortcut menu.)

e. Add values to the data labels. (*Hint*: Double-click a data label and select the Value checkbox in the Format Data Labels pane.)

f. Select the Bachelor's degree pie slice by clicking the chart, then clicking the Bachelor's degree slice. Change the slice color to the light green Standard color.

g. Add a shape style of Subtle Effect - Blue Accent 5 to the chart area. Compare your chart to FIGURE J-22.

FIGURE J-22

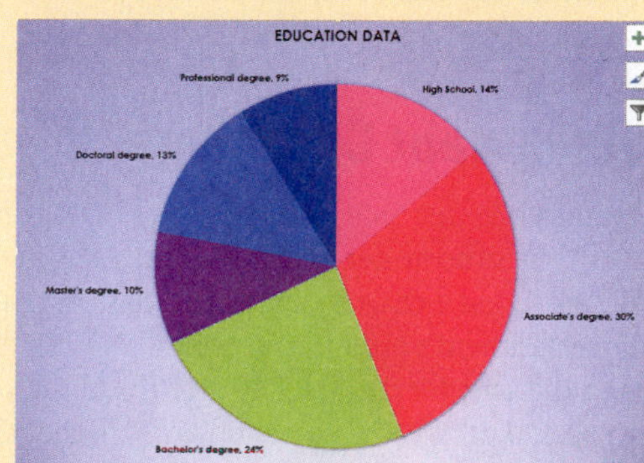

h. On the Income Data worksheet, use the data in A2:B6 to create a clustered column chart.

i. Place the chart on a new sheet named **Income Chart**. Format the chart using chart Style 16.

j. Add a chart title of **Income Data** above the chart, and format the title using WordArt Style Gradient Fill - Dark Purple, Accent 4, Outline - Accent 4.

k. Format the title in 28 point font.

l. Add horizontal and vertical axes titles. Change the title of the horizontal axis to **Income**. Change the title of the vertical axis to **Percent of Customers**. Format both axes' titles in 18-point bold. (*Hint*: Right-click the title and select Font from the shortcut menu.)

m. Enter your name in the center sections of the footers of the Income Chart and Education Chart sheets.

n. Save the workbook, preview the Income Chart and the Education Chart sheets.

o. Close the workbook, submit the workbook to your instructor, and exit Excel.

Independent Challenge 2

You manage the Atlanta Sports Club, which offers memberships for swimming, tennis, and fitness. You also offer a full membership that includes all of the activities at the club. The club owner has asked you to assemble a brief presentation on the membership data over the past 4 years while it has been under your management. You decide to include a chart showing the memberships in each category as well as an analysis of trends in memberships.

a. Start Excel, open the file titled EX J-4.xlsx from the location where you store your Data Files, then save it as **EX J-Memberships**.

b. Create a clustered bar chart on the worksheet, comparing the membership enrollments in the four types of memberships over the years 2013 - 2016. Format the chart using chart Style 12.

c. Change the row and column data so the years are shown in the legend.

d. Add a chart title of **Membership Data** above the chart, and format it using WordArt Style Gradient Fill - Dark Green, Accent 4, Outline - Accent 4.

Independent Challenge 2 (continued)

e. Move the chart to the region A9:H24.

f. Add Line sparklines to cells F4:F7 showing the membership trend from 2013 to 2016.

g. Format the sparklines using Sparkline Style Accent 5, (no dark or light).

h. Add high point markers to the sparklines with the color Red, Accent 2 from the theme colors.

i. Add a new membership type of **Family** in row 8 of the worksheet with the data in this table:

Year	Membership
2013	1449
2014	1881
2015	1937
2016	2546

j. Add the data to the chart. Copy the sparklines to cell F8.

k. Move the chart to a sheet named **Membership Chart**.

l. Add a horizontal axis title of **Number of Memberships**, and format it in 18-point bold font. Delete the vertical axis title placeholder.

m. Add a data table with legend keys to the chart. Delete the chart legend.

n. Compare your chart to FIGURE J-23.

o. Add your name to the footers of the Membership and Membership Chart sheets, save the workbook, preview the Membership Chart and Membership sheets.

p. Close the workbook, submit the workbook to your instructor, and exit Excel.

FIGURE J-23

Membership Data

	Full	Swim	Tennis	Fitness	Family
2016	1667	655	894	2001	2546
2015	1544	854	799	1796	1937
2014	1337	984	733	1881	1881
2013	1224	1022	697	1667	1449

Number of Memberships

Independent Challenge 3

You manage the East Side Golf Club. You meet twice a year with the store owner to discuss store sales trends. You decide to use a chart to represent the sales trends for the department's product categories. You begin by charting the sales for the first five months of the year. Then you add data to the chart and analyze the sales trend using a trendline. Lastly, you enhance the chart by adding a data table, titles, and a picture.

a. Start Excel, open the file EX J-5.xlsx from the location where you store your Data Files, then save the workbook as **EX J-Golf Sales**.

b. Create a clustered column chart on the worksheet showing the May through July sales information, using the first suggestion in the chart recommendations. Move the upper-left corner of the chart to cell A8 on the worksheet.

c. Format the May data series using the Lime, Accent 1, Lighter 40% color from the theme colors.

d. Add the Aug, Sep, and Oct data to the chart.

e. Move the chart to its own sheet named **May - Oct**.

f. Add the following profit data to the Sales sheet:

Cell	Data
A7	Profit
B7	$2,010
C7	$1,742
D7	$2,450
E7	$1,975
F7	$1,020
G7	$1,814

Independent Challenge 3 (continued)

g. Add the new profit data to the chart, then change the row and column view so the sales items are in the legend.

h. Create a combination chart placing clubs, apparel, footwear, and cart rentals in clustered column charts and profit in a line chart.

i. Add a chart title of **May - October Sales** in size 28-point font above the chart. Format the chart title using the WordArt Style Fill - Lime, Accent1, Shadow.

j. Add a title of **Sales** in 20-point to the vertical axis. Format it in the same WordArt style as the chart title. Delete the horizontal axis title placeholder.

k. Change the value axis scale to a maximum of **6000**, then save your workbook.

l. Add data labels to the profit data series. (*Hint*: Select the profit line chart before adding data labels.)

m. Compare your chart to FIGURE J-24.

FIGURE J-24

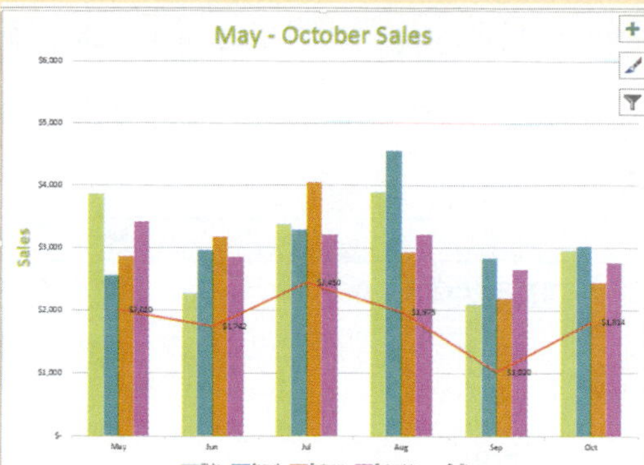

n. Enter your name in the center footer section of the chart sheet, save the workbook, then preview the chart.

o. Close the workbook, submit the workbook to your instructor, then exit Excel.

Independent Challenge 4: Explore

As the sales manager of Smith Motor Group you are interested in how sales at your company correlate with vehicles' fuel economy. Your administrative assistant has entered the January sales and mpg data in a worksheet and you decide to chart the data to visualize this relationship. You will use a combination chart because of the different types of data.

a. Start Excel, open the file EX J-6.xlsx from the location where you store your Data Files then save the workbook as **EX J-Car Sales**.

b. Create a clustered column chart using the data in cells A3:B10. Move and resize your chart to fill the range D1:L20.

c. Link the chart title to cell A1. (*Hint*: With the chart title selected, enter = in the formula bar, click cell A1, then press [Enter].)

d. Format the chart title text in WordArt style Fill - Blue, Accent 1, Shadow.

e. Add a vertical axis title and link it to cell A3. Format the axis title using a shape style of Subtle Effect - Blue, Accent 1. Add a shape effect of circle bevel.

f. Delete the horizontal axis title.

g. To improve the visibility of the combined MPG series, place it on a line chart and assign it to a secondary axis. (*Hint*: Change the chart type to Combo and select Secondary Axis for the Combined MPG line chart.)

h. Change the text in cell B3 from Combined MPG to MPG and verify that the legend changed.

i. Change the chart title link to cell A2 and verify the change in the chart title.

j. Change cell A5 to 52,500 and view the chart animation of the second bar to reflect this data change.

k. Add data labels to the MPG data series. (*Hint*: Select the MPG line chart before adding data labels.)

l. Assign the same shape style to the chart title that you assigned to the vertical axis.

m. Compare your chart to FIGURE J-25.

n. Enter your name in the center footer section of the worksheet, save the workbook, then preview the worksheet.

o. Close the workbook, submit the workbook to your instructor, then exit Excel.

FIGURE J-25

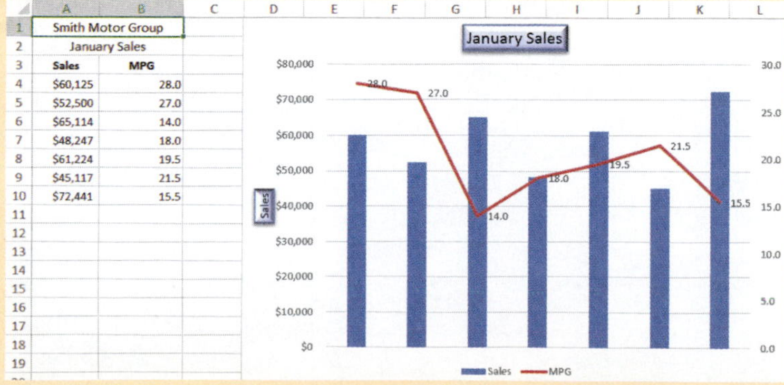

Excel 2013

Visual Workshop

Open the file EX J-7.xlsx from the location where you store your Data Files, and create the custom chart shown in **FIGURE J-26**. (*Hint*: The trendlines forecast three periods forward and use the standard line colors red and purple.) Save the workbook as **EX J-Organic Sales**. Study the chart and worksheet carefully to make sure you select the displayed chart type with all the enhancements shown. Enter your name in the center section of the worksheet footer, then preview the worksheet in landscape orientation on one page. Submit the workbook to your instructor.

FIGURE J-26

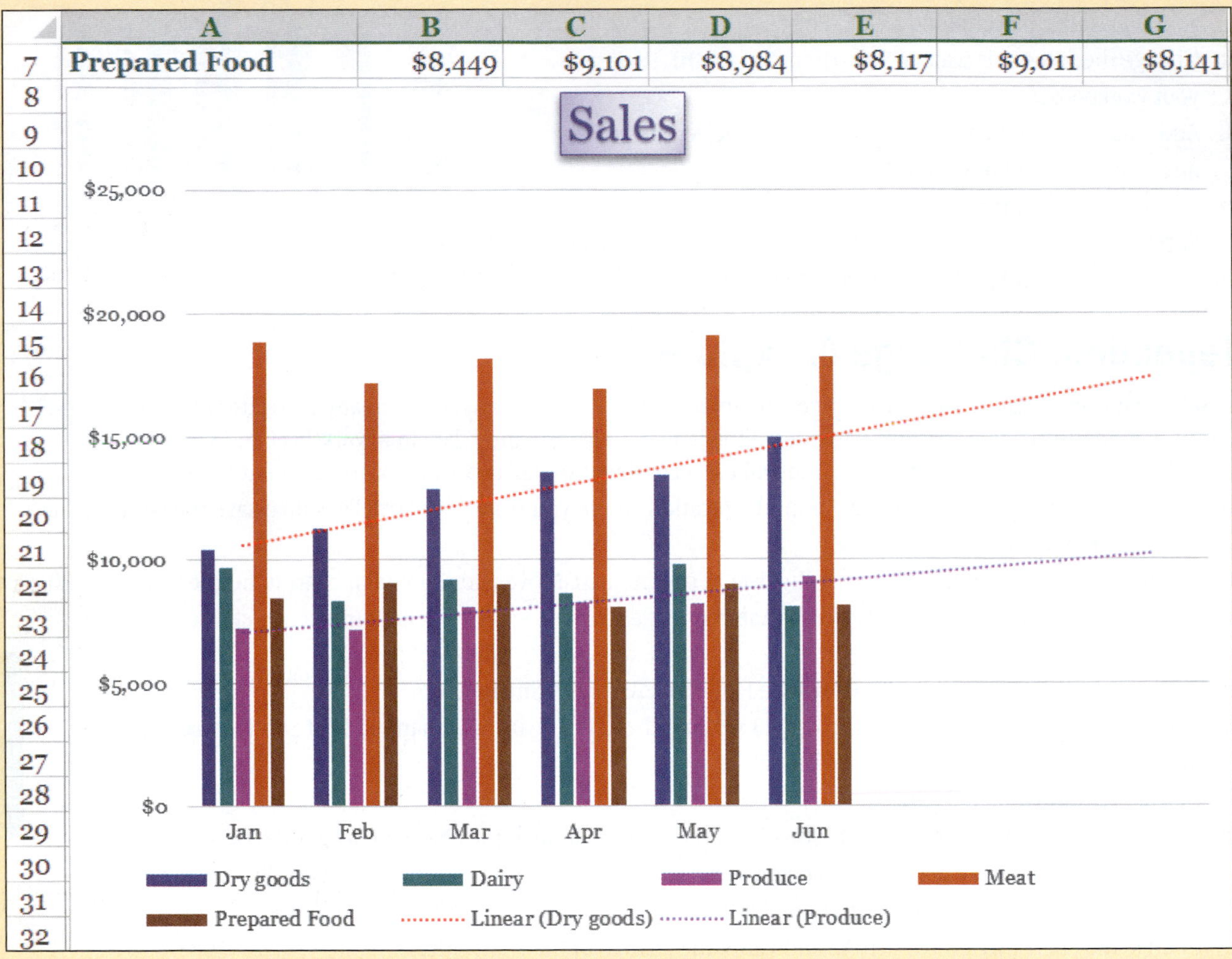

Using What-if Analysis

CASE Kate Morgan, the vice president of sales at Quest, is meeting with the U.S. region manager to discuss sales projections for the first half of the year. In preparation for her meeting, Kate asks you to help analyze the U.S. sales data using what-if scenarios, data tables, goal seek, Solver and the Analysis ToolPak.

Unit Objectives

After completing this unit, you will be able to:

- Define a what-if analysis
- Track a what-if analysis with Scenario Manager
- Generate a scenario summary
- Project figures using a data table
- Use Goal Seek
- Set up a complex what-if analysis with Solver
- Run Solver and summarize results
- Analyze data using the Analysis ToolPak

Files You Will Need

EX K-1.xlsx
EX K-2.xlsx
EX K-3.xlsx
EX K-4.xlsx
EX K-5.xlsx
EX K-6.xlsx
EX K-7.xlsx

Define a What-if Analysis

Learning Outcomes
- Develop guidelines for performing what-if analysis
- Define what-if analysis terminology

By performing a what-if analysis in a worksheet, you can get immediate answers to questions such as "What happens to profits if we sell 25 percent more of a certain product?" or "What happens to monthly payments if interest rates rise or fall?". A worksheet you use to produce a what-if analysis is often called a **model** because it acts as the basis for multiple outcomes or sets of results. To perform a what-if analysis in a worksheet, you change the value in one or more **input cells** (cells that contain data rather than formulas), then observe the effects on dependent cells. A **dependent cell** usually contains a formula whose resulting value changes depending on the values in the input cells. A dependent cell can be located either in the same worksheet as the changing input value or in another worksheet. **CASE** *Kate Morgan has received projected sales data from regional managers. She has created a worksheet model to perform an initial what-if analysis, as shown in* **FIGURE K-1**. *She thinks the U.S. sales projections for the month of January should be higher. You first review the guidelines for performing a what-if analysis.*

DETAILS

When performing a what-if analysis, use the following guidelines:

- **Understand and state the purpose of the worksheet model**
  Identify what you want to accomplish with the model. What problem are you trying to solve? What questions do you want the model to answer for you? Kate's Quest worksheet model is designed to total Quest sales projections for the first half of the year and to calculate the percentage of total sales for each Quest region. It also calculates the totals and percentages of total sales for each month.

- **Determine the data input value(s) that, if changed, affect the dependent cell results**
  In a what-if analysis, changes in the content of the data input cells produces varying results in the output cells. You will use the model to work with one data input value: the January value for the U.S. region, in cell B3.

- **Identify the dependent cell(s) that will contain results**
  The dependent cells usually contain formulas, and the formula results adjust as you enter different values in the input cells. The results of two dependent cell formulas (labeled Total and Percent of Total Sales) appear in cells H3 and I3, respectively. The total for the month of January in cell B7 is also a dependent cell, as is the percentage in cell B8.

- **Formulate questions you want the what-if analysis to answer**
  It is important that you know the questions you want your model to answer. In the Quest model, you want to answer the following question: What happens to the U.S. regional percentage if the sales amount for the month of January is increased to $109,667?

- **Perform the what-if analysis**
  When you perform the what-if analysis, you explore the relationships between the input values and the dependent cell formulas. In the Quest worksheet model, you want to see what effect an increase in sales for January has on the dependent cell formulas containing totals and percentages. Because the sales amounts for this month is located in cell B3, any formula that references that cell is directly affected by a change in this sales amount—in this case, the total formula in cell H3. Because the formula in cell I3 references cell H3, a change in the sales amount affects this cell as well. The percentage formulas will also change because they reference the total formulas. **FIGURE K-2** shows the result of the what-if analysis described in this example.

FIGURE K-1: Worksheet model for a what-if analysis

	A	B	C	D	E	F	G	H	I	J	K
1	2017 Projected Sales										
2		Jan	Feb	Mar	Apr	May	Jun	Total	Percent of Total Sales		
3	U.S.	$91,475	$67,189	$69,423	$61,664	$103,926	$100,244	$493,921	31.08%		
4	Canada	$64,868	$75,326	$77,244	$71,688	$67,015	$67,388	$423,529	26.65%		
5	U.K.	$61,573	$62,756	$64,681	$72,988	$61,191	$40,334	$363,523	22.88%		
6	Australia	$37,043	$57,657	$61,539	$60,708	$45,868	$45,224	$308,039	19.39%		
7	Total	$254,959	$262,928	$272,887	$267,048	$278,000	$253,190	$1,589,012			
8	Percent of Total Sales	16.05%	16.55%	17.17%	16.81%	17.50%	15.93%				
9											
10											
11											
12											
13											

Data input value

Dependent cell formulas

FIGURE K-2: Changed input values and dependent formula results

	A	B	C	D	E	F	G	H	I	J
1	2017 Projected Sales									
2		Jan	Feb	Mar	Apr	May	Jun	Total	Percent of Total Sales	
3	U.S.	$109,667	$67,189	$69,423	$61,664	$103,926	$100,244	$512,113	31.86%	
4	Canada	$64,868	$75,326	$77,244	$71,688	$67,015	$67,388	$423,529	26.35%	
5	U.K.	$61,573	$62,756	$64,681	$72,988	$61,191	$40,334	$363,523	22.62%	
6	Australia	$37,043	$57,657	$61,539	$60,708	$45,868	$45,224	$308,039	19.17%	
7	Total	$273,151	$262,928	$272,887	$267,048	$278,000	$253,190	$1,607,204		
8	Percent of Total Sales	17.00%	16.36%	16.98%	16.62%	17.30%	15.75%			
9										
10										
11										
12										
13										
14										
15										

Changed input value

Changed formula results

Track a What-if Analysis with Scenario Manager

Learning Outcomes
- Create scenarios to analyze Excel data
- Analyze scenarios using Scenario Manager

A **scenario** is a set of values you use to observe different worksheet results. For example, you might plan to sell 100 of a particular item, at a price of $5 per item, producing sales results of $500. But what if you reduced the price to $4 or increased it to $6? Each of these price scenarios would produce different sales results. A changing value, such as the price in this example, is called a **variable**. The Excel Scenario Manager simplifies the process of what-if analysis by allowing you to name and save multiple scenarios with variable values in a worksheet. **CASE** *Kate asks you to use Scenario Manager to create scenarios showing how a U.S. sales increase can affect total Quest sales over the 3-month period of February through April.*

STEPS

1. **Start Excel, open the file EX K-1.xlsx from the location where you store your Data Files, then save it as EX K-Sales**

   The first step in defining a scenario is choosing the changing cells. **Changing cells** are those that will vary in the different scenarios.

2. **With the Projected Sales sheet active, select range C3:E3, click the DATA tab, click the What-If Analysis button in the Data Tools group, then click Scenario Manager**

   You want to be able to easily return to your original worksheet values, so your first scenario contains those figures.

3. **Click Add, drag the Add Scenario dialog box to the right if necessary until columns A and B are visible, then type Original Sales Figures in the Scenario name text box**

   The range in the Changing cells box shows the range you selected, as shown in FIGURE K-3.

4. **Click OK to confirm the scenario range**

   The Scenario Values dialog box opens, as shown in FIGURE K-4. The existing values appear in the changing cell boxes. Because you want this scenario to reflect the current worksheet values, you leave these unchanged.

5. **Click OK**

   You want to create a second scenario that will show the effects of increasing sales by $5,000.

6. **Click Add; in the Scenario name text box type Increase Feb, Mar, Apr by 5000; verify that the Changing cells text box reads C3:E3, then click OK; in the Scenario Values dialog box, change the value in the $C$3 text box to 72189, change the value in the $D$3 text box to 74423, change the value in the $E$3 text box to 66664, then click Add**

   You are ready to create a third scenario. It will show the effects of increasing sales by $10,000.

7. **In the Scenario name text box, type Increase Feb, Mar, Apr by 10000 and click OK; in the Scenario Values dialog box, change the value in the $C$3 text box to 77189, change the value in the $D$3 text box to 79423, change the value in the $E$3 text box to 71664, then click OK**

   The Scenario Manager dialog box reappears, as shown in FIGURE K-5. You are ready to display the results of your scenarios in the worksheet.

8. **Make sure the Increase Feb, Mar, Apr by 10000 scenario is still selected, click Show, notice that the percent of U.S. sales in cell I3 changes from 31.08% to 32.36%; click Increase Feb, Mar, Apr by 5000, click Show, notice that the U.S. sales percent is now 31.73%; click Original Sales Figures, click Show to return to the original values, then click Close**

9. **Save the workbook**

QUICK TIP
You can delete a scenario by selecting it in the Scenario Manager dialog box and clicking Delete.

QUICK TIP
To edit a scenario, select it in the Scenario Manager dialog box, click the Edit button, then edit the Scenario.

FIGURE K-3: Add Scenario dialog box

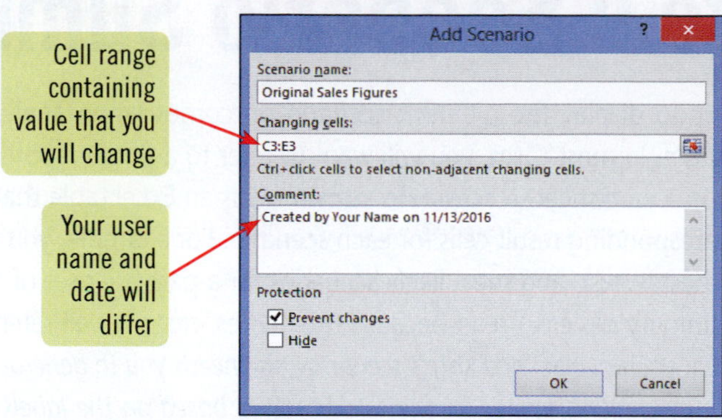

FIGURE K-4: Scenario Values dialog box

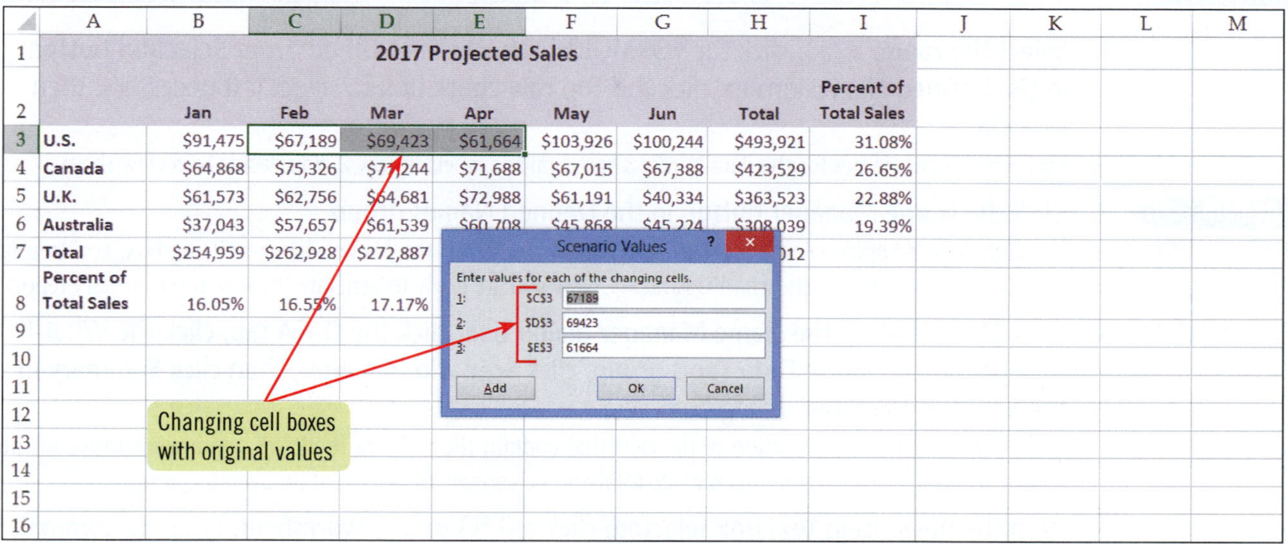

FIGURE K-5: Scenario Manager dialog box with three scenarios listed

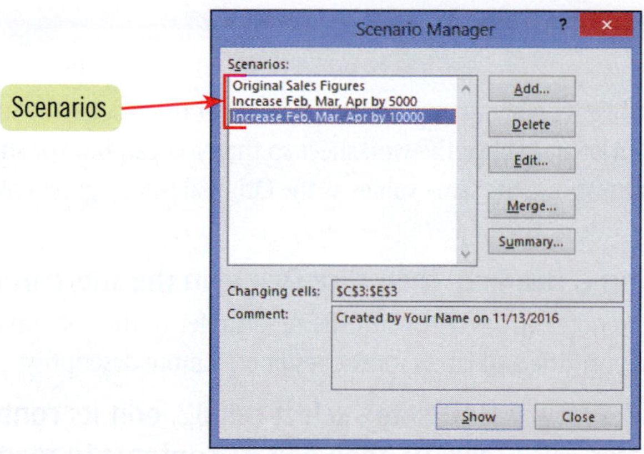

Merging scenarios

Excel stores scenarios in the workbook and on the worksheet in which you created them. To apply scenarios from another worksheet or workbook into the current worksheet, click the Merge button in the Scenario Manager dialog box. The Merge Scenarios dialog box opens, letting you select scenarios from other locations. When you click a sheet name in the sheet list, the text under the sheet list tells you how many scenarios exist on that sheet. To merge scenarios from another workbook, such as those sent to you in a workbook by a coworker, open the other workbook file, click the Book list arrow in the Merge Scenarios dialog box, then click the workbook name. When you merge workbook scenarios, it's best if the workbooks have the same structure, so that there is no confusion of cell values.

Generate a Scenario Summary

Learning Outcomes
- Display scenarios in a scenario summary report
- Format a scenario summary report

Although it may be useful to display the different scenario outcomes when analyzing data, it can be difficult to keep track of them. In most cases, you will want to refer to a single report that summarizes the results of all the scenarios in a worksheet. A **scenario summary** is an Excel table that compiles data from the changing cells and corresponding result cells for each scenario. For example, you might use a scenario summary to illustrate the best, worst, and most likely scenarios for a particular set of circumstances. Using cell naming makes the summary easier to read because the names, not the cell references, appear in the report. **CASE** *Now that you have defined Kate's scenarios, she needs you to generate and print a scenario summary report. You begin by creating names for the cells in row 3 based on the labels in row 2, so that the report will be easier to read.*

STEPS

1. **Select the range B2:I3, click the FORMULAS tab, click the Create from Selection button in the Defined Names group, click the Top row check box to select it if necessary, then click OK**

   Excel creates the names for the data in row 3 based on the labels in row 2. You decide to review them.

2. **Click the Name Manager button in the Defined Names group**

   The eight labels appear, along with other workbook names, in the Name Manager dialog box, confirming that they were created, as shown in FIGURE K-6. Now you are ready to generate the scenario summary report.

> **QUICK TIP**
> You can also click the Name box list arrow on the formula bar to view cell names.

3. **Click Close to close the Name Manager dialog box, click the DATA tab, click the What-If Analysis button in the Data Tools group, click Scenario Manager, then click Summary in the Scenario Manager dialog box**

   Excel needs to know the location of the cells that contain the formula results that you want to see in the report. You want to see the results for U.S. total and percentage of sales, and on overall Quest sales.

4. **With the Result cells text box selected, click cell H3 on the worksheet, type , (a comma), click cell I3, type , (a comma), then click cell H7**

   With the report type and result cells specified, as shown in FIGURE K-7, you are now ready to generate the report.

5. **Click OK**

   A summary of the worksheet's scenarios appears on a new sheet titled Scenario Summary. The report shows outline buttons to the left of and above the worksheet so that you can hide or show report details. Because the Current Values column shows the same values as the Original Sales Figures column, you decide to delete column D.

> **QUICK TIP**
> To see the Comments for each scenario, which by default contain the creator name and creation date, click the plus sign to the left of row 3.

6. **Right-click the column D heading, then click Delete in the shortcut menu**

   Next, you notice that the notes at the bottom of the report refer to the column that no longer exists. You also want to make the report title and labels for the result cells more descriptive.

7. **Select the range B13:B15, press [Delete], select cell B2, edit its contents to read Scenario Summary for U.S. Sales, click cell C10, then edit its contents to read Total U.S. Sales**

8. **Click cell C11, edit its contents to read Percent U.S. Sales, click cell C12, edit its contents to read Total Quest Sales, then click cell A1**

   The completed scenario summary is shown in FIGURE K-8.

> **QUICK TIP**
> The scenario summary is not linked to the worksheet. If you change the values in the worksheet, you must generate a new scenario summary.

9. **Add your name to the center section of the Scenario Summary sheet footer, change the page orientation to landscape, then save the workbook and preview the worksheet**

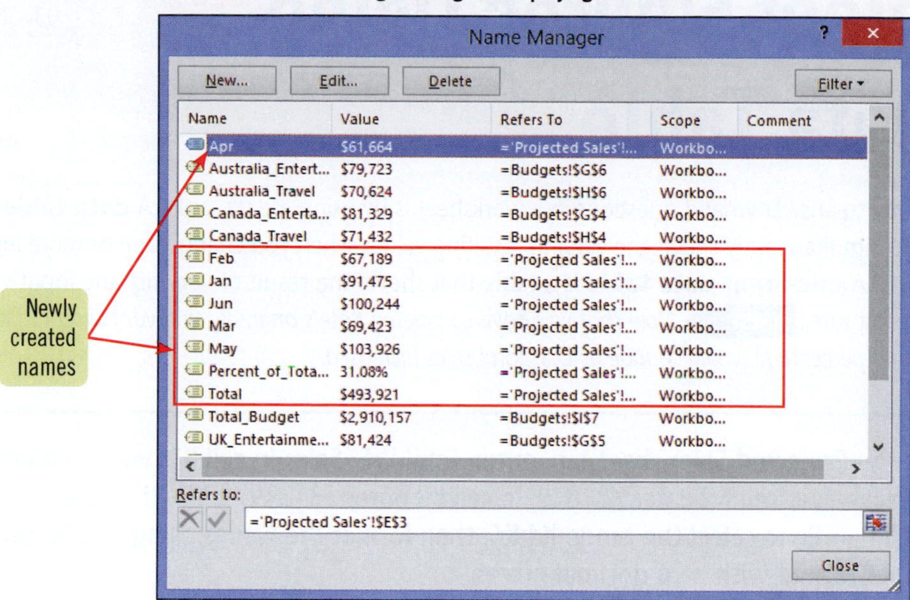

FIGURE K-6: Name Manager dialog box displaying new names

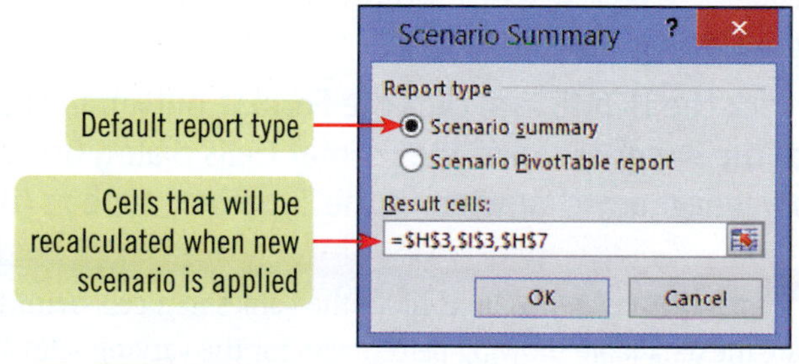

FIGURE K-7: Scenario Summary dialog box

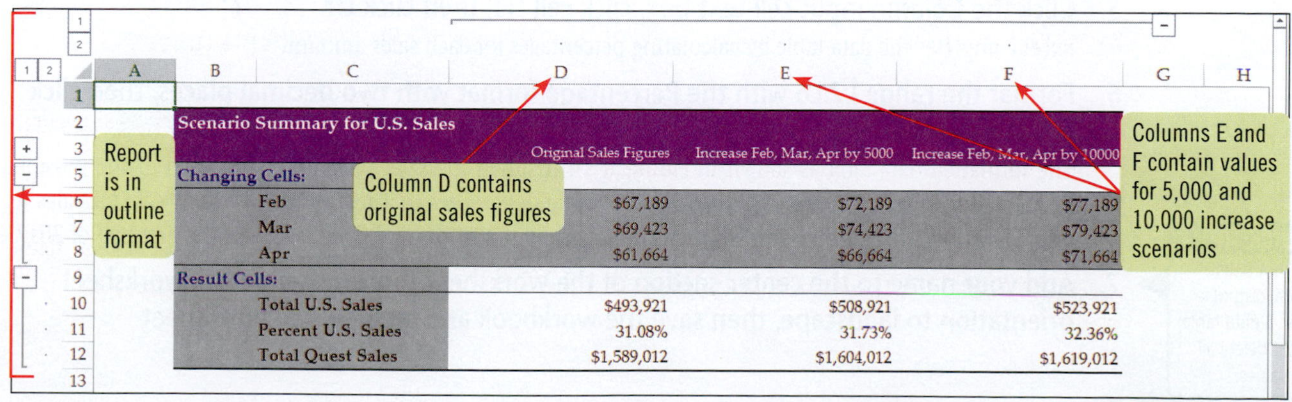

FIGURE K-8: Completed Scenario Summary report

Excel 2013
UNIT K

Learning Outcomes
- Develop a data table structure
- Analyze options using a data table

Project Figures Using a Data Table

Another way to answer what-if questions in a worksheet is by using a data table. A **data table** is a range of cells that simultaneously shows the varying resulting values when you change one or more input values in a formula. A **one-input data table** is a table that shows the result of varying one input value, such as the interest rate. **CASE** *Now that you have completed Kate's analysis, she wants you to find out how the U.S. sales percentage would change as U.S. total sales increased.*

STEPS

1. **Click the Projected Sales sheet tab, enter Total U.S. Sales in cell K1, widen column K to fit the label, in cell K2 enter 481819, in cell K3 enter 531819, select the range K2:K3, drag the fill handle to select the range K4:K6, then format the values using the Accounting number format with zero decimal places**

   You begin setting up your data table by entering total U.S. sales lower and higher than the total in cell H3 in increasing amounts of $50,000. These are the **input values** in the data table. With the varying input values listed in column K, you enter a formula reference to cell I3 that you want Excel to use in calculating the resulting percentages (the **output values**) in column L, based on the possible sales levels in column K.

2. **Click cell L1, type =, click cell I3, click the Enter button ✓ on the formula bar, then format the value in cell L1 using the Percentage format with two decimal places**

   The value in cell I3, 31.08%, appears in cell L1, and the cell name =Percent_of_Total_Sales appears in the formula bar, as shown in FIGURE K-9. Because it isn't necessary for users of the data table to see the value in cell L1, you want to hide the cell's contents from view.

> **QUICK TIP**
> You can create your own custom format by clicking a format that resembles the one you want and customizing it in the Type text box.

3. **With cell L1 selected, click the HOME tab, click the Format button in the Cells group, click Format Cells, click the Number tab in the Format Cells dialog box if necessary, click Custom under Category, select any characters in the Type box, type ;;; (three semicolons), then click OK**

   Applying the custom cell format of three semicolons hides the values in a cell. With the table structure in place, you can now generate the data table showing percentages for the varying sales amounts.

> **TROUBLE**
> If you receive the message "Selection not valid", repeat Step 4, taking care to select the entire range K1:L6.

4. **Select the range K1:L6, click the DATA tab, click the What-If Analysis button in the Data Tools group, then click Data Table**

   The Data Table dialog box opens, as shown in FIGURE K-10. Because the percentage formula in cell I3 (which you just referenced in cell L1) uses the total sales in cell H3 as input, you enter a reference to cell H3. You place this reference in the Column input cell text box, rather than in the Row input cell text box, because the varying input values are arranged in a column in your data table structure.

5. **Click the Column input cell text box, click cell H3, then click OK**

   Excel completes the data table by calculating percentages for each sales amount.

6. **Format the range L2:L6 with the Percentage format with two decimal places, then click cell A1**

   The formatted data table is shown in FIGURE K-11. It shows the sales percentages for each of the possible levels of U.S. sales. By looking at the data table, Kate determines that if she can increase total U.S. sales to over $700,000, the U.S. division will then comprise about 40% of total Quest sales for the first half of 2017.

> **QUICK TIP**
> You cannot delete individual output values in a data table; you must delete all output values.

7. **Add your name to the center section of the worksheet footer, change the worksheet orientation to landscape, then save the workbook and preview the worksheet**

FIGURE K-9: One-input data table structure

L1 =Percent_of_Total_Sales

	A	B	C	D	E	F	G	H	I	J	K	L
1				2017 Projected Sales							Total U.S. Sales	31.08%
2		Jan	Feb	Mar	Apr	May	Jun	Total	Percent of Total Sales			
3	U.S.	$91,475	$67,189	$69,423	$61,664	$103,926	$100,244	$493,921	31.08%		$ 481,819	
4	Canada	$64,868	$75,326	$77,244	$71,688	$67,015	$67,388	$423,529	26.65%		$ 531,819	
5	U.K.	$61,573	$62,756	$64,681	$72,988	$61,191	$40,334	$363,523	22.88%		$ 581,819	
6	Australia	$37,043	$57,657	$61,539	$60,708	$45,868	$45,224	$308,039	19.39%		$ 631,819	
7	Total	$254,959	$262,928	$272,887	$267,048	$278,000	$253,190	$1,589,012			$ 681,819	
8	Percent of Total Sales	16.05%	16.55%	17.17%	16.81%	17.50%	15.93%					
9												
10												

Value displayed in cell I3

Varying sales totals

FIGURE K-10: Data Table dialog box

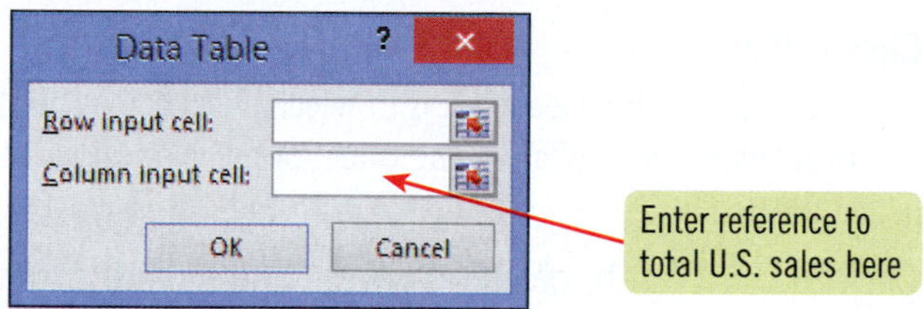

FIGURE K-11: Completed data table with resulting values

	A	B	C	D	E	F	G	H	I	J	K	L
1				2017 Projected Sales							Total U.S. Sales	
2		Jan	Feb	Mar	Apr	May	Jun	Total	Percent of Total Sales		$ 481,819	30.55%
3	U.S.	$91,475	$67,189	$69,423	$61,664	$103,926	$100,244	$493,921	31.08%		$ 531,819	32.69%
4	Canada	$64,868	$75,326	$77,244	$71,688	$67,015	$67,388	$423,529	26.65%		$ 581,819	34.70%
5	U.K.	$61,573	$62,756	$64,681	$72,988	$61,191	$40,334	$363,523	22.88%		$ 631,819	36.59%
6	Australia	$37,043	$57,657	$61,539	$60,708	$45,868	$45,224	$308,039	19.39%		$ 681,819	38.37%
7	Total	$254,959	$262,928	$272,887	$267,048	$278,000	$253,190	$1,589,012				
8	Percent of Total Sales	16.05%	16.55%	17.17%	16.81%	17.50%	15.93%					
9												
10												
11												
12												
13												

Input values in column K

Percentages (output values) in column L

Completed data table

Creating a two-input data table

A **two-input data table** shows the resulting values when two different input values are varied in a formula. You could, for example, use a two-input data table to calculate your monthly car payment based on varying interest rates and varying loan terms, as shown in **FIGURE K-12**. In a two-input data table, different values of one input cell appear across the top row of the table, while different values of the second input cell are listed down the left column. You create a two-input data table the same way that you created a one-input data table, except you enter both a row and a column input cell. In the example shown in **FIGURE K-12**, the two-input data table structure was created by first entering the number of payments in the range B6:D6 and rates in the range A7:A15. Then the data table values were created by first selecting the range A6:D15, clicking the DATA tab, clicking the What-If Analysis button in the Data Tools group, then clicking Data Table. In the Data Table dialog box, the row input value is the term in cell C2. The column input value is the interest rate in cell B2. You can check the accuracy of these values by cross-referencing the values in the data table with those in row 2 where you can see that an interest rate of 4.5% for 36 months has a monthly payment of $594.94.

FIGURE K-12: Two-input data table

	A	B	C	D	E
1	Loan Amount	Interest Rate	# Payments	Monthly Payment	
2	$20,000.00	4.50%	36	$594.94	
3					
4		Car Payment for $20,000 Loan			
5			Term		
6		36	48	60	
7	4.00%	$590.48	$451.58	$368.33	
8	4.25%	$592.71	$453.82	$370.59	
9	4.50%	$594.94	$456.07	$372.86	
10	4.75%	$597.18	$458.32	$375.14	
11	5.00%	$599.42	$460.59	$377.42	
12	5.25%	$601.67	$462.85	$379.72	
13	5.50%	$603.92	$465.13	$382.02	
14	5.75%	$606.18	$467.41	$384.34	
15	6.00%	$608.44	$469.70	$386.66	
16					
17					

Excel 2013
UNIT K

Use Goal Seek

Learning Outcomes

- Determine input values for a desired result using goal seek
- Answer questions about data using goal seek

You can think of goal seeking as a what-if analysis in reverse. In a what-if analysis, you might try many sets of values to achieve a certain solution. To **goal seek**, you specify a solution, then ask Excel to find the input value that produces the answer you want. "Backing into" a solution in this way, sometimes referred to as **backsolving**, can save a significant amount of time. For example, you can use Goal Seek to determine how many units must be sold to reach a particular sales goal or to determine what expense levels are necessary to meet a budget target. CASE *After reviewing her data table, Kate has a follow-up question: What January U.S. sales target is required to bring the January Quest sales percentage to 17%, assuming the sales for the other regions don't change? You use Goal Seek to answer her question.*

STEPS

1. **Click cell B8**

   The first step in using Goal Seek is to select a goal cell. A **goal cell** contains a formula in which you can substitute values to find a specific value, or goal. You use cell B8 as the goal cell because it contains the percent formula.

2. **Click the DATA tab, click the What-If Analysis button in the Data Tools group, then click Goal Seek**

   The Goal Seek dialog box opens. The Set cell text box contains a reference to cell B8, the percent formula cell you selected in Step 1. You need to indicate that the figure in cell B8 should equal 17%.

3. **Click the To value text box, then type 17%**

   The value 17% represents the desired solution you want to reach by substituting different values in the By changing cell.

4. **Click the By changing cell text box, then click cell B3**

   You have specified that you want cell B3, the U.S. January amount, to change to reach the 17% solution, as shown in FIGURE K-13.

5. **Click OK**

   The Goal Seek Status dialog box opens with the following message: "Goal Seeking with Cell B8 found a solution." By changing the sales amount in cell B3 to $109,667, Goal Seek achieves a January percentage of 17.

6. **Click OK, then click cell A1**

   Changing the sales amount in cell B3 changes the other dependent values in the worksheet (B7, H3, I3, and H7) as shown in FIGURE K-14.

7. **Save the workbook, then preview the worksheet**

QUICK TIP

Before you select another command, you can return the worksheet to its status prior to the Goal Seek by pressing [Ctrl][Z].

FIGURE K-13: Completed Goal Seek dialog box

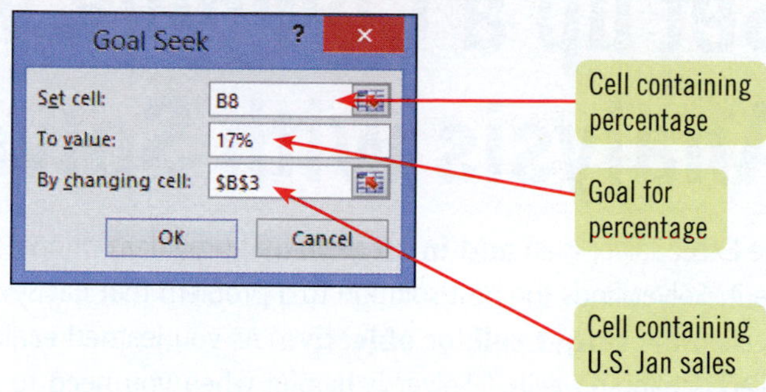

FIGURE K-14: Worksheet with new dependent values

	A	B	C	D	E	F	G	H	I	J
1	2017 Projected Sales									
2		Jan	Feb	Mar	Apr	May	Jun	Total	Percent of Total Sales	
3	U.S.	$109,667	$67,189	$69,423	$61,664	$103,926	$100,244	$512,113	31.86%	
4	Canada	$64,868	$75,326	$77,244	$71,688	$67,015	$67,388	$423,529	26.35%	
5	U.K.	$61,573	$62,756	$64,681	$72,988	$61,191	$40,334	$363,523	22.62%	
6	Australia	$37,043	$57,657	$61,539	$60,708	$45,868	$45,224	$308,039	19.17%	
7	Total	$273,151	$262,928	$272,887	$267,048	$278,000	$253,190	$1,607,204		
8	Percent of Total Sales	17.00%	16.36%	16.98%	16.62%	17.30%	15.75%			
9										
13										
14										
15										

New target values calculated by Goal Seek

New dependent values

Excel 2013

Set up a Complex What-if Analysis with Solver

Learning Outcomes
- Develop an understanding of the solver terminology
- Set up a worksheet analysis using the Solver Parameters dialog box

The Excel Solver is an **add-in** program that provides optional features. It must be installed before you can use it. Solver finds the best solution to a problem that has several inputs. The cell containing the formula is called the **target cell**, or **objective**. As you learned earlier, cells containing the values that vary are called "changing cells." Solver is helpful when you need to perform a complex what-if analysis involving multiple input values or when the input values must conform to specific limitations or restrictions called **constraints**. **CASE** *Kate decides to fund each region with the same amount, $775,000, to cover expenses. She adjusts the travel and entertainment allocations to keep expenditures to the allocated amount of $775,000. You use Solver to help Kate find the best possible allocation.*

STEPS

TROUBLE
If Solver is not on your DATA tab, click the FILE tab, click Options, click Add-Ins, click Go, in the Add-Ins dialog box click the Solver Add-in check box to select it, then click OK.

1. **Click the Budgets sheet tab**
   This worksheet is designed to calculate the travel, entertainment, and other budget categories for each region. It assumes fixed costs for communications, equipment, advertising, salaries, and rent. You use Solver to change the entertainment and travel amounts in cells G3:H6 (the changing cells) to achieve your target of a total budget of $3,100,000 in cell I7 (the target cell). You want your solution to include a constraint on cells G3:H6 specifying that each region is funded $775,000. Based on past budgets, you know there are two other constraints: the travel budgets must include at least $83,000, and the entertainment budgets must include at least $95,000. It is a good idea to enter constraints on the worksheet for documentation purposes, as shown in **FIGURE K-15**.

2. **Click the DATA tab, then click the Solver button in the Analysis group**
   If the Solver Parameters dialog box opens, you indicate the target cell with its objective, the changing cells, and the constraints under which you want Solver to work. You begin by entering your total budget objective.

QUICK TIP
If your Solver Parameters dialog box has entries in the By Changing Variable Cells box or in the Subject to the Constraints box, click Reset All, click OK, then continue with Step 3.

3. **With the insertion point in the Set Objective text box, click cell I7 in the worksheet, click the Value Of option button, double-click the Value Of text box, then type 3,100,000**
   You have specified an objective of $3,100,000 for the total budget. In typing the total budget figure, be sure to type the commas.

4. **Click the By Changing Variable Cells text box, then select the range G3:H6 on the worksheet**
   You have told Excel which cells to vary to reach the goal of $3,100,000 total budget. You need to specify the constraints on the worksheet values to restrict the Solver's answer to realistic values.

5. **Click Add, with the insertion point in the Cell Reference text box in the Add Constraint dialog box, select the range I3:I6 in the worksheet, click the list arrow in the dialog box, click =, then with the insertion point in the Constraint text box click cell C9**
   As shown in **FIGURE K-16**, the Add Constraint dialog box specifies that cells in the range I3:I6, the total region budget amounts, should be equal to the value in cell C9. Next, you need to add the constraint that the budgeted entertainment amounts should be at least $95,000.

QUICK TIP
If your solution needs to be an integer, you can select it in the Add Constraint dialog box.

6. **Click Add, with the insertion point in the Cell Reference text box select the range G3:G6 in the worksheet, click the list arrow, select >=, with the insertion point in the Constraint text box click cell C11**
   Next, you need to specify that the budgeted travel amounts should be greater than or equal to $83,000.

7. **Click Add, with the insertion point in the Cell Reference text box select the range H3:H6, select >=, with the insertion point in the Constraint text box click cell C10, then click OK**
   The Solver Parameters dialog box opens with the constraints listed, as shown in **FIGURE K-17**. In the next lesson, you run Solver and generate solutions to the budget constraints.

FIGURE K-15: Worksheet set up for a complex what-if analysis

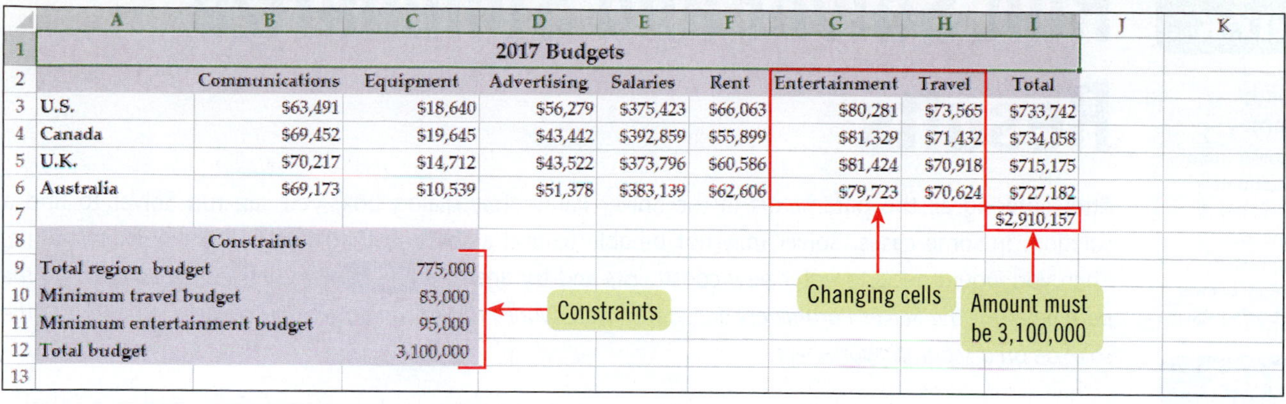

	A	B	C	D	E	F	G	H	I	J	K
1	2017 Budgets										
2		Communications	Equipment	Advertising	Salaries	Rent	Entertainment	Travel	Total		
3	U.S.	$63,491	$18,640	$56,279	$375,423	$66,063	$80,281	$73,565	$733,742		
4	Canada	$69,452	$19,645	$43,442	$392,859	$55,899	$81,329	$71,432	$734,058		
5	U.K.	$70,217	$14,712	$43,522	$373,796	$60,586	$81,424	$70,918	$715,175		
6	Australia	$69,173	$10,539	$51,378	$383,139	$62,606	$79,723	$70,624	$727,182		
7									$2,910,157		
8	Constraints										
9	Total region budget		775,000								
10	Minimum travel budget		83,000								
11	Minimum entertainment budget		95,000								
12	Total budget		3,100,000								
13											

FIGURE K-16: Adding constraints

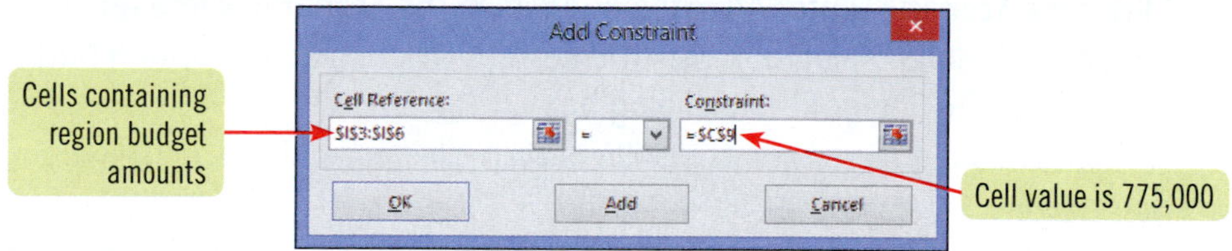

FIGURE K-17: Completed Solver Parameters dialog box

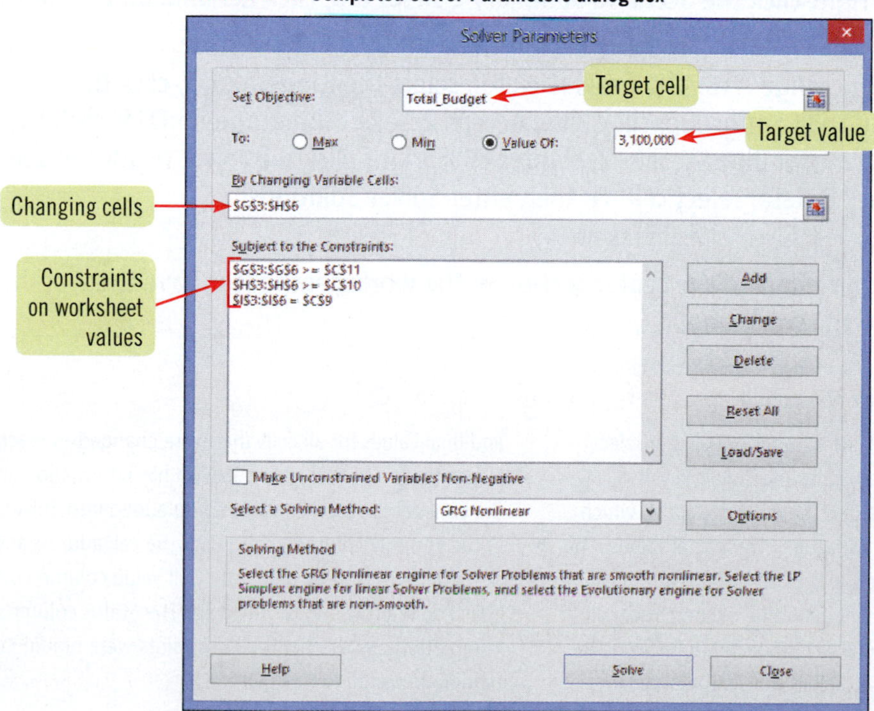

Excel 2013

Excel 2013
UNIT K

Run Solver and Summarize Results

Learning Outcomes
- Run solver using the parameters in the Solver Parameters dialog box
- Create an answer report using solver

After entering all the parameters in the Solver Parameters dialog box, you can run Solver to find a solution. In some cases, Solver may not be able to find a solution that meets all of your constraints. Then you would need to enter new constraints and try again. **CASE** *You have finished entering the parameters in the Solver Parameters dialog box. Kate wants you to run Solver and create a summary of the solution on a separate worksheet.*

STEPS

1. **Make sure your Solver Parameters dialog box matches FIGURE K-17 in the previous lesson**
2. **Click Solve**

   The Solver Results dialog box opens, indicating that Solver has found a solution, as shown in FIGURE K-18. The solution values appear in the worksheet, but you decide to save the solution values in a summary worksheet and display the original values in the worksheet.
3. **Click Save Scenario, enter Adjusted Budgets in the Scenario Name text box, click OK, in the Solver Results dialog box click the Restore Original Values option button, then click OK to close the Solver Results dialog box**

   The Solver Results dialog box closes, and the original values appear in the worksheet. You will display the Solver solution values on a separate sheet.
4. **Click the What-If Analysis button in the Data Tools group, click Scenario Manager, with the Adjusted Budgets scenario selected in the Scenario Manager dialog box click Summary, then click OK**

   The Solver results appear on the Scenario Summary 2 worksheet, as shown in FIGURE K-19. You want to format the solution values on the worksheet.
5. **Select Column A, click the HOME tab if necessary, click the Delete button in the Cells group, right-click the Scenario Summary 2 sheet tab, click Rename on the shortcut menu, type Adjusted Budgets, then press [Enter]**
6. **Select the range A16:A18, press [Delete], select the range A2:D3, click the Fill Color list arrow in the Font group, click Blue, Accent 2, select the range A5:D15, click the Fill Color list arrow, click Blue, Accent 2, Lighter 80%, right-click the row 1 header to select the row, click Delete, select cell A1, then enter Solver Solutions**

   The formatted Solver solution is shown in FIGURE K-20.
7. **Enter your name in the center section of the worksheet footer, save the workbook, then preview the worksheet**

Understanding Answer Reports

Instead of saving Solver results as a scenario, you can select from three types of answer reports in the Solver Results window. One of the most useful is the Answer Report, which compares the original values with the Solver's final values. The report has three sections. The top section has the target cell information; it compares the original value of the target cell with the final value. The middle section of the report contains information about the adjustable cells. It lists the original and final values for all cells that were changed to reach the target value. The last report section has information about the constraints. Each constraint you added into Solver is listed in the Formula column, along with the cell address and a description of the cell data. The Cell Value column contains the Solver solution values for the cells. The Status column contains information on whether the constraints were binding or not binding in reaching the solution.

FIGURE K-18: Solver Results dialog box

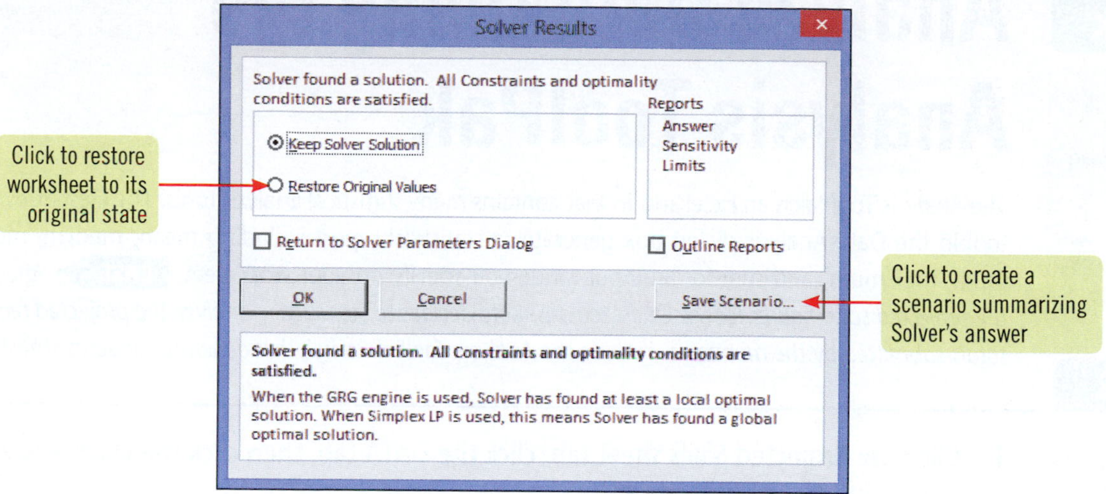

FIGURE K-19: Solver Summary

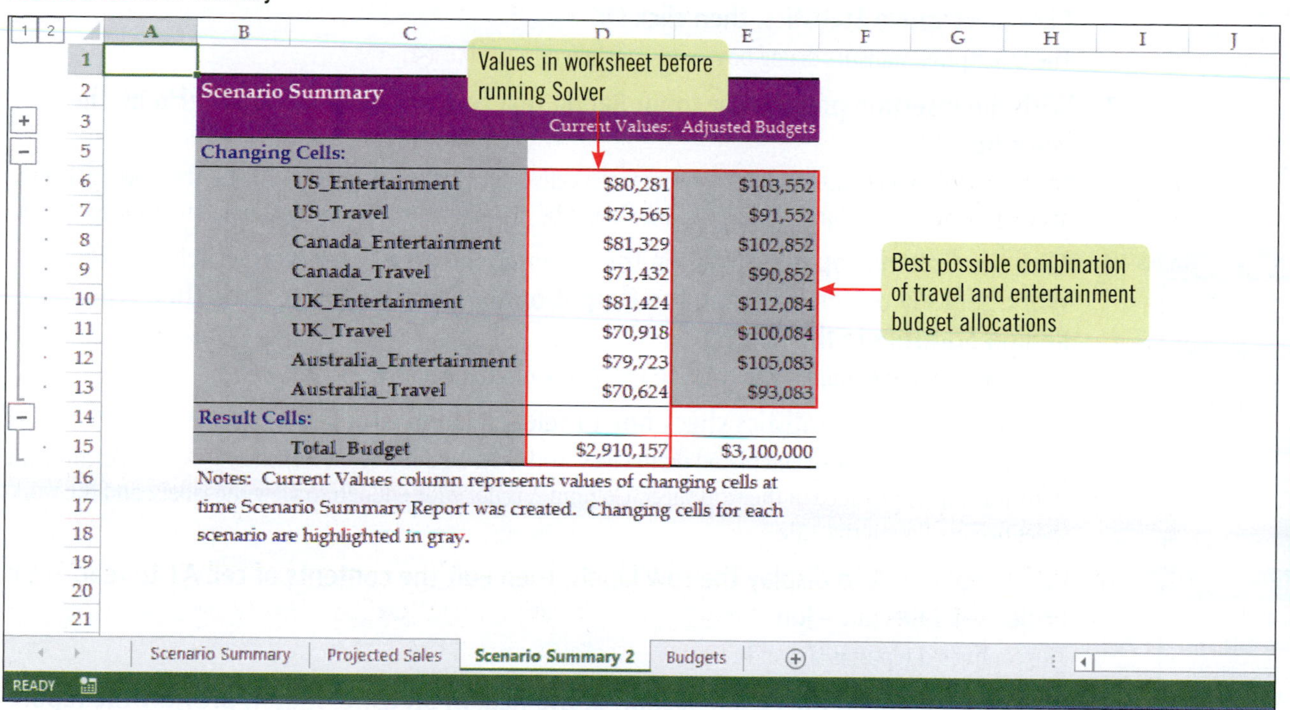

FIGURE K-20: Formatted Solver Summary

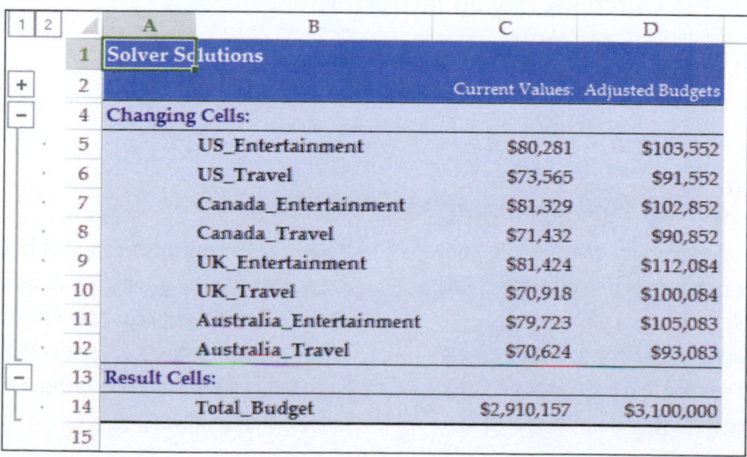

Excel 2013
UNIT K

Analyze Data Using the Analysis ToolPak

Learning Outcomes
- Create a summary statistics worksheet
- Analyze worksheet data using descriptive statistics

The Analysis ToolPak is an Excel add-in that contains many statistical analysis tools. The Descriptive Statistics tool in the Data Analysis dialog box generates a statistical report including mean, median, mode, minimum, maximum, and sum for an input range you specify on your worksheet. **CASE** *After reviewing the projected sales figures for the Quest regions, Kate decides to statistically analyze the projected regional sales totals submitted by the managers. You use the Analysis ToolPak to help her generate the sales statistics.*

STEPS

TROUBLE
If Data Analysis is not on your DATA tab, click the FILE tab, click Options, click Add-Ins, click Go, in the Add-Ins dialog box click the Analysis ToolPak check box to select it, then click OK.

1. **Click the Projected Sales sheet tab, click the DATA tab, then click the Data Analysis button in the Analysis group**
   The Data Analysis dialog box opens, listing the available analysis tools.
2. **Click Descriptive Statistics, then click OK**
   The Descriptive Statistics dialog box opens, as shown in FIGURE K-21.
3. **With the insertion point in the Input Range text box, select the range H3:H6 on the worksheet**
   You have told Excel to use the total projected sales cells in the statistical analysis. You need to specify that the data is grouped in a column and the results should be placed on a new worksheet named Region Statistics.

QUICK TIP
Selecting the New Worksheet Ply option places the statistical output on a new worksheet in the workbook.

4. **Click the Columns option button in the Grouped By: area if necessary, click the New Worksheet Ply option button in the Output options section if necessary, then type Region Statistics in the text box**
   You want to add the summary statistics to the new worksheet.
5. **Click the Summary statistics check box to select it, then click OK**
   The statistics are generated and placed on the new worksheet named Region Statistics. TABLE K-1 describes the statistical values provided in the worksheet. Column A is not wide enough to view the labels, and the worksheet needs a descriptive title.

QUICK TIP
If there are fewer than four data values, the Kurtosis will display the DIV/0! error value.

6. **Widen column A to display the row labels, then edit the contents of cell A1 to read Total Projected Sales Jan – Jun**
   The completed report is shown in FIGURE K-22.
7. **Enter your name in the center section of the Region Statistics footer, preview the report, save the workbook, close the workbook, then exit Excel**
8. **Submit the workbook to your instructor**

Choosing the right tool for your data analysis

The Analysis ToolPak offers 19 options for data analysis. Anova, or the analysis of variance, can be applied to one or more data samples. The Regression option creates a table of statistics from a least-squares regression. The Correlation choice measures how strong of a linear relationship exists between two random variables. A Moving Average is often calculated for stock prices or any other data that is time sensitive. Moving averages display long-term trends by smoothing out short-term changes. The Random Number Generation option creates a set of random numbers between values that you specify. The Rank and Percentile option creates a report of the ranking and percentile distribution.

FIGURE K-21: Descriptive Statistics dialog box

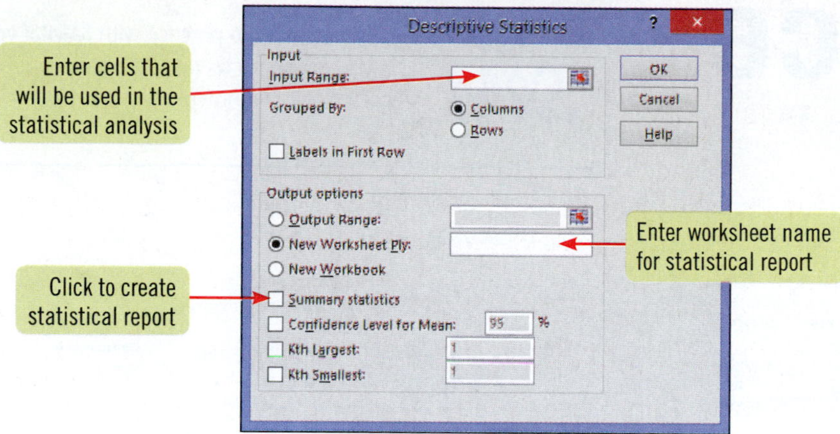

FIGURE K-22: Completed report

Total Projected Sales Jan - Jun	
Mean	401801
Standard Error	43681.95
Median	393526
Mode	#N/A
Standard Deviatior	87363.9
Sample Variance	7.63E+09
Kurtosis	-0.46892
Skewness	0.472144
Range	204074
Minimum	308039
Maximum	512113
Sum	1607204
Count	4

TABLE K-1: Descriptive statistics

statistic	definition
Mean	The average of a set of numbers
Standard Error	The deviation of the mean of your data from the overall population
Median	The middle value of a set of numbers
Mode	The most common value in a set of numbers
Standard Deviation	The measure of how widely spread the values in a set of numbers are; if the values are all close to the mean, the standard deviation is close to zero
Sample Variance	The measure of how scattered the values in a set of numbers are from an expected value
Kurtosis	The measure of the peakedness or flatness of a distribution of data
Skewness	The measure of the asymmetry of the values in a set of numbers
Range	The difference between the largest and smallest values in a set of numbers
Minimum	The smallest value in a set of numbers
Maximum	The largest value in a set of numbers
Sum	The total of the values in a set of numbers
Count	The number of values in a set of numbers

Practice

Put your skills into practice with SAM! If you have a SAM account, go to www.cengage.com/sam2013 to access SAM assignments for this unit.

Concepts Review

FIGURE K-23

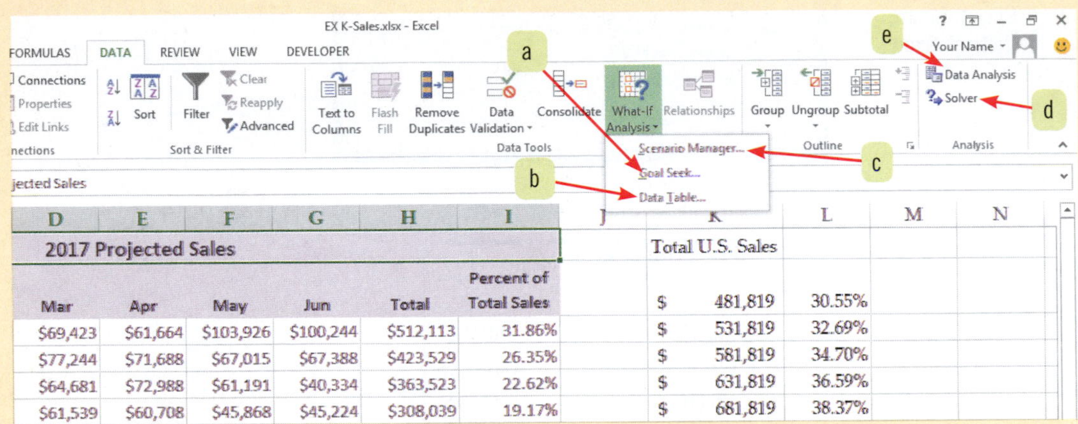

1. **Which element do you click to create a range of cells showing the resulting values with varied formula input?**
2. **Which element do you click to perform a statistical analysis on worksheet data?**
3. **Which element do you click to name and save different sets of values to forecast worksheet results?**
4. **Which element do you click to perform a what-if analysis involving multiple input values with constraints?**
5. **Which element do you click to find the input values that produce a specified result?**

Match each term with the statement that best describes it.

6. Solver	**a.** Add-in that helps you solve complex what-if scenarios with multiple input values
7. One-input data table	**b.** Separate sheet with results from the worksheet's scenarios
8. Scenario summary	**c.** Generates values resulting from varying two sets of changing values in a formula
9. Goal Seek	**d.** Helps you backsolve what-if scenarios
10. Two-input data table	**e.** Generates values resulting from varying one set of changing values in a formula

Select the best answer from the list of choices.

11. To hide the contents of a cell from view, you can use the custom number format:

a. —
b. ;;;
c. Blank
d. " "

12. The __________ button in the Scenario Manager dialog box allows you to bring scenarios from another workbook into the current workbook.

a. Combine
b. Add
c. Merge
d. Import

13. When you use Goal Seek, you specify a ____________, then find the values that produce it.

a. Row input cell
b. Column input cell
c. Changing value
d. Solution

14. In Solver, the cell containing the formula is called the:

a. Target cell.
b. Changing cell.
c. Input cell.
d. Output cell.

15. Which of the following Excel add-ins can be used to generate a statistical summary of worksheet data?

a. Solver
b. Lookup Wizard
c. Conditional Sum
d. Analysis ToolPak

Skills Review

1. Define a what-if analysis.

a. Start Excel, open the file EX K-2.xlsx from the location where you store your Data Files, then save it as **EX K-Repair**.
b. Examine the Auto Repair worksheet to determine the purpose of the worksheet model.
c. Locate the data input cells.
d. Locate any dependent cells.
e. Examine the worksheet to determine problems the worksheet model can solve.

2. Track a what-if analysis with Scenario Manager.

a. On the Auto Repair worksheet, select the range B3:B5, then use the Scenario Manager to set up a scenario called **Most Likely** with the current data input values.
b. Add a scenario called **Best Case** using the same changing cells, but change the Labor cost per hour in the $B$3 text box to **70**, change the Parts cost per job in the $B$4 text box to **65**, then change the Hours per job value in cell $B$5 to **2.5**.
c. Add a scenario called **Worst Case**. For this scenario, change the Labor cost per hour in the $B$3 text box to **95**, change the Parts cost per job in the $B$4 text box to **80**, then change the Hours per job in the $B$5 text box to **3.5**.
d. If necessary, drag the Scenario Manager dialog box to the right until columns A and B are visible.
e. Show the Worst Case scenario results, and view the total job cost.
f. Show the Best Case scenario results, and observe the job cost. Finally, display the Most Likely scenario results.
g. Close the Scenario Manager dialog box.
h. Save the workbook.

3. Generate a scenario summary.

a. Create names for the input value cells and the dependent cell using the range A3:B7.
b. Verify that the names were created.
c. Create a scenario summary report, using the Cost to complete job value in cell B7 as the result cell.
d. Edit the title of the Summary report in cell B2 to read **Scenario Summary for Auto Repair**.
e. Delete the Current Values column.
f. Delete the notes beginning in cell B11. Compare your worksheet to **FIGURE K-24**.
g. Return to cell A1, enter your name in the center section of the Scenario Summary sheet footer, save the workbook, then preview the Scenario Summary sheet.

4. Project figures using a data table.

a. Click the Auto Repair sheet tab.
b. Enter the label **Labor $** in cell D3.

FIGURE K-24

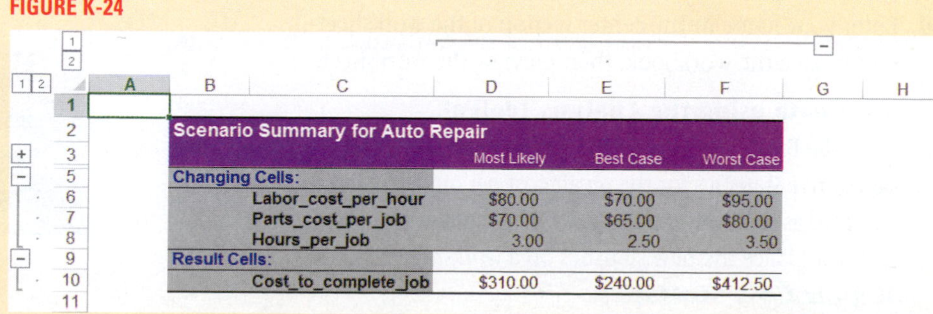

	A	B	C	D	E	F	G	H
1								
2		Scenario Summary for Auto Repair						
3				Most Likely	Best Case	Worst Case		
5		Changing Cells:						
6			Labor_cost_per_hour	$80.00	$70.00	$95.00		
7			Parts_cost_per_job	$70.00	$65.00	$80.00		
8			Hours_per_job	3.00	2.50	3.50		
9		Result Cells:						
10			Cost_to_complete_job	$310.00	$240.00	$412.50		
11								

Skills Review (continued)

c. Format the label so that it is boldfaced and right-aligned.

d. In cell D4, enter **75**; then in cell D5, enter **80**.

e. Select the range D4:D5, then use the fill handle to extend the series to cell D8.

f. In cell E3, reference the job cost formula by entering **=B7**.

g. Format the contents of cell E3 as hidden, using the ;;; Custom formatting type on the Number tab of the Format Cells dialog box.

h. Generate the new job costs based on the varying labor costs. Select the range D3:E8 and create a data table. In the data table dialog box, make cell B3 (the labor cost) the column input cell.

i. Format the range E4:E8 as currency with two decimal places. Compare your worksheet to FIGURE K-25.

j. Enter your name in the center section of the worksheet footer, save the workbook, then preview the worksheet.

5. Use Goal Seek.

a. Click cell B7, and open the Goal Seek dialog box.

b. Assuming the labor rate and the hours remain the same, determine what the parts would have to cost so that the cost to complete the job is $290. (*Hint*: Enter a job cost of **290** as the To value, and enter **B4** (the Parts cost) as the By changing cell. Write down the parts cost that Goal Seek finds.

c. Click OK, then use [Ctrl][Z] to reset the parts cost to its original value.

d. Enter the cost of the parts that you found in step 5b into cell A14.

e. Assuming the parts cost and hours remain the same, determine the fee for the labor so that the cost to complete the job is $250. Use [Ctrl][Z] to reset the labor cost to its original value. Enter the labor cost in cell A15.

f. Save the workbook, then preview the worksheet.

FIGURE K-25

	A	B	C	D	E
1	Auto Repair Model				
2					
3	Labor cost per hour	$80.00		Labor $	
4	Parts cost per job	$70.00		75	$295.00
5	Hours per job	3.00		80	$310.00
6				85	$325.00
7	Cost to complete job:	$310.00		90	$340.00
8				95	$355.00
9					
10					

6. Set up a complex what-if analysis with Solver.

a. With the Brake Repair sheet active, open the Solver Parameters dialog box.

b. Make B14 (the total repair costs) the objective cell, with a target value of 16,000.

c. Use cells B6:D6 (the number of scheduled repairs) as the changing cells.

d. Specify that cells B6:D6 must be integers. (*Hint*: Select int in the Add Constraint dialog box.)

e. Specify a constraint that cells B6:D6 must be greater than or equal to 10.

7. Run Solver and summarize results.

a. Use Solver to find a solution.

b. Save the solution as a scenario named **Repair Solution**, and restore the original values to the worksheet.

c. Create a scenario summary using the Repair Solution scenario, delete the notes at the bottom of the solution, and rename the worksheet **Repair Solution**. Compare your worksheet to FIGURE K-26.

d. Enter your name in the center section of the worksheet footer, save the workbook, then preview the worksheet.

FIGURE K-26

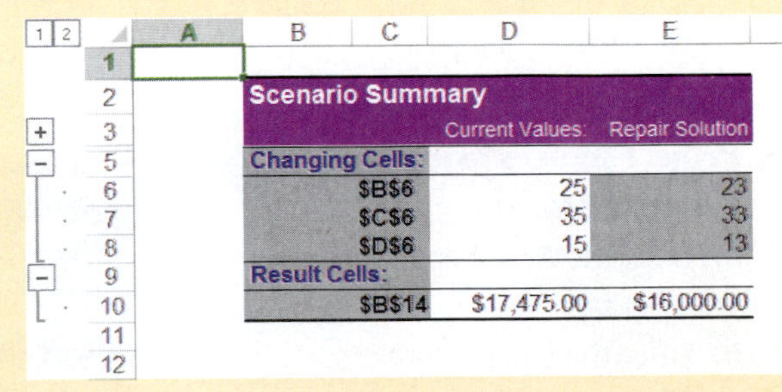

	A	B	C	D	E
1					
2		Scenario Summary			
3				Current Values:	Repair Solution
5		Changing Cells:			
6			$B$6	25	23
7			$C$6	35	33
8			$D$6	15	13
9		Result Cells:			
10			$B$14	$17,475.00	$16,000.00
11					
12					

8. Analyze data using the Analysis ToolPak.

a. With the Brake Repair sheet active, generate summary descriptive statistics for the repair cost per model, using cells B10:D10 as the input range. (*Hint*: The input is grouped in a row.) Place the new statistics on a worksheet named **Repair Cost Statistics**.

b. Widen columns as necessary to view the statistics.

Skills Review (continued)

c. Change the contents of cell A1 to **Repair Cost Per Model**. Delete row 9 containing the kurtosis error information. (This was generated because you only have three data values.) Compare your worksheet to FIGURE K-27.

d. Add your name to the center section of the worksheet footer, then preview the worksheet.

e. Save and close the workbook, submit the workbook to your instructor, then exit Excel.

FIGURE K-27

	A	B
1	Repair Cost Per Model	
2		
3	Mean	5825
4	Standard Error	1517.467737
5	Median	6500
6	Mode	#N/A
7	Standard Deviation	2628.33122
8	Sample Variance	6908125
9	Skewness	-1.0794537
10	Range	5125
11	Minimum	2925
12	Maximum	8050
13	Sum	17475
14	Count	3
15		

Independent Challenge 1

You are the manager for Stern & Jones, an environmental consulting firm based in Boston. You are planning a computer hardware upgrade for the engineers in the company. The vice president of finance at the company has asked you to research the monthly cost for a $200,000 equipment loan to purchase the new hardware. You will create a worksheet model to determine the monthly payments based on several different interest rates and loan terms, using data from the company's bank. Using Scenario Manager, you will create the following three scenarios: a 4-year loan at 6.8 percent; a 3-year loan at 5.75 percent; and a 2-year loan at 5.5 percent. You will also prepare a scenario summary report outlining the payment details.

a. Start Excel, open the file EX K-3.xlsx from the location where you store your Data Files, then save it as **EX K-Hardware Loan**.

b. Create cell names for the cells B4:B11 based on the labels in cells A4:A11, using the Create Names from Selection dialog box.

c. Use Scenario Manager to create scenarios that calculate the monthly payment on a $200,000 loan under the three sets of loan possibilities listed below. (*Hint*: Create three scenarios using cells B5:B6 as the changing cells.)

Scenario Name	Interest Rate	Term
6.8% 4 Yr	.068	48
5.75% 3 Yr	.0575	36
5.5% 2 Yr	.055	24

d. Show each scenario to make sure it performs as intended, then display the 6.8% 4 Yr scenario.

e. Generate a scenario summary titled **Scenario Summary for Hardware Purchase**. Use cells B9:B11 as the Result cells.

f. Delete the Current Values column in the report, and delete the notes at the bottom of the report. Rename the sheet **Hardware Purchase**.

g. Enter your name in the center section of the Hardware Purchase sheet footer. Save the workbook, then preview the scenario summary.

h. Close the workbook, exit Excel, then submit the workbook to your instructor.

Independent Challenge 2

You are a CFO at Bay City Digital, an interactive media consulting company based in Michigan. The company president has asked you to prepare a loan summary report for a business expansion. You need to develop a model to show what the monthly payments would be for a $750,000 loan with a range of interest rates. You will create a one-input data table that shows the results of varying interest rates in 0.2% increments, then you will use Goal Seek to specify a total payment amount for this loan application.

a. Start Excel, open the file EX K-4.xlsx from the location where you store your Data Files, then save it as **EX K-Capital Loan Payment Model**.

Independent Challenge 2 (continued)

b. Use FIGURE K-28 as a guide to enter the data table structure. Reference the monthly payment amount from cell B9 in cell E4, then format the contents of cell E4 as hidden.

FIGURE K-28

	A	B	C	D	E
1	Bay City Digital				
2					
3				Interest Rate	
4	Loan Amount	$750,000.00			
5	Annual Interest Rate	7.80%		7.00%	
6	Term in Months	60		7.20%	
7				7.40%	
8				7.60%	
9	Monthly Payment:	$15,135.61		7.80%	
10	Total Payments:	$908,136.58		8.00%	
11	Total Interest:	$158,136.58		8.20%	
12				8.40%	
13				8.60%	

c. Using cells D4:E13, create a one-input data table with varying interest rates for the loan.

d. Generate the data table that shows the effect of varying interest rates on the monthly payments. Use cell B5, the Annual Interest Rate, as the column input cell. Format the range E5:E13 as currency with two decimal places.

e. Select cell B10 and use Goal Seek to find the interest rate necessary for a total payment amount of $850,000. Use cell B5, the Annual Interest Rate, as the By changing cell. Note the interest rate, then cancel the solution found by Goal Seek. Enter the interest rate in cell B16.

f. Select cell B9 and use Goal Seek to find the interest rate necessary for a monthly payment amount of $13,000. Use cell B5, the Annual Interest Rate, as the By changing cell. Note the interest rate, then cancel the solution found by Goal Seek. Enter the interest rate in cell B17.

g. Enter your name in the center section of the worksheet footer, save the workbook, then preview the worksheet.

h. Close the workbook, exit Excel, then submit the workbook to your instructor.

Independent Challenge 3

You are the owner of Cape Medical, a home medical products company based in Boston. You are considering a purchase of vans, sedans, and compact cars to provide local delivery service. You want to use Goal Seek to look at how the interest rate affects the monthly payments for two of each type of vehicle. Next you want to look at options for expanding the delivery service by purchasing a combination of vans, sedans, and compact cars that can deliver a total of 1500 cubic feet of products. As you review your expansion options, you need to keep the total monthly payments for all of the vehicles at or below $6,500. You use Solver to help find the best possible combination of vehicles.

a. Start Excel, open the file EX K-5.xlsx from the location where you store your Data Files, then save it as **EX K-Vehicle Purchase**.

b. Use Goal Seek to find the interest rate that produces a monthly payment for the van purchase of $1,800, and write down the interest rate that Goal Seek finds. Reset the interest rate to its original value, record the interest rate in cell A19, then enter **Interest rate for $1800 van payment** in cell B19.

c. Use Goal Seek to find the interest rate that produces a monthly payment for the sedan purchase of $1000. Reset the interest rate to its original value, record the interest rate in cell A20, then enter **Interest rate for $1000 sedan payment** in cell B20.

Independent Challenge 3 (continued)

d. Use Goal Seek to find the interest rate that produces a monthly payment for the compact purchase of $650. Reset the interest rate to its original value, record the interest rate in cell A21, then enter **Interest rate for $650 compact payment** in cell B21.
e. Assign cell B8 the name **Quantity_Van**, name cell C8 **Quantity_Sedan**, name cell D8 **Quantity_Compact**, and name cell B15 **Total_Monthly_Payments**. Use Solver to set the total delivery capacity of all vehicles to 1500. Use the quantity to purchase, cells B8:D8, as the changing cells. Specify that cells B8:D8 must be integers. Make sure that the total monthly payments amount in cell B15 is less than or equal to $6,500.
f. Generate a scenario named **Delivery Solution** with the Solver values, and restore the original values in the worksheet. Create a scenario summary using the Delivery Solution scenario and the Total Monthly Payments as the result cells, delete the notes at the bottom of the solution, and edit cell B2 to contain **Total Capacity of 1500**.
g. Enter your name in the center footer section of both worksheets. Preview both worksheets, then save the workbook.
h. Close the workbook, then submit the workbook to your instructor.

Independent Challenge 4: Explore

You are researching various options for financing a new car loan. You haven't decided whether to finance the car for 3, 4, or 5 years. Each loan term carries a different interest rate. To help with the comparison, you will create a two-input data table using interest rates and terms available at your credit union.

a. Start Excel, open the file EX K-6.xlsx from the location where you store your Data Files, then save it as **EX K-Car Loan**.
b. Using FIGURE K-29 as a guide, enter the input values for a two-input data table with varying interest rates for 3-, 4-, and 5-year terms.
c. Reference the monthly payment amount from cell B9 in cell A13, and format the contents of cell A13 as hidden.
d. Generate the data table, using cells A13:D22, that shows the effect of varying interest rates and loan terms on the monthly payments. (*Hint*: Use cell B6, Term in Months, as the row input cell, and cell B5, the Annual Interest Rate, as the column input cell.)
e. Format the range B14:D22 as currency with two decimal places.
f. Enter your name in the center section of the Loan sheet footer, then preview the Loan sheet.
g. Save the workbook, close the workbook, then exit Excel and submit the workbook to your instructor.

FIGURE K-29

	A	B	C	D
1	Car Financing Options			
2				
3				
4	Loan Amount	$20,000.00		
5	Annual Interest Rate	3.50%		
6	Term in Months	60		
7				
8				
9	Monthly Payment:	$363.83		
10	Total Payments:	$21,830.09		
11	Total Interest:	$1,830.09		
12				
13		36	48	60
14	3.00%			
15	3.25%			
16	3.50%			
17	3.75%			
18	4.00%			
19	4.25%			
20	4.50%			
21	4.75%			
22	5.00%			
23				
24				

Visual Workshop

Open the file EX K-7.xlsx from the location where you store your Data Files, then save it as **EX K-Columbus Manufacturing**. Create the worksheet shown in FIGURE K-30. (*Hint*: Use Goal Seek to find the Hourly labor cost to reach the total profit in cell H11 in the figure and accept the solution.) Then generate descriptive statistics for the products' total profits on a worksheet named **Manufacturing Profits**, as shown in FIGURE K-31. Add your name to the center footer section of each sheet, change the orientation of the Profit sheet to landscape, then preview and print both worksheets.

FIGURE K-30

	A	B	C	D	E	F	G	H
1	Columbus Manufacturing							
2	December Production							
3	Hourly Labor Cost	$51.76						
4								
5								
6	Product Number	Hours	Parts Cost	Cost to Produce	Retail Price	Unit Profit	Units Produced	Total Profit
7	NA425	9	$473	$ 938.85	$1,522.00	$ 583.15	425	$ 247,838.73
8	CX877	7	$230	$ 592.33	$ 974.00	$ 381.67	387	$ 147,707.14
9	QA287	2	$421	$ 524.52	$ 776.00	$ 251.48	127	$ 31,937.68
10	TQ894	11	$187	$ 756.37	$1,322.00	$ 565.63	305	$ 172,516.46
11	Total Profit							$ 600,000.00
12								
13								

FIGURE K-31

	A	B
1	*Profit Statistics*	
2		
3	Mean	150000
4	Standard Error	44743.1
5	Median	160112
6	Mode	#N/A
7	Standard Deviation	89486.3
8	Sample Variance	8E+09
9	Kurtosis	1.376
10	Skewness	-0.64908
11	Range	215901
12	Minimum	31937.7
13	Maximum	247839
14	Sum	600000
15	Count	4
16		

Glossary

Add-in An extra program, such as Solver and the Analysis ToolPak, that provides optional Excel features. To activate an add-in, click the File tab, click Options, click Add-Ins, then select or deselect add-ins from the list.

And logical condition A filtering feature that searches for records by specifying that all entered criteria must be matched.

Ascending order In sorting an Excel field (column), the lowest value (the beginning of the alphabet, or the earliest date) appears at the beginning of the sorted data.

AutoFilter A table feature that lets you click a list arrow and select criteria by which to display certain types of records; *also called* filter.

AutoFilter list arrows *See* Filter List arrows.

Backsolving A problem-solving method in which you specify a solution and then find the input value that produces the answer you want; sometimes described as a what-if analysis in reverse. In Excel, the Goal Seek feature performs backsolving.

Banding Worksheet formatting in which adjacent rows and columns are formatted differently.

Calculated columns In a table, a column that automatically fills in cells with formula results, using a formula entered in only one other cell in the same column.

Changing cells In what-if analysis, cells that contain the values that change in order to produce multiple sets of results.

Chart animation The movement of a chart element after the relevant worksheet data changes.

Chart elements Parts of a chart, such as its title or its legend, which you can add, remove, or modify.

Color scale In conditional formatting, a formatting scheme that uses a set of two, three, or four fill colors to convey relative values of data.

Comments In a Visual Basic procedure, notes that explain the purpose of the macro or procedure; they are preceded by a single apostrophe and appear in green. *See also* Cell comments.

Constraints Limitations or restrictions on input data in what-if analysis.

Criteria range In advanced filtering, a cell range containing one row of labels (usually a copy of column labels) and at least one additional row underneath it that contains the criteria you want to match.

Data entry area The unlocked portion of a worksheet where users are able to enter and change data.

Data label Descriptive text that appears above a data marker in a chart.

Data series A column or row in a datasheet. Also, the selected range in a worksheet that Excel converts into a chart.

Data table A range of cells that shows the resulting values when one or more input values are varied in a formula; when one input value is changed, the table is called a one-input data table, and when two input values are changed, it is called a two-input data table. In a chart, it is a grid containing the chart data.

Dependent cell A cell, usually containing a formula, whose value changes depending on the values in the input cells. For example, a payment formula or function that depends on an input cell containing changing interest rates is a dependent cell.

Descending order In sorting an Excel field (column), the order that begins with the letter Z, the highest number, or the latest date of the values in a field.

Dynamic page breaks In a larger workbook, horizontal or vertical dashed lines that represent the place where pages print separately. They also adjust automatically when you insert or delete rows or columns, or change column widths or row heights.

External reference indicator In a formula or macro name, an exclamation point (!) that indicates that a macro is outside the active workbook.

Extract To place a copy of a filtered table in a range you specify in the Advanced Filter dialog box.

Field In a table (an Excel database), a column that describes a characteristic about records, such as first name or city.

Field name A column label that describes a field.

Filter list arrows List arrows that appear next to field names in an Excel table; used to display portions of your data. *Also called* AutoFilter list arrows.

Freeze To hold in place selected columns or rows when scrolling in a worksheet that is divided in panes. *See also* Panes.

Goal Seek A problem-solving method in which you specify a solution and then find the input value that produces the answer you want; sometimes described as a what-if analysis in reverse; also called backsolving.

Header row In an Excel table, the first row; it contains field (column) names.

HTML (Hypertext Markup Language) The format of pages that a Web browser can read.

Hyperlink An object (a filename, a word, a phrase, or a graphic) in a worksheet that, when you click it, displays another worksheet or a Web page called the target. *See also* Target.

Hypertext Markup Language *See* HTML.

Icon sets In conditional formatting, groups of images that are used to visually communicate relative cell values based on the values they contain.

Input cells Spreadsheet cells that contain data instead of formulas and that act as input to a what-if analysis; input values often change to produce different results. Examples include interest rates, prices, or other data.

Input values In a data table, the variable values that are substituted in the table's formula to obtain varying results, such as interest rates.

Instance A worksheet in its own workbook window.

Intranet An internal network site used by a group of people who work together.

Keywords Terms added to a workbook's Document Properties that help locate the file in a search.

List arrows *See* AutoFilter list arrows.

Lock To secure a row, column, or sheet so that data in that location cannot be changed.

Logical conditions Using the operators And and Or to narrow a custom filter criteria.

Logical formula A formula with calculations that are based on stated conditions.

Macro A named set of instructions, written in the Visual Basic programming language, that performs tasks automatically in a specified order.

Metadata Information that describes data and is used in Microsoft Windows document searches.

Model A worksheet used to produce a what-if analysis that acts as the basis for multiple outcomes.

Module In Visual Basic, a module is stored in a workbook and contains macro procedures.

Multilevel sort A reordering of table data using more than one column (field) at a time.

Objective *See* Target cell

One-input data table A range of cells that shows resulting values when one input value in a formula is changed.

Or logical condition A filtering feature that searches for records by specifying that only one entered criterion must be matched.

Output values In a data table, the calculated results that appear in the body of the table.

Panes Sections into which you can divide a worksheet when you want to work on separate parts of the worksheet at the same time; one pane freezes, or remains in place, while you scroll in another pane until you see the desired information.

Personal Macro Workbook A special workbook used only for macro storage.

Personal macro workbook A workbook that can contain macros that are available to any open workbook. By default, the personal macro workbook is hidden.

Plot The Excel process that converts numerical information into data points on a chart.

Print area A portion of a worksheet that you can define using the Print Area button on the Page Layout tab; after you select and define a print area, the Quick Print feature prints only that worksheet area.

Print title In a table that spans more than one page, the field names that print at the top of every printed page.

Program code Macro instructions, written in the Visual Basic for Applications (VBA) programming language.

Properties File characteristics, such as the author's name, keywords, or the title, that help others understand, identify, and locate the file.

Publish To place an Excel workbook or worksheet on a Web site or an intranet in HTML format so that others can access it using their Web browsers.

Read-only format Describes cells that display data but that cannot be changed in a protected worksheet.

Record In a table (an Excel database), data about an object or a person.

Run To play, as a macro.

Scenario A set of values you use to forecast results; the Excel Scenario Manager lets you store and manage different scenarios.

Scenario summary An Excel table that compiles data from various scenarios so that you can view the scenario results next to each other for easy comparison.

Screenshot An image of an open file that is pasted into an Excel document; you can move, copy, and edit the image.

Search criterion In a workbook or table search, the text you are searching for.

Sparklines Miniature charts that show data trends in a worksheet range, such as increases or decreases.

Structured reference Allows table formulas to refer to table columns by names that are automatically generated when the table is created.

T

Table An organized collection of rows and columns of similarly structured data on a worksheet.

Table styles Predesigned formatting that can be applied to a range of cells or even to an entire worksheet; especially useful for those ranges with labels in the left column and top row, and totals in the bottom row or right column. *See also* Table.

Table total row A row you can add to the bottom of a table for calculations using the data in the table columns.

Target The location that a hyperlink displays after you click it.

Target cell In what-if analysis (specifically, in Excel Solver), the cell containing the formula. Also called objective.

Trendline A series of data points on a line that shows data values that represent the general direction in a series of data.

Two-input data table A range of cells that shows resulting values when two input values in a formula are changed.

V

Variable In the Visual Basic programming language, an area in memory in which you can temporarily store an item of information; variables are often declared in Dim statements such as *DimNameAsString*. In an Excel scenario or what-if analysis, a changing input value, such as price or interest rate, that affects a calculated result.

View A set of display or print settings that you can name and save for access at another time. You can save multiple views of a worksheet.

Virus Destructive software that can damage your computer files.

Visual Basic Editor A program that lets you display and edit macro code.

Visual Basic for Applications (VBA) A programming language used to create macros in Excel.

W

Watermark A translucent background design on a worksheet that is displayed when the worksheet is printed. A watermark is a graphic file that is inserted into the document header.

Wildcard A special symbol that substitutes for unknown characters in defining search criteria in the Find and Replace dialog box. The most common types of wildcards are the question mark (?), which stands for any single character, and the asterisk (*), which represents any group of characters.

WordArt Specially formatted text, created using the WordArt button on the Drawing toolbar.

Index

D

I

K

L

M

N

O

P

Q

R

S